this undeserved life

Praises for
This Undeserved Life

"If you've ever wondered if it's okay to be sad, if you're wondering where God is amidst your greatest grief, read this book. Natalie's story is our story."

—Jeff Goins, Bestselling Author of *The Art of Work*

"Some words of advice when you read Natalie Brenner's ***This Undeserved Life***: clear your schedule because you won't want to put it down; start a book club because you are going to want to talk about this book with everyone you know; and try not to bawl after reading because you realize how painful, incredible, stressful, and magical life can be.

Natalie weaves a story about grief, adoption, infertility, heartache, love, and more. Page after page you will be amazed at how one person finds her way through trauma and pain to a beautiful, imperfectly wonderful life.

This is a must-read for anyone looking to find more purpose, beauty, and life."

—Crystal Perkins, Editor-in-Chief of Adoption.com

"Sometimes it seems like the world of writing where real life and Jesus collide is just for women. It would be easy to put this text in that same vein. It is more than that though. As a foster dad figuring out how to love and raise kids that aren't like me, this book spoke to my heart. As someone trying to figure out what it means to love The Church when hurt is everywhere, this book spoke to my heart. As a guy trying to figure out the meaning of life and birth for the women all around me, this book taught me pieces I never before understood. Natalie is exactly what she seems like. Full of hope and kindness even in the darkest of places. There is nothing false or fake hiding between the lines. Grateful for the words of this book."

—Seth King, Refugee Family Support Specialist

"Natalie's words in this book shine light on the darkest, unseen places of the soul. Her raw and honest words extend an invitation for us to give our grief, found in each of our stories, the space and time to heal. These words will speak to deep places in you, I know they have in me."

—Jessica Satterfield, Writer and Speaker at Grace While We Wait

"This book may make you cry while you read it in public spaces. At least that is what happened to me. Natalie leaves her beating heart on these pages so we can all feel safer with baring our own hearts. If you have walked through grief of any kind you will likely feel safe, seen, and heard in these pages. May you no longer feel alone in your grief."

—Josie Corliss, Professional Stay At Home Mom

"Natalie Brenner is courageously transparent. Her new book is no exception. She writes openly and honestly about loss and the importance of grieving what has been lost. As an international adoptee, her story touches me deeply. I know the cost of suppressing grief; the suffering that comes with numbing our pain. *This Underserved Life* gives grief a voice, and thus gives voice to us all."

—**Michelle Madrid-Branch,**
Author, Speaker, and Global Advocate

"In *This Underserved Life*, Natalie Brenner opens her heart wide to let us into her grief and pain. She courageously invites us to feel with her, to weep and moan— to be the broken people we are. Natalie's story will bring you to the One— Jesus— who can birth beauty out of ugliness and joy out of grief.

This is more than a story about loss— it is a story of finding the greatest treasure imaginable."

Diane Comer, Author of *He Speaks In The Silence*
and Cofounder of Intentional

"Like heart-drenched entries from a journal, Natalie's raw reflections show what we all know and yet often fail to understand: True healing comes from entering pain, not shying away from it. These honest glimpses of a young life flipped upside-down by pain, loss, and shame will help many hurting hearts know they're not alone. Natalie's sweet soul shines through her words, taking readers on an intimate journey of what it really means to be joyful in hope, patient in affliction, and faithful in prayer."

—**Kayla Craig, Author of *Just Really Joseph*,**
Co-Host of The Upside Down Podcast,
and Writer at KaylaCraig.com

this undeserved life

UNCOVERING THE GIFTS OF GRIEF
AND THE FULLNESS OF LIFE

NATALIE BRENNER

FIRST EDITION.

Printed in the United States of America
Published by BB Books

For permissions and information:
Natalie Brenner
P.O. Box 220191
Portland, Oregon 97269
natalie@nataliebrennerwrites.com

Cover design by Manda Julaine Designs
Interior design by MartinPublishingServices.com
Author photography by Kersten Green Photography

ISBN-10: 0-9991634-0-X
ISBN-13: 978-0-9991634-0-5

For the brokenhearted:
may you find yourself crashing into oceans of grace.
This is my labor of love for you.

To Jesus, who has never failed
to meet me right where I am:
You are my favorite example of love.

Contents

"Sometimes a book isn't a heartbreaking work of staggering genius. Sometimes it's the only story you knew how to tell."

—Tahereh Mafi

Thank Yous

Life's a trip. I like to think of this book as one of my many, great adventures. Loren, thank you for the joy in joining me. My great ideas are often a little more wild and crazy than you imagined; I don't think anyone lost their lunch along the way. Hard to say. LB, thank you for all the Monday zoo trips and countless nights you bounced both babies into oblivion, at the same time, so I could write. Also, that train ride you sent me on for fifteen hours to finish my manuscript? Who even are you? You believe in me far more than I give you credit; I'm proud to be your wife. We have a lot of fun together, don't we?

To the fierce loving women who spent hours changing rancid diapers, and trying to calm frantic babies down so I could write—Mom, Hannah, Deb, and Danielle to name a few—I certainly owe you some fancy donuts or something. I love your love for my boys.

My family is made up of a whole bunch of humans I don't want to do life without. The older I get, the more I love each of you. Seriously, I adore you. We are loud and wild, our jokes suck, and LB always teases my side of the family for their love of deviled eggs (gross).

To our dearest pals, the Kings: there aren't adequate words to thank you for sharing with us such love for ice cream. Also your friendship is a favorite.

Carrie, my counselor: I can never thank you enough for the hours spent in your office, on your gray Ikea couch. You have invited me to be vulnerable and transparent, raw and honest, exploring what it means to feel fully and fully feel. With you, I have uncovered more of Jesus and stripped away so much unnecessary shame. Thank you.

I am so inspired by the pastors at our church, Imago Dei Community. Ben Thomas, thank you for helping me see that in talking about The Church's brokenness, I can love it more completely. It isn't because I hate The Church that I share of its ugliness. It's because I love it. To Rick, Joshua, Michelle, Bill, Mike Pinkerton, and all the rest of you justice-loving, Jesus-like leaders: you have become the church for us over the last two years. You have provided spaces to heal and grow, and to be known and seen. I am proud to be a part of you.

Thank you to my people and village in Corvallis. You have waded through oceans of pain and grace with me. I love you forever.

To my book team: I hit the jackpot with each of you. Lorna Bailey and Jeff Goins, much gratitude to you for the immense privilege it has been to be guided by you in the writing and publishing process. Thank you for believing in me. Ashley Ormon, my editor, wow. Without you, there would be far too many unnecessary "thats" and hyphens. You are a magic-maker and I could not have done this without you. Amanda Stitcher, this cover? It makes me giddy; you took my suggestions and turned it into so much more. Melinda Martin: your expertise in formatting my manuscript and incorporating the style with the cover blew my mind. You far exceeded my expectations. All of you have gone above and beyond.

To the baristas at the Starbucks on Oak Street: I knew I made it when you started bringing my coffee to me as I walked through the door. You make writing delicious.

Lastly, but never the least, I am so grateful to you, Jesus. Your oceans of grace have saved me innumerable times. The way you love is the way I want to love. Your heart for justice is the heart I want. May my family run into this world saturated in the scandalous grace you've given as we fight for justice in an unjust world.

Welcome, glad you're here.

When I was about ten years old, we lived on a one-acre farm. One day my dad and I walked down our gravel driveway to take one of our llamas on a walk. When we reached the end of the driveway where our thriving garden was, dad handed me the leash to the llama and told me not to let go. He needed to check on the corn stalks. Listen, I am a rule follower. For the most part. If you want me to do something, I will do it and I will conquer. I am determined to do hard things.

The llama snickered and sensed my confidence. I am sure of this. He bolted back toward the open gate, wide open to embrace his welcome; you better bet I was holding onto that leash for most of the journey. So, there I was, ten-years-old and being dragged down a gravel driveway. Finally, I released the leash and the llama went with it. I heard my dad laughing hysterically. Embarrassed, I slowly stood up with blood soaking my ripped-up shirt and rock pebbles stuck into my skin. I was so mad at him for laughing at me that I ran inside to hide.

This is pretty much how I feel about this book: Jesus asked me to write it, so I did everything I could to do so. It was more painful than for what I was ready. It stirred up deep emotions and wild memories. Some were good, others bad.

I wish I would have let go of the llama leash, but I am thankful I listened to Him when He invited me to put words to paper.

Through this writing expenditure, and since that day with the llama, I've learned this: if you're ever handed a leash with a llama, drop it and run. If you don't drop the leash and the llama drags you, bask in the fact you were just dragged through gravel and survived. You can do hard things: including acknowledging the dark, gravelly bits embedded into you during traumatic journey.

PART 1

Memoir

[1]

"He fired me."

Loren's words were quiet and desperate. His face was painted with shades of sadness and shock.

I dropped my mascara into the sink, my mouth gaping as I stared at my husband in disbelief. Putting on makeup was now the last thing on my mind. Sadness registered over Loren's face. "What? Can he even do that? Doesn't he need to consult the elders?" I asked.

"I don't know, but I'm fired. He's sending my termination letter by email. Oh, and we are banned from the church; we have to cancel youth group tonight." Loren's words pushed through gritted teeth and furrowed brows.

Youth Group was our favorite part of this church since helping plant it over four years ago. It was our whole heart, filled with teens so brave and tender. We considered it a high honor to speak into their life, to be considered a part of their safe space. We found ourselves left without the chance to say goodbye. We were being ripped away from them without preparing an exit plan. It was sudden and unexpected.

Staring at each other, the air filled with betrayal and hurt. It was only two weeks ago we found out I was pregnant for the second time this year. Our adoption was moving along. We were active with multiple agencies and awaiting a match. The week before this abrupt dismissal, Loren and our boss, Matthew, held a conversation. We were nervous about sharing our hearts with him regarding moving on to another church and youth ministry position. We feared he would take it personally, so for months we prayed and struggled to find the most opportune moment to tell him. Loren felt the conversation went well, providing hope for a smooth transition. Our journey to gracefully transition from our current church to a new one within a year abruptly shattered.

"In Matthew's words, we are 'unhealthy, toxic, and detrimental to the health of this church,'" Loren said. "So much for a smooth transition," he muttered. Rubbing his eyes with one hand, he lowered his chin to his chest and avoided eye contact with me. It was clear this knocked him off his feet. Nausea gripped me and that morning's oatmeal landed in the toilet.

As we sat on our bed tensely searching the internet for answers, the termination letter came through with flesh-tearing words felt purposefully to rip our hearts. Gentle tears turned into sobs reading the letter. It was filled with lies, stripping us of our dignity, and erasing our integrity as we were planning to shift our growing family to a new church, city, and ministry. Frantically searching for something stable to hold onto, we called Bill who was close to the situation and understood its complexity. He knew how messy the entire staff was, how tired, and *off* the leadership team was. It had been a long few years and he intimately knew.

Church planting was ridiculously fun the first year, but became increasingly harder and demanded more than all of us in the continuing years. It wore us thin, especially in the most important parts of us. It was justified by helping so many people uncover God for the first time. Releasing my sanity for someone's salvation? It seemed like an easy decision for a while.

Furious, Bill told us he would try to figure out how to fix some of the broken pieces. The termination letter stated very clearly we could not speak of the avalanche of unhealthy events leading to this moment, at least not with truth because the truth painted a poor picture of those involved. If we painted poor pictures of the church's leadership—even if that's what the truth revealed—our two months of severance pay would be withheld. I now knew what a gag order felt like.

The day's plans were drastically changed since we were no longer preparing for middle school youth group. Unexpectedly released from planning weird games, picking up snacks, and practicing the prayed-through message, our minds filled up with insecurities and lies. Matthew's words and intense labeling of "*unhealthy, toxic,* and *detrimental*" fabricated themselves into the quilt of our identity, leaving us later the taxing work of uprooting it. Battered at soul level, wondering if he was right—if *we* were the problem—we sought out safe people who could help us process the bomb that just blew up our world.

The shock of such betrayal and damage clung to us like leeches on a mound of raw flesh. Loren and I ping-ponged hurt driven questions as we drove our car to some trusted friends, people who knew us. Questions consumed our minds on our drive over: how could Matthew spew such hateful words; did he mean them and really not care for the lies he was sewing into the quilt of our identity? How could he say we were toxic, unhealthy, detrimental, slanderers? We had given years of ourselves, built our entire marriage and life around this church plant, but suddenly we are so toxic we must be banned?

What was Matthew going to say to people who asked about us? We couldn't even say goodbye to our youth group? They meant the world to us. They hold chunks of our hearts. It isn't like us disappearing was going to delete the imprint we left, our legacy, or the love people had for us. Dismissing us immediately wasn't going to expunge the dysfunction we participated in. How was his story of firing my husband going to unfold for others? Would Loren be depicted as the gracious, teachable leader I knew him to be, or made out to be a horrible, prideful person who doesn't know how to communicate? And what about our adoption? Do we tell the adoption agencies we are currently jobless and unsure of when we'll be receiving income again? This baby inside of me. Would the stress wear on me and cause another miscarriage?

Do we continue pursuing a position as youth pastors, or make a career change? Do we move across the country to somewhere new, or Idaho where Loren's family is, or Portland where it is a bit more diverse? How do we confidently move forward when everything feels so tender, broken, and confusing?

Pulling into our friend's driveway, the car sat idling as we gathered enough pieces of ourselves to walk through Jesse's door. Enough pieces, that is, only to drop them and fall apart again before Jesse and her husband. This situation felt unfair and I was furious. "I will never be the same again," I thought as a burning fury formed into a profound amount of pain. I felt it searing, piercing my heart in a way that would change me forever.

[2]

I was sick of my family faking itself into a picture-perfect image in public. At home no one got along, everyone yelled, and sometimes I didn't even know if one of my parents was there through the night. Sometimes I wished my parents would just divorce and move on with life. Wouldn't them separating for good—surrendering to divorce—make life simpler and easier? There would be less yelling, less anger spewed, less chaos.

We lived in this big, fancy house my mom and dad built with their own hands. It was beautiful. Hardwood floors, more than 3,000 square feet, giant windows, multiple bathrooms, fancy, granite counters. It sat in the middle of a mountain overlooking the tree-filled, countryside of the Willamette Valley. But inside this glorious mansion-like home was anger. Sadness. Can sorrow permeate a building meant to be home?

My family felt anything but glorious. I felt we tried to appear like some sort of ideal Christian family, put together and perfect; it felt like we were always trying to fit into some mold Christian culture expected of us. If we just got along enough in public, maybe everything else would be fine. If we just faked that we were fine, maybe we could convert non-Christian families into Christians. Because that's the goal, right? To convert unbelievers into believers by showing them how perfect our life is? To show them how painless and spotless and joy-filled we are because we have Christ?

Don't get me wrong: I was determined to change this world for Jesus. I was ready to spend my life serving the church or better yet, hopefully be a pastor's wife. I believed there was no higher calling, no better life lived, than one poured out to change people's lives for Jesus. I simply needed to figure out how to get rid of all this hidden pain, how to avoid my discomfort, how to have a better and more perfect family. I needed to figure out how to be strong when my story threatened to tear into my joy. I needed to know how to control my emotions, my reactions, my facial expressions.

Blood dripped down my arm. The piece of sandpaper I dragged across my forearm burned, rocky bits of paper pulling at the softness of my teenage skin. Sunlight tried to peer in through my window, but instead drew my attention to the stormy sections of the sky. I could control this kind of pain, the kind caused to my physical self; I couldn't choose or control the pain in my heart but I could choose the pain on my body.

If only I could scrape myself right out of this skin, escape the shell that holds me in. How do people become okay with the story being written? How do people live in their skin with joy when the world seems so heavy and dark? *Do all thirteen-year-olds feel the weight of their world like me, or am I just cursed?* I wondered to myself as anger and sadness bubbled out of my eyes. *Are all families messed up? Or just mine?*

All this pain and anger, the sadness, welled up inside of me screaming to get out. Pain boils and burns. It was an all-consuming, all-encompassing, weight on my entire soul.

The hidden tunnel I continued to find myself in over the years of middle and high school was dark and lonely; it felt so undeserved. Mom always said we don't deserve anything but Hell; I wasn't sure what I believed about her statement. She meant we don't deserve God's love or invitation to Heaven, but He freely gives it to us because He is a good, good father. I still wondered on the other hand, do we then deserve His wrath and punishment? *What* do *we deserve?* Does He sometimes cause us torment and suffering when we choose to live against His will?

The body holding me captive wasn't disappearing, or setting me free; neither was my broken family. The sandpaper I was kneading into myself was struggling to let the sorrow ooze out, and instead simply turned my skin crimson until little speckles of blood began to show up. With the release of blood does not come the release of tension within: the misery, the irritation, the affliction. The frustration of an imperfect family trying so hard to be something it isn't; a family hiding its pain and sorrow with the hope to appear *fine*. What were we hiding from anyways? If God sees it all, then couldn't He see how messed up we were? Who were we pretending for?

Minutes later there was a four-inch gash bursting my flesh. It was a resemblance of my heart's wounded rawness, but it didn't work how I'd hoped. The pain of my broken family bottled up inside me like a can of soda shaken up and ready to explode. Loneliness clothed me as a cloak. *But no one can or will know—I have my smile down pat. I'm the best Christian girl around: miss goody-two-shoes. I'm happy, kind, seen as a "strong Christian."* I wasn't sure what exactly that meant, but knew it was meant as some sort of compliment.

It was in this soul-shattering space of loneliness I wondered what I did to deserve such darkness inside of me. *Why is there a tornado inside me? What did I do to feel so deeply, the brokenness trapped up inside of me? Why is my hurt pricking me like needles?*

If this is what being a Christian means—a bunch of tornadoes whipping up my soul—and what living "His will" looks like— plastering pieces of what's left of me into a smile—I wasn't sure I liked it. I wasn't sure I wanted it enough to pursue "His plan and will" for "His story" pretending "it is well." But what would my Christian friends think?

[3]

We were standing on a cracked, concrete basketball court at camp. We talked for only two minutes, but I knew I had met the man I would marry. His name? Loren. Maybe I was crazy. And while I don't believe in soul-mates, he is as close as they come.

As he explained his goals of serving as a youth pastor and being present through the broken branches of young people's lives, my heart almost jumped out of my chest. Loren had one year until he graduated with his B.A. in Preaching and Ministry. He was applying to churches and *hopefully* moving back to where he interned (I also lived there), Corvallis. Meaning, we could be married in the next five years. He didn't say this and possibly had no idea I was thinking it; after all, we had just met minutes prior. But my instincts told me he was The One.

I'm unsure if it was the way he talked about the campers, how he interacted with them, or simply the visible purity of his heart, but I knew I would be his wife one day. First things first: I had to breakup with my boyfriend of two years back home.

I had always dreamed of being some sort of pastor's wife. The title seemed so holy and set apart with so much opportunity to encourage others. I had also "dated" too many boys to count by the time I was nineteen, always so sure I would marry each of them, but alas I didn't. They all ended in tears and embarrassment, revealing once again I must be annoying or a burden or simply: *something* was incredibly wrong with me. As I stood there staring

12

at Loren, thinking about how I was going to marry him, I wondered how long it would take him to know the same thing. Maybe he already knew like I did? Probably not.

This was an entirely different experience than the other boys-turning-men I'd fallen for so quickly. This was an out of body moment, you know? It was like I was staring at the two of us standing there so awkwardly, watching the tension and discomfort cover our clunky conversation as we attempted to connect briefly and for the first time. But just as our conversation began, about two minutes in, I felt my face flush red and turned around to walk away. I couldn't let myself feel this way while I was still technically dating someone else, even if "we" were on hold. I needed to end that unhealthy relationship.

On the last day of camp I found myself standing next to Loren by the murky-watered lake. We witnessed middle schoolers be dunked beneath the filthy water for a holy baptism. Everyone was "on fire for Jesus" if you know what I mean; including me. Parents picking up their students spilled into the area while we stood there awkwardly unsure how to hold a comfortable conversation.

"So—" he paused hesitantly, "can I have your number?"

Surprised by his pursuit, my face flushed hot again as the words, "You want *my* number?" fell out of my mouth. I watched him take his phone out his pocket. I never had a guy ask me for my number; I grew up in a tiny town of less than 3,000 people where everyone knew everyone.

It was a hot August day, the 14th, 2011. I drove dangerously fast two hours from the Oregon coast to Harrisburg, my small home town nestled in the valley. It was time to break up with my on-pause-boyfriend for the last time. I had left him with a note before camp saying I thought it was time for us to finally cut off the weird, unhealthy relationship we had built. I put my 1992 Toyota Tercel in park outside his house. I knocked on the door, and we walked up and down the block as I said we needed to be done doing whatever we were doing. For the first time, I didn't cry while talking with him about the end of *us*. I knew it was time. I knew I had met the man I was going to marry, and it wasn't him.

After one last uncomfortably stiff hug, we said goodbye, and I drove back to the town I then made home: Corvallis. I was ready to start fresh, to pray into this budding relationship, to be a big girl dating a soon-to-be-pastor. I begged God for His will to be done; if that meant God stripping me of feelings for Loren, so be it. I didn't want to find myself in a mess of hurting hearts yet again.

Loren and my dating relationship began quickly. It was a long distance, 500-mile commute, making the meat of our conversations through Skype dates and hand-written letters. I knew to the bottom of myself I was going to marry him. It was just a matter of time. For now, we would have coffee over Skype and get to know one another a bit more, before our forever-together began.

I was stationed on my full-size bed in the room I shared with Emily, my soon-to-be sister in law. I had just clocked out of a twelve-hour shift as a CNA when we started our usual date on the computer. I had never used Skype until I met Loren. He introduced me to all the hip and technological things, which is ironic since he now uses nothing technological but a ten-year-old flip phone.

It was a few months before he kneeled onto one knee to pop The Question when I felt an urgency to reveal to him the brokenness of my body, the potential of barrenness. I had to tell him. I needed to invite him into thinking about adoption now or free him to move on to someone whose body worked.

I had a long list of diagnoses and accidents, reports and warnings from years of doctor visits to lay down before him via Skype. I exposed to him my concern of not being able to conceive, to carry a life with our DNA wrapped in love as one little being. My blue eyes and button nose, his long legs and slender build, our light, brown hair: genetics passing through our own bodies and into one baby. I wanted to be sure he had the opportunity to opt-out of life with me if biology was that important to him when it came to family-building. I often had days I could hardly get out of bed because of body aches and nausea threatening to knock me out. Growing up I often believed I was merely a medical bill. Was he ready to sign up for this kind of forever?

Feeling raw and exposed, I was laying it all out before him: my invisible fallibilities. My warm mug of coffee met my lips. I stole sips in between the tense spaces of silence, then placed the cup down. My eyes stared at the light, brown liquid; I liked my half n' half with a dash of coffee. I want to jump into it. I want to hide. It seemed like eternity before I dared to bring my eyes back up to the screen, to lock into his, but when I did he was smiling.

"I wouldn't marry you for your reproductive system, Nat. You're more than that." He said with an err of confidence.

"Oh. Well, that's good. I've always wanted to adopt. Would you adopt with me?" I asked smiling.

"Duh."

And that was that. Adoption was decided: whenever we got married and were ready to grow our family, we would adopt. Our Skype dates were always about something serious and life-altering, deciding about it and then moving on to blue Doritos and sour gummy worms. He sat at his table in Boise; I sat on my bed in Corvallis, and we dream chatted about living in the same city one day. Maybe he would move here to Corvallis? Maybe I would move there to Boise? What if I quit school and pursued my nursing degree in Idaho? What if he applied to churches here?

I was growing a little antsy, wondering when he might ask me to marry him, ready to marry him *tomorrow*. I bought my wedding dress preemptively when shopping for another friend's wedding. I couldn't help it; it was perfect. It was long and vintage, tiers of lacy fabric and sweetheart cuts and pearls. It was a whopping $75 and I couldn't pass up a deal like that! I had about $1,000 saved for our wedding; rumor had it, Loren's parents may be able to help a bit too. But we weren't into fancy and expensive, shiny and showy. I liked vintage and rustic, used and recycled, you know? Why spend thousands of dollars on things you'll only use once?

Really, I was just relieved to finally tell him about my health situation of potentially not creating a masterpiece hewn by the same chisel. This wasn't going to stop him from marrying me, and the relief in knowing this freed my frantic mind.

For the first time, I felt fully myself and fully loved. I felt free and lighthearted. I was no longer sleeping in the small Toyota Tercel that had traveled with me through my younger years. No longer was I in the small town I grew up in with the unhealthy and shame-filled, weird relationships. I was no longer living in the thick of heated arguments between my parents. I had joined the small church plant in my college town, was working full-time as a CNA, and planning my dream wedding. The community I was immersed in was a dream. I was ready to begin building a youth ministry with my soon-to-be husband. Ready to live selflessly, to change lives for Jesus, to show the world how amazing life is as a Christian.

Helping plant a church had been my greatest adventure yet: the people on staff had quickly become family. Matthew and Helen, Bill and Bella, Darth and Melanie - we ate meals together and went on bike rides. We volunteered. The last piece of the leadership team was Loren and we all knew it, awaiting his graduation and decision to move to Corvallis.

Finally he accepted an offer to join the staff in Corvallis. The only catch was he (we) had to raise his own salary; church plant budgets hardly have room for youth ministry.

On the day Loren proposed to me, May 11, he also graduated college. Less than a month later he packed his treasures and moved himself from Boise to Corvallis. I couldn't have been more elated. I continued to ask Jesus, "What did I do to deserve this beautiful life?"

Our long-distance dating to engaged to married relationship was less than twelve months. Some called us crazy, others noted how meant to be we were, most celebrated alongside us. Our wedding was a day to remember, filled with intricate details and precious people. It was a celebration infused with joy and hope and happiness. I giggled my way through the vows, knowing how important they were and how giddy I was to be marrying an amazing man of God. We were going to change this world together. We were going to invite people into an abundant life of freedom. We were going to help bring heaven to earth.

[4]

2012

We lived in a postage-stamp apartment.

That's what Loren called it. But I think he was being pessimistic; many people live in smaller spaces than our 600-square-foot, two-bedroom apartment. Plus, we even had a patio. We'd been married a few months and they were just as blissful and perfect as our months of dating and engagement. Except better because we lived in the same city, in the same home, and never had to say goodbye.

My heart wrapped around Loren fiercer than I expected it to; *how could I love him more than I do now?* I found myself constantly wondering that.

Flowers were frequently left on our round, wooden table and graced with a sweet note written with his child-like scribbles telling me how beautiful I am, or how much he loved life with me. We would often be at our favorite coffee shop meeting with students at separate tables, sipping gallons of coffee all day, studying the Bible and praying for kids. We rode bikes, explored our small town, and showed up early to church to set up every single Sunday. Missing a Sunday was out of the question to us, and we didn't mind. We loved Sundays. We loved the church plant we were building our life around.

Sometimes Loren would just pick a couple of daisies for me and get on one knee to deliver them with a smile. Other times I left lingerie on our bed to spice up the long days of meeting with people. Groups met in our home almost every day to eat and pray, building a community to change the world. Or just the city. Either way, each of our small worlds were changing by living in such close quarters, sharing resources, and breaking bread together.

Living life in the church planting world was fun and enthralling, creating beautiful things out of nothing, inviting people into our life and our space and our home. We shared laughter and friendship. Life was a delicious treat. Living life and doing ministry with Loren was such a blast, I imagined how much fun it'd be to grow a family with him. I couldn't help but picture our future kids running around Sunday mornings, playing with the other kids, and being cherished by this special community.

"I think I want to ditch birth control pills forever." I threw the statement out into the air, nonchalantly, like it was normal chit-chat for us as we laid our heads on our pillows.

The silence felt loud. I didn't know if Loren was scared, shocked, confused, or agreed. It wasn't that I thought we needed babies *now*. Simply, I wasn't sure how long it would take for my body to work right. I explained this to him and to my surprise, he agreed almost instantly. Because we were already really good at doing what needs to be done to make babies, we decided to continue perfecting the art.

I wasn't prepared for how quickly my heart would grab ahold of becoming a mama. I wasn't ready to desire pregnancy with such longing that even my bones felt it. But as soon as I stopped swallowing the tiny pill preventing mini people to be formed, I began envisioning myself holding babies, kissing babies, swaddling babies and living on zero sleep. I pictured my youth girls coming over to help me fold baby clothes and change diapers. Babies popped around in my mind like popcorn.

The first three months of trying to conceive were fun and thrilling. Every month we wondered if my body had worked right, wondered if a surprise was waiting inside of my womb. I was no where near ready to embrace the idea of infertility.

My cycle had already been painful to the point it was debilitating, and they were only increasing in pain and discomfort every month. I was sure if only I could get pregnant, my pain would calm down. After much discussion with our doctor, consents were signed and my tenth surgery was scheduled.

I remember her emerging, screaming like a siren. When my first niece was born it was in the dead of winter: January 2009. Her peaches and cream complexion slowly revealed itself and was framed by thin, blond hair. Then, she grew too quickly for any of our hearts. Her chubby cheeks and squishy legs thinned too soon. From the moment she arrived, she has been a tiny, beauty queen bursting sweetness at her seams. Since that January morning, my heart has beat for her. I tape-recorded her entrance and I caught myself wondering when I would experience the wonders of birthing a baby or loving deeper than I could imagine.

It was one of those defining moments where I knew I loved childbirth; I'm one of *those* weirdos. But being invited into the sacred moments of her birth set me up for years of birth work I did not see coming. I had always envisioned myself as two things: a nurse and a pastor's wife. Of course, my first and initial dream ever conceived was to be a writer, but daring to pursue it seemed too big, impossible, and even narcissistic. *Writer's don't make it. Writing isn't a real job,* I was told.

My first niece held a special place in my heart for many reasons, but helping me conceive the hope of being a mama—long before I was ready—was the greatest. Her birth gave me hope to conquer childbirth and assist others' in labor and delivery. Maybe I would work on the delivery floor as a nurse, become a midwife, or maybe a doula or birth photographer. I didn't know what I would end up doing with this love for birth, but I hoped to serve laboring mothers. Often, I thought back to my first niece's birth, remembering the adrenaline rush I had while my sister labored.

My major was pre-nursing, but I was also thoroughly enjoying this whole church planting thing. Truth be told, I liked doing so many things I didn't know how to pick what to do with my life—and don't you have to pick one thing? I thought about nursing and births and serving expectant families; I thought about church planting and the adrenaline rush I got every time a new young person met Jesus or encountered him on an entirely new level. Subconsciously I began believing there was no higher calling, nothing quite as honorable, as spending a life spilled out for others on behalf of The Church. I began believing the choice to become a nurse was selfishly driven — the paycheck would be nice on earth but maybe I should be storing up treasures in heaven, living my life for Him, which ultimately began meaning solely as a leader in the church.

I was three semesters away from being able to apply to the nursing program when I quit college. I was working forty hours a week at night as a CNA and going to school full-time. Throw in a church plant and a husband and my sanity was out the door. Something needed to go and becoming a nurse was not what I wanted anymore; actually, it was never a genuine priority on my list of hidden dreams to accomplish. Hidden dreams are our truest dreams. They're the vulnerable dreams you would pursue if resources weren't an issue and you didn't care what other people thought.

Decisions were made and I decided to pursue the gory, bloody, beautiful thing of birth-work along with youth ministry in church planting with my husband. Building my birth business quickly became one of my priorities, specifically for women in the church. But it didn't top my responsibility as a youth pastor's wife or my job in the church office. Those titles and responsibilities, those honors, remained in the forefront of my mind. Church work was the most important, so I did my best to couple birth work with church people: this led me to giving away so much of my time and energy as a doula and birth photographer. This led to donated services and zero business boundaries.

As I built my doula and birth photography business, we were immeasurably busy building the youth ministry from the ground up. All we really had were willing hearts and Him. Church plant budgets don't include salaries for youth pastors or youth ministries, so we worked our butts off fundraising our income. We wrote letters and met with potential financial donors, shedding our heart before them, explaining how important our job as youth pastors were. Loren worked part-time at a residential youth facility and what felt like more than a full-time job for the church plant.

I attended and supported way too many births for free, and spent an unlimited amount of hours working for the church. "Working for the church" meant planning outreach events, writing newsletters, inviting countless individuals and couples into our home, visiting people in the hospital, hosting and attending small groups and barbeques and building safe communities. Among many other things.

My title in the church office was "glue;" Matthew came up with it and I wore it like a crown. I attempted to smile with humility every time he bragged about me to others and all that I did for the church. He would often tell people I held everyone together, I picked up all of the pieces that fell to the ground forgotten. I saw things other people didn't see and I was in fact the glue that held the office together. I began to believe God couldn't do what He needed to do without me: I was filled with ambition and believed I was doing noble work. I was helping to hold together a baby church and its leaders. I saw myself as part of the scaffolding for God's kingdom being built in Corvallis.

I met with girls of all ages from eleven to ninety years old; we all learned from one another's unique perspectives. Time squeezed itself into our life, making ministry and work and marriage happen.

Yet, tired was an understatement and I was perpetually telling myself not to be prideful or selfish with my time: what else would I do if I didn't do all of this? Lacking boundaries and the inability to say "no," I often asked, "If not me, who else?"

[5]

August 2013

I peed on the plastic stick that would forever-alter our life. It was going to be positive. Results: not pregnant. Loren and I were heading into a week at the sandy-beached camp where we met two years prior. Butterflies chase one another in the cavity of my stomach. So many monumental memories had been made there on those sand dunes. Our drive to camp was full of potential names for our babies; this is nothing new, bouncing names off one another.

Middle School camp hadn't quite yet started when I notice my friend, Bella, wasn't spending as much time with the staff as normal; she was spending a lot of time in her cabin lying down. I knocked on the door, quietly pushing it open, "Are you okay, Bella?"

Her words were gentle and sweet, cautious even, as she shared she is pregnant with their fourth. *Oops.* A twinge of longing, *jealousy maybe*, intertwined with ecstatic celebration crept into my heart as one confusing emotion. I tried to ignore the perplexity of my heart and listen intently. I wanted to love my friend well; this was no time for jealousy. She is my dearest friend.

I walked back to our cabin wondering why my insides felt all twisted up, emotions contorted and curled into braids of pain. *Why do I feel so nasty inside? Why do I feel so sad and so lonely? What is wrong with me?*

The daunting reality that I have truly allowed my reproduction system to be fried like eggs by years of birth control silently ebbed its way into my mind. I put one foot in front of the other on the crab-grass of Winema heading towards the dune. It's like a comatose part of me is fighting its way out to spill over into existence, shouting to me the diagnoses are my actual reality. That I need to stare the loss of fertility straight in the face.

I was nervous to admit I dreaded infertility; would bravery and faith gained during my journey be lost in the character of my story? I worried I would not handle infertility beautifully, heroically, as I envisioned myself doing. What if all those adolescent years of teaching myself to be strong in the face of weakness didn't toughen me up after all? I was scared I was not as strong as I was hoping to be, and as grounded in trusting Him as I claimed. I wouldn't be the picture-perfect pastor's wife. *Was I ready to come to grips with that? Was I ready to plunge into the uncertainty that my body may be barren and never gift me the fullness of a life swelling large, the miracle of pregnancy and the conquer of childbirth?*

I was the girl who said she would be martyred for Him, if it came to it—I desired to be like the inspiring Jen Hatmaker or bravely, gentle Anne Voskamp or vibrant Lara Casey type, revolutionizing our world for Jesus. I wanted to lead many to the feet of the cross, denying all our ego and comfort and consumerism. *That* is the story I craved, but not this one. Not the story of struggling to conceive and carry. *This will not be our story. It is distracting from the one I want to live. This is not the story I deserve*, not when I am willing to go to great lengths as a voice for His grace and justice.

I ended up on the top of my sand dune rather than our sand filled cabin; He was always there in the sand that stares out over the sea. It's the same sand dune where I cried the blue out of my eyes two summers ago when I knew I had met my husband-to-be, and had to go home to break up with the man I thought I would marry. It's the same sand dune that caught snot from those ugly sobs, sending prayers off like a pigeon. It was here, this place, where Jesus chose to set me free from so much. It is where He never fails to meet me, and I seek Him genuinely.

God began whispering to me it was okay to be sad over the uncertainties, the lack of wholeness. He assured me that acknowledging what I desired so deeply wasn't happening was worth grieving. He was trying to give me permission and a space to grieve. I chose, for possibly the first real time, to accept His offer. I chose to sit in the pain as the grains of sand seeped into my clothes and between my toes.

But my honest questions quickly started rattling off and transformed into lies who married fear: *Who am I to believe I can love a child well? Who am I to think I would be a good mama? Who am I to be envious of a thirty-year-old woman who is pregnant with their fourth baby? They are well into life and marriage and family years. We stand at the mere beginning, the prologue of our life, imaginably the beginning of the first chapter. God will grant me this desire when it is time, right? It simply must not be time yet. Isn't that what everyone says? "His timing is perfect; this is His plan?"*

I processed these questions and the sacred space of sitting in the grains of pain was suddenly cast out, shamed. Surely, He is disappointed in the way I am reacting and responding to the way our story is unfolding. So, I judge and criticize and shame myself by allowing other's words to define me, words like silly and entitled, digging into my identity and stripping my dignity: *I am so prideful.*

[6]

October 2013

The operating table was cold on my bare skin. I was lying there before the gas knocked me out, hoping the pregnancy test they made me take would come back positive. I was scheming the various ways I would tell Loren I was pregnant. I had a few ideas for this special announcement, but I needed a positive pregnancy test first.

But that didn't happen. As our doctor had speculated, I had the autoimmune disease endometriosis. They cut into me leaving two, small scars to mark where they initially removed the first batch of agony-inducing endometrial tissue.

Endometriosis is glue-like. It grows sticky all over your organs, destroying any welcome a womb may attempt to offer for new life. I was plagued with it. It causes scars, internal bleeding, and cysts. Many women silently suffer from this disease, and I discovered it is one of the most common reasons for infertility. A hurt like hell was let loose from inside of me, both physically and emotionally. I was so ready to be rid of this disease.

The good news was the doctors could remove all the extra tissues and cysts that weren't meant to reside there. This created a slightly better home for a baby. I felt a million pounds lighter, walking around without the glue-like tissue between my organs. For the first time in years, it didn't feel like someone was carving out my insides like a pumpkin. I could sit, stand, and walk for more than an hour without my back crippling me in pain. I could run without feeling like I might split in half. I could mop and sweep, vacuum and clean, all without fearing the exhaustion this disease brings.

However, the bad news was it could grow back and more rapidly along with some scar tissue. The diagnoses of many doctors rang in my ears like the pain once resounded in my body: *radiation-plagued ovaries, blood clotting disorders, endometriosis.* Diagnoses were real, revealing a reality we were not yet ready to face. Diagnosis frightened me in medical terms, but I believed God was stronger. He was greater. He had to be, right? He had a plan and a future, and that *must* contain Little Brenners running around. Biological. Adopted. *Both.* I *needed* to experience pregnancy, I *needed* to conquer childbirth, I *needed* to understand the women I was serving as a doula.

We were neither ready nor willing to accept infertility as ours, even if diagnosed. Not yet. I had the endometriosis removed, and we put our faith in the God who performs miracles, who authors and creates and perfects life. We believed in a God who does the unexpected, conquers fickle bodies, and places in us the deepest desires of our hearts. We believed in a God who could bring us babies from our womb, wrapped up in our DNA as one. We were determined and infertility was so undeserved; I was unknowingly instilling into myself the belief that the life we were living is deserving of His gifts. A life poured out for Him coupled with mountain moving faith meant He would hand us the miracle of a biological baby if that was our desire, right?

I was subconsciously embedding into my heart that choosing to selflessly pour into lives daily, spreading God's goodness to people, and spending time with God merited an easy fertility. A life of vocational ministry and church planting was not easy, it was hard and demanding and sacrificial on so many levels. Why would He make conceiving and carrying difficult too?

[7]

December 2013

I was grieving but I didn't yet know it; if I knew it, I didn't want to believe it. I ignored it. They call this denial. We invited teens into our home relentlessly, making dinner and baking cookies, sewing crafts and feeding the homeless. With our youth ministry, we picked pumpkins every fall, sipped hot cocoa in the winter, wrote each other valentines, and over-filled our summer with hikes, camps, water games, and bug hunting. We craved in the deepest parts of ourselves to reveal His goodness and grace, even though life is messy and often painful. The teens felt like our kids; some lived with us for short periods of time sleeping on our couches or in our spare bedroom. Community wasn't just a part of our life and marriage, it *was* our life and marriage.

Part of me loved every moment of vocational ministry, how giving it was to others, but the rest of me—the hidden parts—grieved the silent loss of what I imagined the first year of marriage to be.

We were almost never alone as newlyweds. There were always tasks to do, people to be present for, emails to answer, or church teams to form and lead. We were never unplugged and felt entirely guilty if we chose to not check our email for more than twelve hours. Stretching ourselves thinner than thin, we spread our schedules into too many people's lives, people we adored. I subconsciously hoped we were *doing good enough* while also attempting to teach others He loves us simply because we exist, not because of the great life we live. It was a backwards and confusing time, joy suffused with sadness, community suffused with loneliness.

Our home was perpetually filled with people, our energy engulfed and rarely refilled, our value tied too tightly to Matthew's (our boss) opinions of us. Always trying to prove I was worthy to Matthew, I spent my life as a youth pastor's wife silently pleading for his approval. I was confused with how much I loved pouring myself out while also experiencing a hidden sadness from exhaustion; but I loved when Matthew's eyes beamed at me for all I did. Attempting to be a never-ending well for those who are thirsty, I felt utterly alone. The two constant realities continued conflicting, crisscrossing, weaving together one experience. Some days I wished my sole work was at home instead of being out and about with someone constantly, listening to their aches and pains. I cared about the people I sat with, creating for them a safe and sacred space, but never without wondering how God would continue to fill me back up.

I felt this unending pressure to say "yes" to all the demands constantly asked of me. The pressure wasn't only placed on me by my leaders, but by my own expectations. My fear of man and yearning for man's approval controlled me. I could have chosen to say "no," but the freedom to say "no" didn't seem to exist in my mind, or in those of my leaders. I felt if I didn't say "yes" I was being prideful and selfish. Prideful and selfish is not the way of Him; I wanted to be like Him.

There was this sense of loss for the life I wanted to live; I didn't fully realize it at the time, but I felt as though I had very little say in how I spent my days and evenings. I didn't have a real choice in how I lived my life. Sure, we were told to take breaks and enjoy the Sabbath. But we were pressured to enjoy the Sabbath *with* Matthew and his family. Don't get me wrong, we loved them. But we craved for time to ourselves, individually and married. The amount of responsibility our jobs descriptions held were insurmountable and unending. Taking a break or true Sabbath meant getting behind or not caring well for others. If I wanted to do anything on this earth, it was to care well for others.

I didn't yet realize how much more of Him I needed to uncover in order to care wholly. Not knowing how big God was and is, I didn't expect to find Him in the spaces of pain and sorrow, so I ignored those experiences stemming from loneliness and vocational ministry. I thought He simply erased sorrow helping us up and out of the trenches, even trenches of ministry.

While I was rounding with exhaustion and burn-out, many of our friends and family were growing plump and announcing new additions and accidental-oops pregnancies. We celebrated and congratulated, pretending we didn't mind the months of waiting we were in. Who were we to make their excitement about us? Bits of desire for our own announcement and celebration, a growing belly making itself known, would creep up and bubble out of me in the form of tears. But I quickly shoved them back into myself, burying them beneath fear based questions:

What if I became a workaholic mom, holding a finger in my child's face while I answer phone calls and emails? What if the doctors are right and I really can't conceive and carry? What if I miscarry? What if I birth a still baby? What if we can never afford adoption costs? What if I become a mom and mess up the innocent humans in my care, without even realizing it? What if I don't reach as many lives through ministry as I should be, because I'm too caught up in my home and kids? What if I focus too much on ministry outside of the home and my kids suffer?

Fear began its work within my fragile heart: a heart yearning for fertility but wasn't yet ready to grieve easy fertility as a loss. I remained unsure if grieving an unknown experience was merely selfish, stemming from a heart of entitlement. Plus, I was a pastor's wife: I needed to handle this well; I needed to uphold the status of a "strong Christian woman."

"Why haven't you guys been spending as much time with us, since getting married?" Matthew's head tilted as he paused before ending with, "We miss you guys a lot and feel like you are pushing us away. We are supposed to be family."

I nodded along as Matthew spoke, taking in all his words and attempting to see his hurt. My heart rate increased while fidgeting with my hands, I quickly sorted through my memories of recent months and where we must have failed in meeting expectations, *again*: ministry dates upon ministry dates with teens and young adults, doing the work he was asking us and exemplifying us to do. The honorable, good-Christian work of bible studies and coffee dates. My eyes darted around the room as I sifted through all the wrong words in my head looking for the right ones.

I chose my words carefully and slowly, doing my best not to say anything that could be misinterpreted as rejection, but also searching for honest words. The task of dancing around and trying to protect Matthew's heart was exhausting as I attempted to explain myself: "It hasn't been our intent to avoid you, I promise. We have just been trying to build all these different ministries and try to spend our Sabbath together. Loren and I spend our day off together to rejuvenate, you know?" My eyes widened as I realized my words weren't cutting it. Matthew covered his face with his hands, then pressed his fingers into his temples.

I felt the color drain from my face as he shook his head in disappointment, his pain filled eyes boring into me refusing to break eye contact. My stomach twisted. My mouth felt dry. I felt trapped in this constant battle of us not spending enough time with Matthew's family and us not doing enough ministry and us not truly resting.

This wasn't the first time we had this conversation. It continued to resurface, time and time again, with Matthew. The man who introduced us to one another with excitement and taught us how to raise funds for income. The man we looked up to in so many ways, who led us fearlessly, determined to change the city for Jesus.

Every time we continued this exact conversation, it was like we were taking steps backwards. Deeper into an uncomfortable relationship, a relationship where expectations were skewed and unhealthy. I felt squirmy in my skin, unsure how to escape the discomfort, but desiring wholeness. I was sure we weren't doing anything hurtful on purpose, we were being misread, but Matthew seemed confident we were purposefully withdrawing. Our intent wasn't to hurt anyone, but the impact we had was just that: hurtful.

We weren't withdrawing. We were attempting to figure out life as a Youth Pastor and His Wife, as newlyweds. There were hidden losses here, the loss of wholeness in not only our relationship with our boss, Matthew, and his family, but also in the life we were hoping to live. We had hoped to live fully and without fear, but we found ourselves constantly fearing Matthew and his disapproval of where our time was spent. It was confusing: were we supposed to spend our time building communities and growing this church plant, or with him and his family? What about our marriage? As fear slowly embedded itself into our hearts, shame did too.

Shame and fear, a formula infused with hidden loss. Hiding fear from even ourselves seemed like the right thing to do though, but hiding anything always invokes shame. Shame and fear, the very feelings and experiences that led this world into the way of brokenness and loss in the Garden.

[8]

January 2014

My heart was racing and I didn't know how to respond.

One of our youth ministry volunteers, Kay, looked at me shyly from behind the protection of her bangs. She picked at her nails and quietly but firmly, almost with poison, spat out, "I'm pregnant."

The little university coffee shop buzzes with chatter, papers shuffling, coffee brewing. We regularly have coffee dates to catch up on life, pray for one another, and talk about Him in it all. Earlier that particular morning I wrote a blog post, "Not Yet a Bunch." It was my first blog post about us battling possible infertility. It wasn't too raw, not too vulnerable—I wasn't quite ready for harshness in criticism towards my gaping wound. Writing too vulnerably for the world can incite a whole lot of pain because writing vulnerably means exposing brokenness, and let's face it: Christian culture is uncomfortable with seeing genuine pain. I wasn't ready to hear another slew of, "In His timing" or "This is God's plan."

I wanted to celebrate with Kay: sing and dance and celebrate a new life created. But as I noted her downcast expression, I realized how terribly unhappy she was. Devastation was written all over her face. Wound up and bound up by the fear and frustration of an unplanned pregnancy, this dear friend was still a university student and had no desire for this—no longing, no aching, no hoping. She had eight years of plans and dreams separating her from even thinking about wanting kids.

And here she was, pregnant.

Part of me wanted to punch her in the face for not jumping with joy, the other part of me broke for her: what an intense discovery to rock your life and plans. What a life-altering experience to feel it a slap in the face when you least expected or planned it.

Kay unravels the last week and a half telling me she had been in denial and cannot accept this as reality. Frightened and scared, her eyes are a fierce blender of emptiness, fullness, sadness, anger, but mainly confusion. I let her words work themselves into me, wedging their sharp edges between my already gaping wounds.

Her eyes mirror parts of my heart: anger, sadness, confusion, emptiness. How can she be so upset to have a miracle, a life, a human wrapped in her and her husband's DNA, growing within herself? How can she possibly receive such a gift, a *blessing*, and be utterly upset while I remain desolate, hidden, and depressed? At the time, I couldn't see past my own pain to sit in the shoes of another.

It seemed ironic I had hit publish on a blog post only hours earlier about trying to be patient as we waited to grow our family. I found myself drenched in jealousy and impatience.

The unplanned and unwanted pregnancies were some of the most difficult pieces of this infertility journey to process. Why is it people who don't want children become pregnant? Why do those who desire it most don't conceive, or experience humiliating and costly ways while those who do not want to conceive become pregnant "on accident," and sometimes despite the use of contraceptives? *God, where are you in this mess and why does this happen? Are you torturing us to teach us a lesson, to force us to lean into you? What's your plan, God?*

Every time someone announced their unplanned, unwanted or now wanted pregnancy, my legs wobbled. The ground beneath me was no longer solid and replaced what was a firm foundation. I trembled to my core, silencing whatever thoughts were initially rummaging through my mind and replacing them with, *"But why her and not me?"*

Immediately following these unanswered questions ushered in guilt and shame, the remorse for feeling sad and jealous. Once again, I sat in self-hatred for ungratefulness, embarrassment that I would have anything other than pure joy for those who receive the privilege of pregnancy.

A Facebook post was being shared and spread around the community of our little town. It was initially posted by the local pregnancy resource center. I read the simple yet significant request on the screen for a mama who came in for her free ultrasound: prayer she would choose life over abortion. *"Pray that she bravely chooses love and life, even though it is painfully difficult and entirely sacrificial. Pray for resources to be provided to her."*

My mama heart leapt and a thought burst. I called Loren. "Can we go in and ask them where they send the mamas who are looking to make an adoption plan?"

With his agreement, we made some phone calls and set an appointment in the calendar to meet the local adoption and pregnancy counselor.

Tomorrow couldn't pass into today quick enough, but when it did we found ourselves sitting in the back corner of a Starbucks downtown. All jitters, the coffee not helping our nerves, a tall woman with blonde-white hair carrying a bag full of binders came toward us. My mind began racing and I felt the desire to jump up and down. This felt so right, this pursuit of adoption and babies and family building. Why hadn't we started this earlier?

My heart palpitated excitement. The woman, now sitting with us, began the conversation with introducing herself, what she does, her heart for adoptive families and birth families. She pulled out papers filled with potential adoptive families' pictures, all bound together by plastic and hope. Families anticipating to be chosen. Turning pages, unveiling faces of couples and families who bubbled optimism, her words revealed a truth I didn't yet understand or even care to: *open communication between birth families and adoptive families is good and desired, healthy and ideal, best for all involved.*

Adoptive families communicating with their child's birth family was of utmost importance to her, and seemed like an unattainable and alarming step for us to take. Skeptical and scared, we nodded and listened pretending to understand what she was saying.

We walked away from the meeting, my heart slumping with the heaviness of our self-centered yet honest questions: *Why so expensive? Why would we pay for an expectant mom's rent and food and clothes and counseling? What if she takes advantage of us? And then legal fees, too? Why so open in communication? Why would I dare to give my child's birth mom my email, phone number, or even address? That seems weird and unhealthy and dangerous for the child, won't our child be confused?*

The questions continued, pointing towards Him: Why such a weighty wait to grow our family? Why not now, God? Why are all the paths closed and out of control? This feels entirely unfair, difficult, uncomfortable. Am I just an entitled brat?

We walked back to our car quietly, refraining from expressing our frustration and fear. Pulling into the driveway, Loren states quietly but firmly what we were both wrestling with, "I don't know if I can adopt if we have to hold contact with the birth family."

I stare out the passenger window thinking of this as another loss. This hope for adoption as if it was never a part of our plan. I wasn't willing to let go of hope for adoption. Not yet. I was determined to bring his heart back into this space of pursuing it. Maybe there was still a possibility for a closed adoption, maybe there was more to this than we knew.

[9]

January 2014

The clumps of red falling from my body seemed unnaturally sized and even textured.

I explained them to the on-call nurse and she said unvarnishedly, "Well, that *is* odd. You may be having a miscarriage and just didn't know you were pregnant; those clumps may be fetal tissue. You are probably fine. Just use pads and treat yourself as though it were a normal period. Call back if it gets worse and we can get an ultrasound and remove any leftover tissue if necessary. We can prescribe you some medication for pain."

When I hit the end button on my phone, the world was spinning, the small bathroom walls were closing in, and the words she pragmatically spat at me through the tiny earpiece of my phone echoed. I felt dizzy. Nauseous. Out of control. The pregnancy test two weeks earlier blared one line, clearly negative, a needle popping my many bubbles of hope. I didn't really know what was going on, or if this was real; what was happening to me? I assumed the pregnancy test was trustworthy, but knew it could have lied or I could have done something wrong. My heart weighed heavy, and a lump lodged in my chest.

Loren was not ready to move forward towards adoption, I was possibly having a miscarriage, we were nearing burn-out from vocational ministry. It hadn't even been five years of church planting or trying to conceive and we were tired. I felt like a wimp. Nothing was going the way I envisioned it a few years earlier; everything felt out of control the moment I let my heart hope for kids.

Dazed and confused, I got up from the ceramic bowl and laid down on my bed to rest for twenty minutes before Loren came home. We had plans to meet a dating couple for dinner who were new to our church. It was our job to spend time with them, to build community, to love them.

Would I rather lay in bed and mourn the loss of what could have just happened? Yes. But that meant I would have to cancel on this new couple. I would have to say "no." I would let multiple people down. It meant I would have to feel really deeply and acknowledge my body is not only potentially barren but very, very broken. Plus, what if it wasn't a miscarriage? Then I am just overreacting and feeling all sorts of feelings in vain. What's the use in feeling crazy?

I am a people-pleaser, someone who subconsciously believes she needs to earn her salvation and grace, no matter what is happening in my reality. My job is to serve God by loving others, not myself. Since life isn't and wasn't about me, I was sure I needed to suck it up and pretend pain did not occur in my life. I continued to believe seeking God meant finding Him in all the good parts, not the broken ones. Having great faith meant pretending sadness away, erasing it. God is bigger than sorrow, therefore I can access supernatural strength to move on as though it doesn't exist—right? Living in His will as a Christian meant ignoring sorrow, ignoring even myself, so that others could be served and loved, right?

[10]

April 2014

My parents signed divorce papers the day before my wedding. Growing up, I knew they would divorce eventually. It was a long time coming and their marriage blew up in rough ways. Part of my adolescent self always wondered when it would happen: would life be easier if they divorced? I always wondered, and sort of wished. Maybe the yelling would end. Maybe the drinking would calm down. Maybe life would be a bit more peaceful; all the pain I harbored inside, hidden from the world and my church friends, would dissipate. I wouldn't have to deal with it.

The answer is no. It isn't easier. It's still messy. Family is made up of humans; people doing the best they can with what they have. Dysfunctional or not, all families are imperfect in some way.

My siblings and I sat down at Papa's Pizza in Corvallis with our mom and a man none of us knew. "We are getting married!" She announced with happiness. I felt like I was hit on the side of my head with a brick. *But we don't know this man, do you even know him? How can you be sure? Are you crazy?* My thoughts ran their silent course.

"When? Like...this fall?" One of my siblings asked, hoping they are at least waiting a few months. They had just met.

"In three weeks," mom replied.

My sister threw her chair down. There is yelling, and we began making quite a scene at Papa's Pizza. I found myself staring at the wall, unsure who to look at. Disappearing sounds nice right about now. I am supposed to see this man as my future children's grandfather? I don't even know him.

Three weeks passed quickly. We dressed up fancy, rented a beautiful house on the Oregon coast, and celebrated their union of becoming one. Everyone was sick to their stomachs, unsure of how to process what was unfolding. We were asked to celebrate something we were unsure of how to celebrate. It felt like so much all at once.

A month later, a text from my dad popped into my phone. I opened it to see a picture with him and a lady I knew growing up. A second text reads: "We got married!" A rock drops in my stomach. *What is happening?* Everything was so out of control and I needed unavailable space to process it all. I wondered: is it godlier to process it—even if I don't like it—or to smile and say congratulations, even if I don't mean it? Is it "Christian" to pretend I am happy for everyone, though inside I am being eaten alive with discomfort? I found myself grappling with God, sifting through selfishness and loss.

Wednesday nights were prayer and worship nights for our church plant. Loren led them with our friend Aaron. Sometimes there were four of us gathered while other times there were thirty. This evening there were around thirty people and my mom and her new husband were among them. I found myself face down, tears pooling on the hardwood floor of Odd Fellows Hall. I grabbed ahold of God's presence and asked Him questions. I ached in the deepest parts of myself but was determined to be candid.

Do You care about my hurt, Lord? Am I supposed to swallow sorrow and accept this story as mine without grieving this loss? Pretend I am fine? Are You interested in the throes of my sadness or are You disappointed I am sad?

I wanted to love well. I wanted to love like Him, and see these new additions into our family as family. But it hurt. I wasn't sure if I wanted to hate the people who suddenly replaced my parents, or the divorce itself.

I always assumed my parents divorcing would make life easier. Now that it has happened holidays and other family events became emotionally taxing. I laid there face down nodding into the floor, talking with Him. I don't hate the people my parents married. I hate the depths of brokenness our family has fallen to. I hate the sorrow we each carry and the pain we've inflicted upon one another, and how we continue to ignore it as if it doesn't exist. I hate the exhausting toll it takes to act like everything is normal when nothing seems right.

My parents are humans too. This has been one of my greatest awakenings in adulthood: my parents being regular people, too. They have baggage and losses, grew up in imperfect homes with imperfect families just as I did. Life hasn't been easy on either of them between the mixture of poor decisions and bad breaks; this world lacks perfection for us all.

Sitting on the wooden floor, knees bent and face bowed, I asked the question I still needed an answer to: Is living like Him really ignoring my pain in these new marriages and forcing a smile? Is a full life choosing joy, denying grief and loss? I don't believe it. Christian culture tells me to swallow my pride, and to get over myself because "life isn't about me." I should be happy for my parents and support them—they are finally finding people again—but the pain demands its space right along with the joy to eventually come. Yes, I believe there will be joy in these relationships, even if it takes years. God promises joy in the morning, but this is the middle of the night.

Matthew's voice is one I respected and revered. He challenged me to access some form of fast forgiveness. He made the situation all about my pride: to love better I must humble myself. This particular ideal of being humble seemed to completely ignore the hurtful parts of me. I had to devalue any feelings other than joy I may have had. God's voice was beckoning me, however; it kept

43

inviting me to give the loss I carried a space to be recognized, and dealt with as needed. His gentle whisper invited me to love bigger than fast forgiveness ever could.

I wanted to forgive my mom and my dad so badly for the deep hurt they caused, the fear their broken marriage invoked in me, but I also didn't want to pretend anymore. Pretending is exhausting. Ignoring the grief from their broken marriage and our dysfunctional family made me weary. My parents choosing to remarry so quickly and suddenly brings about much discomfort in my heart. Matthew pulls me aside after this Wednesday's evening prayer service. He must have seen me weeping on the floor with my face down.

We walked down the stairs and stood on the sidewalk. The night sky dimly lit itself and was accompanied by a few street lights. Matthew looked into my eyes and said, "What would Jesus say to your unhappiness towards your mom's new marriage? Jesus is celebrating with your mom, you should be too. Think about where your heart should be towards her."

It felt like there was a measuring stick being held next to me, and here I am miles below where he says I should be. I snapped at him, saying I *am* trying but I think Jesus can handle my honesty. I curtly tell him he doesn't know where my heart is. Quickly, I jump into our car beyond frustrated, and hurt. Matthew doesn't know the intimate conflictions in my heart, how I wrestled with Him through service, how painful my surrender is. He seems to just see I am not beaming with joy and giddiness; therefore, my faith is little and my pride is huge. I sat in the car shaking with anger and fear; *tomorrow, would I be reprimanded for the way I spoke to him?*

My short conversation with Matthew begged for me to continue asking scary questions: can I truly forgive my parents for the sorrow their choices bring? Am I allowed to see and name their sin and brokenness, my suffering, as well as move toward forgiveness? Or does living like Him demand I ignore losses and suffering, ignore how others have hurt us, and forgive quickly as though nothing has happened? How can I wipe away these stains like there never was one?

[11]

Life began to be calculated by cycles. Cycles consume time. Questions loomed, challenging what we knew as true: *isn't the growth of our family supposed to just happen rather than become this obstacle of distraction and waiting? God is a big miraculous God, isn't He?* It happens for many others, two, three, four times over. Everyone in the world is pregnant except us. *Why do we have to remain in this painful limbo of patient suffering and weighty waiting? Has God forgotten us? Has He cursed us? What ever happened to, "God will give you the desires of your heart?" Isn't that what He did when He convicted us of our birth control, our fight to control when we had babies? Didn't He place a new desire into our hearts, a desire for babies, for life, for the chaos of family-growth? He replaced our fear of them with a conception of longing for them. When will that conception be birthed into reality?*

We kept this waiting-ache mostly to ourselves, wondering if we were worried for no reason and being dramatic as we remained without *blessed expectation.* Without promise. Without child. Without the experience of what all our friends were receiving in being, *"blessed."* It had only been a little over year or so since we started trying.

Often, I found myself walking through life covered in a silent, isolated shame because I felt sad about how long it was taking. Shameful that I cared about experiencing a pregnancy, when I knew adoption was a valid way to create a family. I was so tired of fearing people's words and opinions; the product of most people's response to our wait was more hurt. I was tired of that pain, of surface level well-intentioned responses. I was tired of being sensitive to these well-meant phrases that feel like bayonets to the heart:

> *You're too young*
> *You've barely been married*
> *You're so young you have years of fertility*
> *You barely know one another*
> *"Just" adopt*
> *You idiot, enjoy the silence and the sleep, take a vacation*
> *while you can*

and on and on. These frequently spewed statements kept us from sharing our lonely wait with many. Together in the confines of our bedroom we eagerly prayed for my womb to welcome babies. *Twins? Maybe even twins, God.* We prayed life and healing over my body, day after day, tear after tear, cycle after cycle.

Part of me was tempted to feel wronged by Jesus, which was embarrassing and humiliating to admit to even myself. I knew how selfish that thought process was, so I judged and criticized how wrong I was to feel anything other than gratitude for the life I lived. *I don't deserve the life I am living,* I often shamed myself. There are people being beheaded across the ocean. There are millions starving and lacking clean water. I am not being trafficked, I am not being beaten, I am not being murdered. The shame I felt for feeling wronged was insurmountable. I felt like a spoiled brat. The voice of our pastor, Matthew, whispered in my heart: "you are prideful and entitled," and therefore not Christlike.

I wanted to be a mama more than anything else. I wanted to create and birth life between my husband and I, to not have a barren and broken body. I wanted to make big dinners and

47

mickey-mouse pancake breakfasts and convivial calendars for the summer days. Right along with the long nights rocking in the chair, the tears soaking my shirt along with the puke and poop, the constantly cold coffee. I longed to feel the miracle of a life inside of me, the kicking, the swelling, the stretching. I craved to conquer birth. I wanted the magical-meeting moment, to experience those first breaths of oxygen, as the shriek of a first cry escapes, and the sweet closeness of skin to skin immediately, my tears soaking my baby's head, daddy cutting baby's cord. I wanted to live the magical moment of meeting the baby I birthed, the moment I had assisted so many times as a doula and documented as a birth photographer. I wanted it to be my turn. I wanted the beautiful mess of motherhood but instead was counting life by cycles, bearing the weight of the wait.

[12]

2014

For a time, our church met in an old dance studio downtown. One wall was covered with brick, the other with mirrors. The floor was old wood which spoke to you in creaks and cracks if you traveled on its soft spots. I loved it here.

One Sunday morning when our worship leader was praying, I gazed across the room full of humans who I love so dearly. I cherished these people: my community. Some of them were divorced, or walking through divorce's messiness, widowed, single, or experiencing serious health challenges. Others had not yet tasted the sour life's lessons squeezes out, but most had. We all taste the sour during our life journey. We all at some point endure the dark night of the soul; the valleys and droughts of rollercoasters life inevitably brings.

I was constantly sure of being pregnant. One Sunday morning when I poured my coffee, I couldn't help but wipe the sleep from my eyes: I had just gotten off a seventeen-hour shift serving a birth as a doula. Being a doula and birth photographer was nothing short of an honor. Serving laboring mama's felt like a gift; rubbing feet and legs, temples and necks. Retrieving cool rags to wipe the beads of sweat off her forehead, pulling hair back into buns, rooting moms on and reminding them of their strength.

There weren't always amazing husbands or partners to support the laboring mama, but last night's birth team was inspiring. Her husband's deep love for her made my heart leap, observing the way he cared for her so gently, so purely, so tenderly. I could not help but envision my own husband as I do during every birth, serving me with such attention, such awareness, such panic and such love while awaiting the arrival of a tiny human.

I would grab her a hot compress for her contraction-pains, ice for her head; I lowered the lights and quieted the room. We squeezed and compressed her hips during the most arduous contractions, relieving pressure. I was all over those pressure points and massaging techniques. We read scriptures to her: passages about children being a blessing, about labor being difficult, but the reward being great, about God the Father with us during trials, about His presence.

She was conquering birth. Jesus was so present as the night rolled on. Over and over and over again, I thanked Him for the fascinating way He brings children into this world. These precious moments of witnessing labor and birth and servanthood...they captured my heart and I grabbed ahold of the extravagant way He loves us through childbirth. I wanted more, I hungered for this experience. Life itself was being birthed, brought forth, and my heart cracked open wider to love deeper than I ever had; I wanted to swell with life, a full womb.

As the dark night slowly transformed into daylight, she pushed her baby out and into her own arms. The moment she had been waiting for, the sigh of relief, baby's first cry, the magic of meeting her little one she fought so hard for: it was here. She conquered birth. I want to conquer birth.

[13]

October 2014

I hated who I had become. We pushed the stroller through the crunchy leaves to Tim Horton's to get iced double doubles—it's the drink around there. We ended up at the park, spending time watching her toddler play in the wood bark. I was feeling okay; but I also didn't think it was okay to not be okay. I love these people and as much as I tended to envy their life, I was okay. They have their own hard things they were walking through, their own Exoduses and trials; we all do. We picked up and headed back home to start the dinner preparations. Canadian Thanksgiving was the day before, so the meal was easy: leftover turkey and cranberry sauce.

One of the things I always looked forward to most when visiting was the fire warming my cheeks, the dimly lit room made cozy. I felt almost safe from the threats of swelling bellies. I sat on my friend's couch in Edmonton. We had just finished our evening stroll through the path of yellow leaves, walking and talking.

FaceTime rang on my phone declaring my sister-in-law calling. She is one of my very best pals. Not knowing why nervousness bubbled in my chest, my sweaty palm answered the call. We chatted a bit and I watched her sixteen-month daughter do what she does best: be wild. She has short dark thin hair, deep brown eyes, a smile to steal anyone's soul. That little girl is fearless. My sister mentioned a doctor visit and a weight of coal dropped in my stomach. I hated the weight of coal more than I hated the wait—it resembled the confusing emotions making up the mess that was me, it reminded me I was not handling this journey well. She responded with a "no" when I did my best to enthusiastically and uncomplicatedly ask her if she had any exciting news.

About three minutes after our FaceTime call I received a long text message explaining she was indeed pregnant and wanted to give me time to process before coming back to the states. I would see her in less than 24 hours. I felt entirely honored she would share with me, cared for, and thought of. And yet, my heart hurt. Why so many conflicting experiences?

A sob escaped my throat as tears stung my eyes; I felt the ugly cry threatening my trembling lips.

I hated who I had become: the person people didn't want to tell they were pregnant. My heart pounded as more blood rushed to my cheeks, teeth clenched, body tense. I looked my friend and her husband in the eyes and they clearly knew I need time to myself. But it also felt like their eyes laid into me like an oppressive weight threatening to crush me, begging the question: *am I ever going to get passed this?* They had no idea what this is like, how could they? How could I expect or want them to understand? I wouldn't wish this wait on anyone.

I was crumbling beneath the weight of this plague not being lifted. This disease of infertility, desolation, isolation. This hoping for pregnancy. The physical pain of endometriosis constantly reminding me my body is so very broken and I was not handling it beautifully nor what most Christians would deem heroically. The phrase, "this must be His plan" was bouncing around my head like a beach ball and I wanted to pop it with my sorrow, I wanted to vomit on it, I wanted to blow up the phrase with fiery anger.

The barrenness of my womb and soul threatened any hope, created in me a hunger, opened me up wide for needing Him. Barrenness endangers hope and joy. But it also creates a space for Him to move, to reside, to become salve for our desolate, tired souls. I found Him repeatedly in the pages of Isaiah; chapter 51:3b promises "Her barren wilderness will become as beautiful as Eden—the garden of the Lord. Joy and gladness will be found there. Lovely songs of thanksgiving will fill the air."

I wasn't there yet; I wasn't finding joy and gladness or thanksgiving in my barrenness, but I believed I would. I believed He would make my barren soul as beautiful as His perfect garden. But I wasn't going to force myself there; I was committed to being genuine in this process, at the expense of appearing unChristian or faithless. I craved to make my faith as real as possible, which meant being recklessly honest in His presence.

I wanted so desperately to be purely and only happy for my brother and best friend, but my wounds were gushing a thickness, bloody and hell-like, distancing me from joy and peace. I didn't know what healing these wounds would look like. Confusing thoughts coursed through me feeling selfish and self-centered while happy for them, but continuing to wonder if I could have permission to honestly grieve my broken body. Wounded and whimpering, unable to even pray, I called my sweet husband to ask him to pray.

He suggested we see a fertility specialist and begin interventions. It was much less expensive than beginning the infant adoption journey and we still had thousands to add to our adoption savings account. In those moments, I loved him so much more than I ever had. He was willing to enter an even more painful journey to grow our family and experience pregnancy. A place of humiliation and costly interventions.

Nervous and scared, I saw a flicker of hope peeking out from the weary, dark soil in my heart. I wanted so badly to cling to Jesus and not place my hope in a baby, or a pregnancy. I wanted and tried to place hope in Him, His plan (whatever it would be), and in His presence and grace. But I also desperately wanted to grow our family, to enter the next season of our marriage and family life. Was that selfish?

[14]

December 2014

My life felt like a nightmare. But only on the inside of me. The cold of December invited the mold in our small apartment and I scrubbed it away as usual, praying for a place to move to with a washer and dryer and no mold. But who are we to think we deserve to move somewhere nicer? There are plenty of people in this world living in shacks and under bridges. Right back to criticizing myself, telling myself how prideful I was, because certainly we didn't deserve to live in any other way except by barely-scraping-by but always-scraping-by. He provided just enough to cover it all. He still hadn't failed us and I was convinced He never would, even if my view of failed was off and skewed. I trusted Him with my heart and was working out the kinks of what I believed the phrase "His plan" meant.

We had entered the beginning round of our first fertility enhancement drug. I had discovered a support group online to secretly observe and learn about it, spying on the lives of those using this said-drug and wondering if it would work for us. My sister-in-law had mentioned the drug months prior, but I was certain at the time me choosing intervention would be me trying to take control. Now here we were, medically intervening to conceive. My doctor said I should be pregnant by the third round in February, if not sooner. It affected me dramatically, but I kept telling myself, "It will be worth it when I see those two pink lines."

We had a tight budget and $33.61 for the fertility drug, clomid, was a lot to move around. However, Loren and I both agreed a baby would be worth it and was nothing compared to the giant cost of infant adoption fees. I swallowed the drug in the evenings with gulps of tap water after I brushed my teeth pearly, hoping to subside any major side effects.

Plagued with nightmares, their vividness increased and caused sleepless nights. I often woke up sweating and crying, afraid to close my eyes again. I had nightmare after nightmare about becoming pregnant only to lose our baby; dreams of never getting pregnant, and friends throwing unthoughtful words toward me to avoid entering my hurt. I envisioned my friends being pregnant with twins (one of my most secret and hidden desires) while I remained barren forever, unable to authentically grieve. My nightmares were gnarly and nasty, vivid and too real. Was I allowed to grieve this process?

Horrid dreams created a deep longing for the morning. There was an ache to stay awake until day-break. Fear threatened to haunt me through the night and became debilitating. I kept praying for Jesus to carry me through the darkness. It seemed no matter how badly I wanted to live from morning to morning, skipping nighttime, I could not. I had to endure the shadows to experience the sunrise.

They say joy comes in the morning, but I had yet to fully experience it. Maybe my morning hasn't arrived yet, I thought to myself. Maybe my morning is those two pink lines. A positive pregnancy test. But likely it is simply finding peace in the story being written, even if it isn't the one I would have written. Maybe it's okay to acknowledge I have not reached the morning's joy yet.

By the end of December's cycle, which had pushed itself into January 2015, I was one-hundred percent certain I was pregnant. I must be because the sickness and nightmares are only worth it for the life created in me. After all, some people said to will it into happening, by wanting it; so, there I was imagining a baby into existence.

I pulled out the pregnancy test which was purchased with confidence. I was ready to read positive. Except, it was negative. December's cycle did not work and I was not pregnant. My heart plummeted below sea level and I wasn't sure I could continue swallowing this nightmare, inducing drug. Pregnancy tests had essentially become push-pin needle points: popping the bubbles of hope flying onward for the second half of my cycle. If I can pop the bubbles and halt the pregnancy-hoping, certainly I wouldn't hurt as badly. Right?

Our church had been meeting in that dance studio for about a year. We initially started off in a cafeteria, moved to the Odd Fellows Hall, and were abruptly moving to the theater a couple blocks down. We didn't hear this news from Matthew, nor were we consulted whatsoever about this monumental move.

"We didn't have time to consult you guys; if we want to move, we had to jump on it. I need you guys to have my back; you're my main staff." Matthew tells us when we ask him about it. To say we felt hurt and frustrated is an understatement. If he wanted us to have his back—if we were his "main staff"—shouldn't we be included in such huge decisions regarding the church we were helping to pastor? "Your pushing back is just your pride from not being included," he continued.

Questioning if he was right—if we were being prideful, spoiled little brats—I shut up. I didn't say anything further, but instead buried my frustration hoping it didn't turn into bitterness.

Bitterness doesn't help anyone and I was determined to uproot it in my quiet time.

Flipping through my Bible's pages, I searched with an unsettled heart for Jesus's words, words I had come to know so well. Misquoting Jesus is something I didn't want to do, and I needed His words for the letter I was crafting for Matthew. I believed he cared about us deeply, more than most people do for each other, so I wanted to be sure I did this right *and* well.

I folded the paper with words scrawled onto it, tucking it into my small Bible, and checking the time: one hour until our meeting. It seemed too long. I wished it were happening now, allowing me to move on. I got up from my table, packed my bag, and walked out the kitchen to head to the car. My heart raced. Every breath seeming shorter than the last driving to the church office. When I arrived, the hour seemed to come faster than I was prepared. My surroundings came into existence and part of me regretted setting up this meeting. It would be easier to ignore the pain inflicted, to not be so easily hurt by his words, to not confront or be honest. It would be easier to suck it up and take his blows without mentioning their effect.

He's always very honest with us, I thought. I should be the same. He always told us it isn't his fault if we are offended by something he has said and done, and it is our responsibility to approach him with hurts and offenses. It's always our choice to be offended, he reminded us often. So that is exactly what I am doing. I am being an adult. Adults talk, right? Even when it's scary?

I pressed the Keurig pod into its place, pulled down the lid, and hit the button. Restless, I reached for the letter with words carefully crafted to share my heart. I heard him and his wife, Helen, rounding the corner. I smiled, not too big, but attempting to seem approachable and unangry. My heart raced. Had I eaten or was I running on just coffee? We began with small talk and I caught myself speaking rapidly, unsure of where and how to initiate the conversation. And then the moment arrived. We sat down at the round table, all in mix-match seating, he in his fold up chair and she in her rocker; I found myself sitting in an orange chair as bold as the words I needed to speak.

We all smile. We loved each other, and wanted the best for another. *I think.* Prayers soar through my mind. Prayers for confidence, strength and peace. Peace. *Give me peace, Jesus.*

"You called the meeting, what's up?" He asks, calm and steadily but also clearly exhausted.

"Well," I start with a shaky voice, "I wrote up a letter to read so I don't forget anything..." I trail off, close my eyes, and suck in a calming breath. Suddenly I feel silly for writing this entire letter; these are my friends, pretty much *family.* A letter feels so formal, but I begin reading it anyway. I looked down at the paper with my hands slightly trembling. I begin reading:

"Matthew, first and foremost, you know I love you. You have meant so much to us, you are more than a boss and more than a pastor. You have stepped into our life and loved us unconditionally. I am in a space of life where I am growing weary, especially weary of hearing constructive criticism. It feels as though every time there is an issue between us all, it is Loren's or my fault. It feels as though you always point to us, telling us it is our fault because we don't spend enough time with you. That feels unfair because we are working so hard to help build this church. You keep telling us we are distancing ourselves and it's our choice to not spend time with you because you are always inviting us over. We are just so

tired after a full day of ministry. We see our Sabbath as a time to be spent together, husband and wife; we barely have alone time together. I feel tired from feeling like it is our fault for messing up our entire relationship with you. I have heard the label 'prideful' thrown at me so many times, it has become primary to my identity. I can hardly see past the word all day, every day, and it hurts. I do my best to live a life of humility and yet, all I can see is my pride and how inadequate I am. Even now, I recognize I am focusing on myself and that is pride."

I pull open my Bible once again, sharing verses with pure intentions, reading Paul's words of thanksgiving for the church. "You encourage me a lot, and I thank you for that. But right now, I just need some space from hearing how prideful I am."

I am shaking by the end. Somewhere in the middle of reading my word-pace picked up to top notch, rapidly trying to convey my message to him and get the heck out of there. I felt nauseous when I looked up at his face. I felt the muscles in my face twitch as I tried to best arrange my features, but the quivering was in control and I could not force my face to appear any sort of way no matter how hard I focused.

He was staring at me; his eyes boring into me. Then he brought his hands up to his scruffy cheeks, rubbed them up and down, landing his hands over his eyes, elbows on his knees. I moved my widened, nervous eyes to his wife, silently questioning her on what to do or say next. She shrugged her shoulders.

He finally responded, "If you knew my heart, you would know how much I love you. If you spent more time with our family, like you used to, you would know my heart and know that when I give you constructive criticism, it is out of pure love for you." As he stated the facts for me to hear, his hands moved from covering his eyes which continued to lay into me. I felt soul-heavy. The tables were turning, and somehow, again, this was my fault.

My already empty stomach felt emptier as I sat there as still as possible. I wanted to disappear. I felt so small. I felt so foolish. I felt stupid. Defeat was settling into me, exhaustion threatening weariness of the soul.

His face was red. His eyes were weary. I wasn't sure if I ruined his day, or if he had something else going on that was adding to it. Whatever the case, I was very aware of his frustration. My cheeks burned hot and I hoped my face was blank. I began questioning whether I should have brought anything up. Maybe honesty isn't welcomed. Maybe I am stuck in a nightmare. Can you be stuck in a nightmare?

[15]

January 2015

"I don't know if I'm ready to start the adoption process," my husband shared vulnerably. I could tell something was up.

I asked him carefully, "Are you afraid you won't be able to love a child that isn't biological?"

"I mean, yeah, kind of. What if we keep trying fertility treatments?"

I shook my head, "No. Honey, you don't give yourself enough credit. I don't think you know yourself very well. Think about how much you love the kids in our community: you love them like your own as you play games with them and throw them around. You love kids. All the kids."

He was quiet, picking at his fingers, "Maybe you're right. I am just nervous."

"That's okay. I am confident in your ability to love. You're going to be the best dad."

We were lying in bed when I read to him story after story from an adoption consultant's blog I found. I wanted to be on her blog, a family featured as an adoption "success." I had spent countless hours learning from her blog. Loren and I laid side by side, his arm under my neck, when I sent her an email:

Hi!

My name is Natalie. I have been married almost 3 years to a wonderful man, Loren. We have been saving 5% of our income each month since our first paychecks as married couple, for adoption. It's still a very low amount of money, as we are on a lower salary, but it reveals our hearts to adopt!

We have been feeling the itch to learn more about adoption. Last January we met with an open-adoption counselor in our area. Since then we haven't had much contact or research until recently!

I discovered this consultant agency through a blog online. We have bounced back and forth the idea of going through DHS and it's possible we will do that in later years. But we are really intrigued by the mission and heart and real connection to their clients. From what I have read, your consultants really help educate adoptive parents and that is what we need!

So, my question is: can you explain the breakdown of each package available?

I hit send and my heart about exploded its seams. Only hours later her response was in my inbox. She sent me an email with clear information; Loren and I decided to make a space to chat Saturday. I was ready, he wanted to process. That's how we roll. Before Saturday arrived, I had more questions for Susan. She was quick to respond and I wanted to come to our husband-and-wife meeting fully prepared for my husband.

Hi again,

My other question is, how do we go about paying for adoption? Is it in chunks? I saw that there are grants and loans available. But this is the main thing we are waiting on. We almost have enough saved up to purchase the consultant package through the client agreement. But would it be unwise to begin pursuing it without $15-20 grand in our savings account? Is this something we should talk about over the phone?

Thank you for your time!

Natalie

Hi Natalie!

Yes, adoption payments are usually in chunks, but they are in BIG chunks. At matched it's typically 2/3 of the adoption with the remaining due when baby is born. But, most families don't wait to start until they have all that in savings. In fact, starting out can create the momentum needed to fundraise in addition to having me help you with grant, loans, and fundraising!

Please let me know if you have any more questions - I'm happy to help!

I was ecstatic. Family growth was in sight. We didn't have many people in our life and no one in our direct circle who had adopted yet. Loren and I read through all the information she had sent, excited and ready. He was in process and recognized the ridiculous love he already had for kids and teens who didn't share his biology, his doubts were diminishing.

Taking one step at a time, allowing the process to teach us and humble us, we both found ourselves in new spaces of hope. God always moves the hearts of His kids when they allow it; I was learning it's okay to take the time needed to allow His work. He loves providing hope. Plus, He was a great example of an adoptive father; with His help, our hearts could do anything.

[16]

February 2015

It is becoming well with my soul. The February sunrise beckoned, and I answered walking around the short, few blocks encircling our small apartment. The skies turned from deep blue to pink, orange into light blue. A cool crispness rested in the air. Something about *today* had brought me to a place of genuine peace.

I had been emailing back and forth with an adoption consultant. We decided last month it was time to reconsider what adoption could look like for us. The fertility medication was taking its toll on me and I was finally facing the reality of not being in control of my body. No one is. Adoption feels right as it always had, but we simply felt it was the right time to get serious about it despite our lack of funds. If God had been teaching me anything about His provision, it is that He is trustworthy.

I am made in His image, but I am broken. I am a beautiful mess of broken bits because I am here instead of there: Heaven. I am coming to terms with this and I am learning to admit it's a beautiful and permissible thing to be a human in process. Jesus doesn't expect anything more.

I experienced this boundless burden to recite this specific song's, *It Is Well*, lyric repeatedly, so its message could sink its teeth into my identity. It is these words I wanted to become embedded into my heart: "Whatever my lot, thou has taught me to say it is well with my soul." It takes time to really believe them; I knew I would grab ahold the lyrics for my life eventually. I rounded the corner of Highland Drive breathing in the air so brisk, it burnt my lungs. I told Him I was okay. I nodded to Him, to myself, and I smiled: *it is well with my soul*. Finding this space of assurance and peace had taken time. I had experienced grief through an array of repeated layers: anger, denial, depression, and bargaining. Finally, a space of acceptance was coming:

If I must walk the face of the earth with physical pain from endometriosis all the days of my life, *it is well with my soul*. If I must wait years to experience the miracle of pregnancy, a baby delivered to my adrenaline shaking arms as tears flow from my eyes and my husband's, *it is well with my soul*. If I must wait to experience labor and delivery, to be humbled by parenting, *it is well with my soul*. If I *never* get the utmost honor and privilege of experiencing a life bud and bloom, growing and flourishing within me, created between my husband and I and God, I think I can say: *it is well with my soul*. If I am called to live a life that does not belong to me in which I am always giving and pouring out, *it is well with my soul*.

I possibly had decades of life ahead with no idea what would be thrown at me. The possibilities are endless, yet God's steadfast love, strength, and safety will be present through it all. I believe this to my core and knew it in my heart. He is good even in the suffering, the deep valleys of longing. He is present even in the sorrow. He is safe even when my world is crumbling. I recalled a verse I'd meditated on countless times: "This is what the LORD says: 'I will go before you and level the mountains. I will smash down gates of bronze and cut through bars of iron. And I will give you treasures hidden in darkness—secret riches. I will do this so you may know that I am the LORD, the God of Israel, the one who calls you by name,'" (Isaiah 45:2-3).

It seemed so much easier to give in to the bitterness, the wishful thinking that this is not the life or journey I had been handed. The asking, "What did I do to deserve such sorrow, such barrenness?" But it is in the long-lasting moments of darkness and night He beckons for me to see Him. God sits right there with me while I grapple, wrestling through the process of surrendering to Him. It is in these dark and hidden spaces I find treasure: Him. *Jesus, I see you. I see you with me as I cling and surrender to sadness. You are peace in the sadness.*

[17]

The instant the second pink line arrived, I blinked disbelief. Gawking, I picked up the tiny little stick changing the course of our life forever. I stared at it from all possible angles. *Can this be real? Is it really happening? With only two rounds of fertility drugs?*

I quickly pulled together a few gifts I had stashed away over a year ago, purchased for this very moment. I wrote on a mug, prepared my sweet announcement for Loren, set up my phone recorder, then woke him up. Wiping the sleep from his eyes, dressed in just his pajama bottoms, he yanks the red tissue paper out of the gift bag. He pulls out and unfolds the shirt I had custom ordered. His face was puzzled as he tried to piece together what this cheesy gift was for. "Is this because we are adopting? Or are you….?" His eyes widened and he stared at my midsection.

I nodded, "Yes. I am."

"No, you can't be...but...what?!" The tears welling in his eyes reveal his desire was as deep as mine.

We were just about to announce to our family we decided to officially step into the adoption process, but the pink lines halted that. Who were we to pursue two babies at once? We didn't know how to be parents. We were due in November and figured if we started the process back up around August, we would "spread the babies out."

I sent off a quick email to the adoption consultant we were about to hire:

Hi again!

So something miraculous happened and I am pregnant! 2 years and 2 fertility treatments later..
But we are still wanting to move forward with adopting and hiring you as our consultant. However we were wondering if we could move our start time and package purchase to this next fall? I'm due November. We want to ensure the little precious babies are spread out even slightly in newborn age.

Let me know your thoughts! Thank you!!

Natalie

We celebrated with tears and dancing and hugs and kisses and all the good things two people can do together. He put his ear up to my not so barren womb and pretended to listen to the four-week life within. I loved him more for it. "Baby Brenner is created!" I finally shouted and declared. I could finally gift my husband the gifts I had been hiding for nearly two years in our second bedroom closet.

Lists were written: who to tell first, how to tell whom, what gifts to make. Containing celebration was the joke of the century and there was no denying the double lines. I had proof of five positive tests. Doctor's appointments were made, congratulations shared, family members were told in creative ways because *we were expecting.*

November 2015, we would expect a bundle of Baby Brenner. Chub and sleepless sleeps, and snuggles so squishy. By November, six of my friends would have had their (second and third rounds of) babies and we could begin baby dates and stroller walks and chitchat about discolored breastmilk and deprived sleep. November would hold family walks with three, strapping Baby in close. Christmas would be monumental. It didn't matter how we did what we did. What mattered was that we were a family of three.

Our home was immediately affected. Selling books and shelves, dishes and dressers, excess was to get out of there as soon as possible. We built more efficient shelving, and organized our chaos to prepare for our newest family member. Pregnancy math was immediately written out: *soon I will be throwing up and eating a lot of rice crackers; by March 8 I will need to be on blood thinners and also get to see our baby on an ultra sound screen. I will be pregnant on our trip to Europe! Maybe we will reveal our pregnancy to the social media world in Germany or Paris or something so fantastic; by June, I will be noticeably showing like I ate a couple of burritos. We will find out the gender of this little baby in July and August. I will take those fun bump-shots with my friend Jesse. September will mark my third trimester, and in October our nursery will be ready. Then finally, we will kiss our baby for the first time in late October or early November; we will conquer birth and I will be sweaty and bloody and the gory will be glory. Christmas at the in-laws has some extra toes to count; spring break vacation to Arizona will entail a little more time in the airport and I'm sure, oogles and gawks from strangers; we will need a second car. What if I'm pregnant with twins?!*

The dreaming was unleashed with abandon. This baby had been prayed for, wished for, hoped for, longed for, and was entirely cherished and wholly loved. This baby *was* proof my body was not entirely broken and ugly within. It didn't contain only pain and sorrow, but had conceived life. A promise and life conceived within my not-so-barren womb.

My mother-in-law took me to our favorite clothing store and bought me a beautiful dress with a stretchy waistband. I ever so quickly envisioned wearing it when we were with them on the coast that summer; I would have a rounded belly, swelling with life, stretching my skin fat and beautiful.

Life before paled in comparison to these current moments. Nothing is as life-altering as seeing those two, pink lines.

[18]

March 2015

Love once appeared beautiful and whole to me, deep wells that were free and generous, courageous and brave. The caverns of my soul began expanding showing me how to love beyond measure. When I looked down to see the spots pink and too bright and red covering the stark, white soft paper my soul plummeted into the water below me with a splash. Death is so quick, and grief is the price for such love.

I experienced an overwhelming emptiness, mouth gaped, gaze stuck in the toilet. The flooding tears were the only moving part of me as I stared. My breath felt short, absent, time stopped. All in one moment of desperation I felt frozen and hot. Desolation hit like a dart, grief overtaking my being. The sears of cramping were nothing compared to the ripping my heart was undergoing. A numbing and grief-filled sorrow hit me like a train. I felt empty, yet heavy. Weighed down, but somehow floating as if I was nothingness.

Flushed down a toilet meant for feces, vomit and urine, my baby and my desire for existence left me. Collapsing beneath the heaviness is all I could do. I felt myself crumbling into bits and pieces. Concrete emotions blended in the whirlpool of my feelings fluidly flying through a fickle and fearful existence. I became a bigger mess than I knew possible. My feet found the floor and walked me to the door; as I rounded the corner I stared into the bathroom for a prolonged second and then headed to tell my husband my body just rejected our baby.

"No, you couldn't have." He shook his head, confidence attempting to replace fear.

With empty eyes I stared into his, my face resembling defeat. How do you breathe when the world stops? He began searching the internet, baby boards on baby boards, rewording the same question in a million ways in search of hope: *can I bleed a lot and have cramps and still be pregnant?* You can find anything you want to find on the internet. We found success stories, stories of moms bleeding abnormal amounts along with cramps, and their babies surviving. But I knew. I knew in my gut there was no more baby. My husband was in the denial phase, and I let him run the course of the frantic search for hope.

The monster of grief, loss and death, writhed in the empty space where my heart and stomach should have been. Lost and disoriented, I didn't have the energy to even grasp anything good. When my baby passed my will escaped me too.

I was feeling all the things I didn't yet know, but thought I knew, until then. How did I deserve such irrevocable loss? This could not be happening. My baby could not be dead. Oceans of tears flooded my vision and blurred my thinking the next few days. I was in a tunnel of darkness. The tears washed away protective heart walls along with strength and dignity. I didn't believe I would ever breathe right again. My ribs felt cracked beneath the gravity of thick air moving slowly in and out of my lungs. Each breath stung. My heart was breaking everywhere, yet it is in that brokenness my baby's love dwells within me forever. It's in the spaces of pain and sorrow that love resides.

Like the wells I drink water from, the wells of my heart were deeply engrained into themselves around this baby. Love unfolded and twisted around, a hurricane damaging my now fragile soul. Grief is the very, real price I was paying for love. Grief hurts and it changed me quickly to reveal a new layer of self.

The entire first week of goodbye overflowed with tears and despair; Loren and I were entangled together on our bed for many hours, sobbing and sinking into one another. Our hearts were crushed, our bodies weak, our hope ripped from our hands. I was still asked and expected to attend a few different staff prayer meetings; I wish I didn't attend. I wish I was gentler with myself. I wish I had better boundaries. But the voices in my head told me I was selfish if I stayed home to cry or rest, told me I was prideful.

No one really told me my heart would be ripped right out with my baby. Society didn't give me permission to lay around and grieve; to many, our baby was invisible. But he existed. He was very much a part of me and forever will be. I later learned I cannot live by society's rules; not when I realized how incredibly human I am. Humanity demands space to be: human.

I did, however, have a few very thoughtful friends during our fresh time of loss. Bella dropped off a small bear with a "B" charm necklace draping across its soft neck. "B" for Baby, or Blake, or Brenner. Whichever one it was perfect. Bella also sent me the book *Empty Arms: Coping with Miscarriage, Stillbirth and Infant Death* by Sherokee Ilse.

The way I entered the grieving process was a way I'm not sure I had ever fully chosen: in raw honesty and with abandon. I didn't want to bottle this pain up only to explode later. I couldn't. But there was still some temptation to hesitate. I feared allowing someone step on the raw, bleeding tender parts of me if I invited them into the darkness of grief with me. We chose a name for our baby; we purchased an expensive garden stone with the words engraved, "Baby Brenner, forever in the hearts of those he left behind," topped with baby feet in a heart; we planted a primrose. I had an entire corner set up for him in our family room: his bear, a vase with flowers, the two books I gave Loren when I found out I was pregnant, and a little Bible with his name engraved on it. He existed, even if briefly, and I needed his life validated. So, I chose to validate it myself, no matter how vulnerable it made me.

[19]

March-May 2015

I was furious, and felt betrayed. The days unfolded one at a time, slowly and painfully, holding horrors I never imagined experiencing. When doctors warned me of the possibility of miscarriage, I had no idea the toll it would take on me. I had not the slightest hint of an idea I would be wrecked completely, stripped of my will to keep going. I thought I wasn't handling infertility and the wait well? Compared to this ugly process of anger and loss, I handled the wait like a hero: miscarriage made me a train wreck. I felt un-Christlike at best. *Some pastor's wife I am, smiling through the storm—not.*

Every Sunday for months, I sobbed the entire way through church service. For weeks, I hid in the light booth of the theater and read grief books to distract myself from people. My job to minister to others was put on pause with my own permission; I had no will or strength or desire to be of service to others. I was out of commission and I felt fine if that disappointed people. There was nothing in me to pour out. Empty didn't scratch the surface of my heart.

Praying was confusing. I knew He was with me. He was steady and there, quiet but there. I didn't know how to talk to God. I didn't know if I wanted to or didn't want to. At times, His presence was welcome and warm. Other times, I avoided Him, afraid of feeling safety and peace, afraid to feel secure when I thought I should feel sad, afraid my vulnerability and sorrow were bad things. Overall, I grew confident that He could handle whatever feelings I had bottled up inside me. Even if that meant being angry and upset at Him, pointing my finger and enraged, without a doubt He could handle it.

Believing He could handle my ugly rawness, my frustration and fury along with my disappointment, freed me to feel wholly loved by Him. It unleashed this great understanding of His scandalous grace. As I learned He was giving me permission to grieve—even if it didn't look pretty—I found a deeper sense of belonging to Him. I uncovered a closeness to Him I had never experienced, a closeness I rarely noticed in others. Experiencing His permission to grieve set me free to be broken. I didn't realize how deeply I needed to *just be broken* in order to inch towards healing.

I wrote two verses in my journal which I carried around with me everywhere: "You keep track of all my sorrows. You have collected all my tears in your bottle. You have recorded each one in your book." Psalm 56:8. If God collected my tears and recorded each one, surely, He invited me to shed them. Surely, He knew sorrow was inevitable on this life journey. Surely, He cared.

The second was, "Where once there were thorns, cypress trees will grow. Where briers grew, myrtles will sprout up. This miracle will bring great honor to the LORD's name; it will be an everlasting sign of his power and love." Isaiah 55:13. I felt caught up and entrapped in the thorns of loss and grief. Briers pricking my heart, holding captive my joy. But I was not without hope; though heavy and downtrodden, I knew He would come through. I knew He would come through without me pretending I was okay. His faithfulness and promises didn't depend on my ability to smile through the thorns and storms of life.

Matthew's wife Helen, whom I highly revered, tried encouraging me not to be mad. This notion to "let go and let God." She was the picture perfect pastor's wife, submissive and beautiful, home cooked meals and multiple kids. She was quiet and kind, gentle and loving. The implication was I could magically be okay and not care, move on, not be frustrated with God. The pressure I felt was to let go of my anger and sorrow, because those things make life about me which is selfish. But for one of the first times, I felt confident to boldly declare He could handle my anger. My goal in this process was to be candid before God. I believe pretending to be something I wasn't was when resentment would start to dig its roots.

Pretending I was okay when I wasn't began to feel inevitable; living life raw and vulnerably isn't popular. At least not in the Christian culture. Pretending I was fine seemed inevitable when "pastor's wife" somehow translated into the expectation of a super woman who isn't phased by pain.

People would tell me to take my time in healing, but soon after gave me sympathetic pity-looks, wondering why I was still moping around. *Couldn't I just get over it?* I read in their facial expressions. Forgetting was far from my mind, and yet it seemed everyone else had forgotten before I could barely begin the grief process.

From the same book, Isaiah 29:13, I clung to His words confident He wanted my broken heart instead of my forced attitude. He would transform my attitude over time as needed, but what He desired was my heart, raw and honest. Even if that meant anger, bitterness, sorrow. "And so, the Lord says, 'These people say they are mine. They honor me with their lips, but their hearts are far away. And their worship of me amounts to nothing more than human laws learned by rote.'" From this verse, I figured He wanted me close; for me to be close to Him, I had to be honest with Him. There was no other way.

One day at a time, I breathed, and asked Him honest questions that pressed into me: *How do I keep walking through grief when no one seems to give me permission? Do I give in to culture and societal expectation or do I fall into Your arms where it's safe to be vulnerable?*

Why did we conceive only to miscarry right when we felt free to move into adoption? I felt halted up, confused, heavy, but I knew He could handle the heaviness consuming me.

[20]

March–May 2015

Grief hits hard in waves turbulent, violent emotion. A few days following the confirmation of miscarriage, I stood over the kitchen stove stirring soup, fighting the urge of meltdown. I could melt right into the surface of the pot, bubbling and boiling liquid, scorching the skin that held me in. I leaned over the steam, eyes closed, distant from the present.

Tears poured out of me, layers and layers of secrets and feelings and emotions were shed, peeled, and distributed into taco soup. My heart beat so wildly it marked more than each second for me; my limbs were numb. A cold feeling surrounded my chest that formed into a weight hanging over my head. *My baby died; my precious and so wanted baby who I endured fertility treatments for died.* Beginning with the deepest parts of me I crumbled into my soup. The stones in my stomach didn't hunger. They wanted to escape.

Grief seeped into my skin, settling into my bones, rocking my core until any strength I thought I had was stripped bare. Grief stole from me. Fear replaced confidence and my joy. Fear is more powerful than pain.

The weeks and months following felt hollow and empty, but heavier than a freight train. Breathing was a task. Quiet was unnatural as air wheezed from my lungs. I did my best to engage in forward motion, to move my legs, though they seemed unable to support the weight I carried. Tremors terrorized my body throughout the night; sleep became a foreign concept. I was in a tunnel of darkness.

The memory of an invisible presence hung in the air perpetually, always reminding me of what I lost. Thick sadness evaded me. When I wrestled sleeplessness, I walked out to the small, patio garden we created for ourselves as a haven. I took in the breeze's freshness, the steadiness of the stars showering the night. But sorrow had moved into my soul and took what seemed a permanent residence. There was no sign signaling its plan of departure; it made its home cozy and prickly, permanently poking my wounded heart.

Loss steals what could have been, what may have been, and replaces it with what can never be. Loss is losing a million tiny things. Freezing life into a snapshot, loss sticks us with what was, even if for but a moment, instead of what could have been. Loss halts life, brings us into darkness, uncovers the vapor that life is. Loss imprints irrevocable incisions upon our earth's forever.

As I walked through the tunnel-moments, feeling heavy and hollow, the all too familiar experience of darkness tugged at me. The tunnel I was walking in changed day-by-day: sometimes I laid in bed and wondered how I'd ever get back up again. Every part of me kept aching and breaking, crying over the loss of dreams and the life we would never see. *Where are you God? Why this?*

I had to quit my doula and birth photography business. I had three births lined up and made the decision to disappoint people, to drop their births and their business. My heart was hardly able to fathom the idea of serving a laboring mother while grieving the loss of our baby.

I sent off vague emails, prayed over each one, hoping for grace. Each client extended more grace than I expected, offering relief. Being a doula and birth photographer felt like the only thing that was mine outside of ministry life and being a pastor's wife. I enjoyed it despite the pain it brought me while we waited, but during this time of grieving our miscarriage, I knew there was no way I could be fully present to serve a mother. Attending and attempting to serve births as I grieved wouldn't be fair to her or her family. Or me. It wouldn't be fair to me and I was trying to decipher the difference between self care and selfishness. And so the losses stacked, one on top of the other, burying me beneath them.

And yet, life carried on around me. I still needed to shower, grocery shop, clean, and work. People still smiled and laughed and were living their lives. *Don't they know how sad I am? Don't they know just because I am made in His image and just because I wear the label Pastor's Wife, my brokenness does not cease to exist?*

[21]

April-May 2015

For a moment grief and loss, and death and its barrenness were nearly forgotten. I was in Europe. I walked to the middle of the breakfast buffet island, and waited in the omelet line as I let the atmosphere engulf me. Desiring to escape the aches that threatened to suffocate my joy, I fought to be fully there. Right where I was. My eyes closed and I listened. I felt, for the real first time in months, I existed *presently*. I breathed. People mulling, sounds buzzing, self-soaking. Pianist playing perfectly. Shoes pounding. Silverware chinking. Toes tapping. Bowls stacking. Coffee brewing. Countless languages. People choosing the courses of meals they wished to consume.

I opened my eyelids softly and I saw him, my husband, sitting in the corner. His gray beanie loosely wrapped around his disheveled hair, face down towards his plate, melting my heart as he did the first few times I laid eyes on him.

The cloud of chaos was lifted for a brief moment as I stood still, intentionally existing in the present moment. My mind felt clear, my eyes were fresh, and for but a brief moment I experienced peace in the middle of our hotel restaurant in the Czech Republic.

But to perpetually exist *now*, in the present, would be to sacrifice *then*. It would be to sacrifice remembering every moment of every day, the life that was lost. It would be to sacrifice the future hopes lost when our baby's life passed. "Then" is the past, the moments of miscarriage. "Then" is the future, the moments of what will never become. In order to live presently, I have to think about present things, not about the past or the future.

To fully live in the present, I must empty my arms of the past, the constant reminders of our baby's existence. I must move forward from the memories of holding [plastic] joy in my hands, positive pregnancy tests, only to be ripped right out. I must empty my arms from a fearful future: fearful of friends who do not understand, of people who do not care, of forgetting what *was*. Fearful of people forgetting our baby. How can one purely hope again without the glint of terror?

We planned this trip to Europe the previous fall. I was once so excited to be on that trip, rounding with a baby for the first time. But those cards weren't played; I was empty and flat stomached. Many women would pay to have my stomach. Not to brag or anything. I am supposed to be squishy by this point, and not from popcorn and poptarts.

Vacation traveling is odd because I left in another country all of my people and most of the things I hold so dearly, but my heart and brokenness were packed into me. There was no leaving my head and heart hidden at home. They traveled with me across the world and greeted me when I walked back over the threshold. Grief, hiding in wounded places of my heart, did the same: remained. I was there again, in the space of pain bottled up, begging to escape, but I was determined to do it right this time. Scraping the skin that held me in never offered the release I had always hoped it would: shame always crept in, piling atop the agony and pain from the brokenness of my family. I was sure it would do the same with this broken piece of the story. Shame is good at secretly creeping in.

Even the most beautiful European buildings and unique people and romantic languages were blurred by the stinging reality of *was*. My baby *was* existing, *was* alive; I *was* pregnant.

I vacillated between the emotions of fear and hope: *maybe I won't start my cycle this week in Germany.* Part of me wanted it to not appear that week and be pregnant; another part of me was scared to my wits end it would happen. *Maybe I will have a birthday present of double lines again. Maybe I will have the scariest moment of seeing those double lines again; maybe we will lose the baby while we are in Europe. I should be twelve weeks pregnant by now and this is sad.*

Secret, hidden grief feels the worst. It is a grief without words, abounding in difficult pain—stabs and throat throbs to the lungs—making it troublesome to breathe. Grief turns the leaf of time over and back, back and over, confusing the past with the present. Is the past already passed or did it continually flow into now? The latter feels right as our lives unfold from pages to chapters. Which means sorrow and loss don't just disappear; they become a part of us whether we want them to or not. We can choose whether to be honest and acknowledge this, or do our best to ignore our pain spots.

We are all living novels flowing together chapter by chapter. Entire stories of our own to which we have no ownership. Could it be possible we are a fragment to a Greater Story than that of *ourselves?* Could it be maybe God is writing something glorious I am still yet to see from the unfortunate, broken pieces being handed to me? What if He really does make beautiful things from the ashes? What if God is taking this undeserved and wretched pain to become something beautiful?

[22]

May 2015

I want to hide until this day passes into the next. Just two months and nine days ago, I was informed that my baby died, my body broke, rejecting a precious life. Yesterday our plane touched down into American territory to conclude our three-week Europe trip. When those two lines had appeared two months ago, one of the bazillion thoughts swarming my heart was, "I won't ever have to endure another childless Mother's Day again. This year marks my first."

The first full day we returned to America from our European extravaganza—to life at home, to routine and work and friends and church and family—is Mother's Day. An entire Sunday to swallow my pain and celebrate all of the mothers who have healthy wombs and living children or finances to fund adoption; proof they are indeed, *Mother*. Proof they can keep their children alive. Proof their bodies are not broken and barren.

I woke up numb. Loren told me he loves the way I love kids; he is proud of me for being a mom and wearing the name so well, even if we didn't get to meet our first baby. *Bless your soul.* I sure didn't feel like a mom; I most definitely don't wear the name well. Not now. Not today, not on Mom's Day. I am bitter, broken, beaten down, and missing the baby who should be inside of me.

Facebook support groups and good friends celebrated me, reminding me they saw me. This meant the world to my slumping soul, because it meant *they remembered*. My brother and sister-in-law gave me the perfect gift: a necklace with a heart inside of another engraved with "Always in my heart." My friend Bella gifted me with my new, favorite coffee mug; it's engraved with, "MOMMA LOVE is nothing to mess with."

But I knew I held my baby in my heart in heaven, not in my arms or our home. My infertile, barren womb and empty arms screamed the ugly and painful truth of me not being a mother. We weren't in any process of adopting. We were not expecting. We had nothing to expect.

Mother's Day screamed sorrow to my soul. The days leading up to it are unavoidably gruesome. I could not avoid Mother's Day, though sleeping through the entirety of it was appealing. I daydreamed I slept through the whole day on our flight home. Sometimes I wonder if the grief leading up to these monumental days is just as bad, if not worse, than the day itself. Grief is clunky and unpredictable.

The agony of this day is unexplainable. Which leads me to feel entirely selfish, self-seeking. *How could I make a day that isn't about me, about me entirely? How can I wrap my identity and heart around such a day as this when I should be celebrating and honoring those who are actual mothers?* To come to grips with the way I viewed this day and how it affected me was humiliating. I criticized myself harshly, attempting once again to shame myself into a better attitude.

Mother's Day was forcing me to face how fickle I was. The waves of life had tossed me around and beat me up but who was I to complain? I was sure I had not been growing upward and more Christlike, but fallen backwards and been twisted around in the ocean. Slid backwards, away from the goal of who I wanted to be.

I didn't often feel like the journey of infertility—the wait—and irrevocable loss—grief—was helping me grow. More than growing healthily and radiant, I was sure I was wilting. I was sure I was a sore thumb to the Christian community, unable to handle any of this pain and sorrow well.

But then grace ushered itself in by the blood and power, the love of Jesus Christ. Psalm 90:1 sneaks its way into my heart, "Lord, You have been the place of comfort for all people of all time." His grace is His comfort. Grace screams *covered*. Grace screams safety. Grace screams, "I don't expect perfection, I solely desire your heart regardless of how much it bleeds. Give it to Me to hold. While it breaks and aches, I want to rake grace through your heart." Grace gave me permission to experience grief—to own it and to feel unashamed in it—even if this seemed to be the "non-Christian" way of living.

[23]

May 11, 2015

I woke up with a gloomy Mother's Day hangover feeling an urgency to shake off the heaviness of invisible weights. For months, I was shattered to my core; I felt like I had nothing to offer God. Nothing. Neither the lift of my head nor heartfelt words. Prayers rarely left my lips. My heart was guarded from releasing my hurt and sadness because I feared being trampled, unknown, misunderstood. Warnings of being condemned and looked down upon crossed my mind. I didn't want to be "ungodly."

The first few vulnerable prayers I bravely released were on our travels through Europe. It was two months after our baby left my body. Exploring old churches brought my heart to its knees, and prayers escaped from those giant cathedrals. Even if it was simply, "God, you know my desires. Please heal my heart." But those prayers were scary; I remember standing in front of a stone statue of Jesus on the cross feeling so much shame for the depth of despair I carried with me. Jesus died, shed His blood, endured hell and I was the one who was covered in despair. *How messed up am I?* As if degrading and making myself feel worse helps; doing so only puts the focus back on me.

Often, I sat in silence before the sun rose to let God wrap His arms around me, His presence sweeping 'round about. It's complex, but I felt numb at the same time. I knew God existed, but He felt far away. My attempt in allowing Him to love me was effortless; I just sat. I began realizing it was okay to just sit with Him instead of always reading and journaling prayers or hustling off to the next bible study. It was okay to just be still. It was possible to find Him in the immense stillness, the hidden parts of my heart. He was always there in my hiddenness.

On this specific Mother's Day Hangover, I walked back inside our apartment and saw an email from the adoption consultant pop up onto my phone screen. She was letting us know of a week-long Mother's Day discount they were running. *No pressure,* since she is aware of our miscarriage, *but just in case.*

Then it was like a light snapped on. Adrenaline rejuvenated me, and hope kept filling my heart. I was so excited I couldn't think straight and my thoughts began to scatter. I quickly pulled up our bank account information to check our adoption fund balance. With the discount, we would only need another $100 to hire her. Our checking account held $150. We would drain our adoption savings, possibly making an irresponsible decision, but what if it's time? What if He continues to be bigger than money?

Tears started streaming down my face seeing the numbers matching up perfectly. I called out to Loren from the other room. My imagination was running wild with all the possibilities that could begin unfolding.

Maybe He was calling us out upon on the waters, shaky and unknown. *What if we find Him there, in the mystery of oceans deep? What if He is in spaces I had yet to venture into, spaces of adoption waiting and fundraising? Will our faith stand, or will it crumble? Will I be able to trust Him? Will my soul rest in His embrace? Will He fail us or continue to be faithful, present, and with us? Was this pursuit of adoption about more than just growing our family?*

"Let's do this," Loren's eyes glowed as we leaned forward together into the desktop, reading the numbers of our bank account. He was fiddling with the pen in his hand, jotting down notes for himself to keep his thoughts steady. We kept talking over one another with slight giggles, and offering the other to continue. My stomach felt fluttery, but *this* felt so right.

"The consultant said she has plenty of families who sign on with her who lack funds for their adoption. She is confident if God is going to write a story, He will write it, including the financial part. I believe that. Think of our fundraised income and how much He continues to blow our mind." I spat the words out with wide eyes and few blinks, too excited about the very reality we were living. We had uncovered a secret more people needed: you can start domestic infant adoption even if you don't have tens of thousands of dollars.

"So how will it work?" Loren asked. "How do we know we will have enough money when fees need paid?" He suddenly became still, the answer to his question weighing heavily on any forward movement. It was as though he momentarily forgot all else waiting for the answer.

"Well, we sign on with the consultant and announce to the world we are adopting and we need their help. People will be excited. People will rally. A village will form!" The words flew from my mouth and my adrenaline spiked with each statement. I could be a motivational speaker, I was sure. My breath felt short and there was a giddiness I hadn't experienced in months.

"And we have enough to hire her?" He voiced his wonder for what felt like the millionth time.

"YES. TODAY!" The anticipation was unreal.

"Let's talk about this, too. What if we get pregnant again? Do we keep going with both?" Loren asked plainly. I couldn't tell which way he leaned, so I went with what felt right to me.

"I vote yes. One-hundred percent yes. I have never felt so right than I have now as we talk about adoption. If that's the story

Jesus has for us, let's live it. I crave crazy." I said with confidence. He smiled and nodded, pulled me in for a kiss.

My chin raises with my determination, and I couldn't help but clap and bounce around the kitchen. A slight shiver ran down my spine and I suddenly envisioned two babies by Christmas 2016. *Calm down*, I coached myself.

There in those moments, I felt frozen in time but an urgency to move forward. It was time to do this. We replied to the consultant telling her we were ready. I immediately contacted my friend Angie from Heartstrings Photography to ask if she would be able to do a photoshoot for us, announcing to the world we were beginning the infant adoption process. It would be our "paper pregnant" announcement. I scoured Pinterest as if my life depended upon it to find the perfect pictures, poses, and props for our photoshoot.

We sat on our couch, signing papers and reading through material sent to our email. We checked boxes regarding race, gender, openness, substance exposure, and fees. We hardly understood what we were signing up for, our thoughts scattered from excitement, thinking we were on a journey just to find our baby. We would later realize how backwards our thinking was, bathing in blissful ignorance. Adoption is so much bigger than we expected, and much less about parents finding babies than it is families being available for vulnerable children. Still we sat together preparing paperwork, hiring a photographer, and writing a blog post to announce our adoption pursuit.

We continued reading and educating ourselves regarding communication in openness. We were slowly realizing it is in the best interest of all involved if there is at least some form of communication or contact. He was beginning to work in us, humanize birth families, and change our hearts in unexpected ways.

As we finished filling out our first rounds of paperwork, my heart weighed heavy about our relationship with Matthew and his family. I wanted to leave the city altogether, but Loren felt like he couldn't yet make that decision. As we signed off on hiring an adoption consultant, investing all of our pennies into making this journey official, I craved a safe space for our family to grow. I needed time to find Him in the hidden spaces of my grief and brokenness, I needed an identity separate from the church. Surprising to myself, I needed to step away from being on staff.

"I need to withdraw my official position as a staff member." I sucked in a deep breath both before and after this statement left my mouth. I had practiced it in the mirror, before coming to this meeting. Despite how confident I felt in this decision, a pit still moved its way into my stomach. I feared Matthew's disapproval of me. He either expected this, was relieved, or didn't believe me; it was entirely hard to tell. But our conversation was short, concise, and to the point. I thought.

We sat around a round wooden table, peering through the glass coffee shop window downtown.

"Okay. But you'll still be a part of the youth ministry, right?" He wasn't bad at making eye contact, that was for sure. His eyes made me feel bare, exposed, like he saw straight through me and to my fear.

"Of course. I can't not, I love those kids way too much." I was addicted to watching teenagers and young adults meet Jesus or uncover new parts of His heart. I felt as though I was critical to His work; more subtly, I thought anyone not spending their life in ministry was wasting it. Also, I wasn't about to ditch my titles altogether.

"And you'll still volunteer by writing the newsletter and

volunteering on Sundays for setup and teardown?" He asked this coolly, but his eyes pierced me with expectation.

I avert my eyes, replaying in my head what I had planned to say, paranoid he thought I was selfish and prideful. "No, actually. I trained and passed off the Sunday responsibilities and Emily said she would do the newsletter." My voice felt quivery despite how hard I tried to be confident. "I need to focus on fundraising for our adoption and preparing my heart and home for our future baby." This, I was certain of. Being a mama, becoming a mama, this is what I was made to do.

But somehow it felt *less-than*. For some reason, it felt as though I was being lazy, selfish, and prideful. My days should be filled up with meetings and saving lives. My time and life should be spent pouring out, not filling up my soul in my home alone where I wanted to be. The battle of the voice inside my head continued, whispering to me that I was prideful by taking time to myself. My rawest fear bounced around my head: I was unlike Him.

Yet I knew He was calling me to live slower paced; I knew He was preparing me for the season ahead, whatever it looked like. I needed space to grieve our loss and simultaneously prepare to grow our family. He was inviting me into those spaces and I had to trust He was big enough to equip other people to step into my roles at the church. I was learning to trust in His bigness: the world wasn't going to fall apart if I took a bit better care of myself.

[24]

June 6, 2015

I went to support group for the first time: a support group set up for any mama grieving pregnancy and infant loss.

It was refreshing in an unexpected sort of way. There were four ladies there, all who have living children, all who have endured miscarriages and unforeseen stillborn losses. They shared their stories with us, they walked us through the moments and lives needing remembered, they talked about their babies. Babies who died before or during birth.

When it was my turn to share, my heart was racing and my voice was wavering as I choked out, "You are all so brave."

Lame is an understatement to how I felt. I was here grieving the loss of my baby who I knew for but a few weeks as they shared stories about losing their full term little loves. One of the rules of grief group was "no interjecting" when other's are sharing: you don't respond except to nod and validate. But they immediately broke the rules and interjected when I spoke that statement.

"We aren't brave. None of us are. We didn't choose this. Bravery is when someone chooses to be strong in the face of something *they choose*. We didn't choose this. If we had a choice, we wouldn't be walking through this. Your child was just as much a child as ours were. Your loss is just as much a loss."

My mouth opened, tears welled, and I felt safe, known, and validated.

I remained pretty quiet through the entirety of the meeting.

They all knew each other from meeting for years on end, walking this terribly pain-filled journey together. The f-word was spoken a few times; this was a space of rawness where no judgement was allowed, no criticism, no fixing. Just rawness. Realness. Authenticity. Zero shame resided in the spaces of this hidden grief group.

I craved this space more than I knew. My heart needed a safe space like this.

There weren't strong enough words to relay the deep anguish I felt, and yet somehow I felt fully seen here in the brokenness of these stories.

"How is your husband doing?" one lady asked, staring at me with kind eyes.

"The first week, he mourned very intensely with me. That meant a lot. To know he had tear ducts and he wanted our baby. Wow. It means so much to me. I am still struggling with a bit of grief, though. I feel bad I still think about it so much. It's been almost three months. I struggle with self-hatred when a wave of grief crops up." I pick at my nails, breaking eye contact. They each assured me I'll most likely wade through thick grief until my due date; the grief is normal and three months was barely any time.

Beverly, pregnant and round at the time, lost her first baby at 9 weeks gestation. She lost her second child at 35 weeks and 8 days, stillborn. She shed a lot of tears through the meeting, a constant stream leaving streaks on her cheeks. Her lips quivered as she spoke, shoulders tight, her voice shrill. Her fear was undeniable.

"Every single day I think to myself, 'This is the last day I will get to know my daughter.' I am sure she will die inside of me. I am a planner, but I cannot plan anything past 10 minutes anymore. I try to get through the days reminding myself I am pregnant right now and I can celebrate right now."

Mary explained she has one living five-year-old. Maybe he was six. She shared about her little daughter, who was stillborn at

41 weeks. Soon after losing the baby, she was pregnant again. A rainbow baby. "Each milestone I meet with Jo, my secondborn, it feels like another dagger to my heart to remind me of the many milestones I will never get to meet with my rainbow baby. I am so busy, feeding mouths, changing diapers, running around the house all day, surviving life. It feels like my rainbow baby is stuck inside a little box in my heart. It's impossible to have time to grieve or mourn the loss of her, but it feels like it's also all I think about. When I have a moment alone in the shower or in the middle of the night, I begin sobbing, shaking with grief. Mourning the loss of our little baby girl. There is so much grief in raising a child after you've lost one. It's not the same as raising a child when you've never lost one. Once you lose a child, you are changed forever. Everything changes. Your priorities change, the way you plan changes, your demeanor changes."

Their words were a confusing blend of encouragement and discouragement. I felt a mixture of agony yet understanding; this brought me hope. Hope that I wasn't crazy, hope that I wasn't stupid, hope that I don't have to get over it, hope that I am not a horrible person for feeling sad. I felt like I might be able to walk through this to the other side, whatever the other side looks like. I won't be stuck in this space of ugly-feeling grief forever.

I felt validated in grief support group. I felt seen, truly and nearly fully seen. Validated because I was given permission to be authentic, to be frustrated, to be real, without shame or the expectation to find reasons to be thankful. In choosing to be honest in my spaces of grief and loss, I was choosing to honor my baby. In choosing to be honest, I was finding life and hope. In choosing to be honest, I was finding Him more than I ever had.

Though these women didn't see or know the intimate pieces of my heart, their validation to feel whatever demanded to be felt drove me closer to Him. If mere humans cared about my broken heart, He must care even more. It is in the dark spaces of being seen by Him I continue to unlock grace.

[25]

June 2015

When I had explained to my birth-clients earlier this year that I was unable to emotionally serve them during their births, I decided to keep one birth on my calendar to attend: my niece's. It was too much of an honor to miss out on.

I decided not to sign up for the repeat fifteen-mile trail run Loren and I defeated together last year in case my niece entered the world that day. The night before the run, there was no sign of labor, so I went ahead and signed up for the run and paid the fees. It was 7:00 p.m. About an hour later I received a group text from my brother letting me know his wife, my sister in law, was in labor. Loren and I were already sitting in bed, preparing to have a full night's rest before our big run.

I started packing up my things and prepared my head and my heart for this privilege and pain. I told Loren I was not going to be running with him after all. Seven minutes later, my brother texts the sibling group:

"Everyone is fine. b sy born in the bathroom."

I felt my mouth fall open as I sucked in air, gasping, and jerked my head away from my phone and towards my husband.

"What?" He asked.

"I think...I don't know. Read this. Do you think Avenly was born in the bathroom?"

The shock was so intense I began nervously laughing in disbelief. My adrenaline picked up and I imagined their adrenaline. That had to be a major typo, right? Certainly, she wasn't born in the bathroom?

The text group went crazy, between my sisters and I, waiting for a reply from our brother: "WAS THAT A TYPO?" "WAS SHE REALLY BORN IN THE BATHROOM?" "PLEASE TELL US WHAT IS HAPPENING?" It's not like he was busy or anything.

Disoriented, I sat in limbo, half-dressed and unsure if I was going to drive north. I thought about how my sister-in-law would have been induced earlier that morning and been okay with pretty much any medical intervention to get her so wanted baby out of her. I thought about how she is the last person on earth to want a home-birth, how she loves the epidural, and how I am completely fine with these things for her. I firmly believe we can choose different things and still be really awesome friends. I thought about how I have wanted a home birth for years; how I have envisioned that magical moment of meeting our biological baby, placed on my chest, bare skin to bare skin in the safe space of our home.

"Yes, she was born at home on the bathroom floor. We are heading to the hospital now. The girls are doing great." My brother's text came through and I was unsure if I should drive up now, arriving around midnight, or if I should wait until morning. I didn't want to overwhelm them any further than they were; I knew this had to be traumatizing for them. Maybe if I drove up right then, I could make it back in time for our run. Ultimately, it was whatever they wanted.

I packed up my things, kissed Loren goodbye, and loaded myself into the car. I needed space to be alone and a drive up north was perfect. As I turned the key igniting the engine, a voice devoid of emotion spoke in my head. "Start preparing yourself for this: the story of her unplanned home birth and how you may never have one. You have about an hour to process this; then you're there for your sister-in-law. When you arrive, it isn't about you, okay?" It was my voice, of course, fatigued and lacking energy. I knew once parked I'd be fully excited to meet this little bundle of baby; it's an honor to call this family mine. I turned out of the apartment parking lot and allowed the weighed down feeling to lay on me instead of pushing it away. I embraced the heaviness in my limbs as I drove and talked to God in between tears.

My nose was runny with snot, and for most of the drive, I was unable to see what was going to happen in my very near future: how would I react to seeing my beautiful family? Would I be so caught up in my own sadness, unmet expectations I wasn't swelling with life as I had envisioned months ago before I miscarried? Would I be able to hear her story and validate her very real birth trauma? Will I be able to comfort her if she needs, and be entirely present? Either way, as I drove I allowed myself to feel the full weight of my sadness. I shunned the shame attempting to attach itself to me, rebuking it, reminding myself He was with me in all of this.

[26]

March 2015

"I hope you're not mad at God." Helen's words were expectant, thoughtful even, as we sat on the giant rock staring out over the ocean. Her eyebrows were raised, her posture stiff, a question on her face, imploring if I was indeed mad at Him or not.

In my stillness, I thought to myself about taking caution to respond. I sat in a slouched position with my hands firmly planted beside my legs so I could stare steadily at the ocean. Steady but relaxed, I gave a half shrug and said, "I don't think I'm mad at Him, so to speak, but I do think if I were He could handle it. You know? I think He can handle my anger. He seems pretty big."

She didn't respond immediately. Our pastor's wife was a dear friend in whom, for years, I had confided. A mentor and friend, we had grown close until my miscarriage because I had begun distancing myself. I found myself breaking away from many people since our miscarriage, even if they were gentle and kind; I immediately threw up protective walls around my heart at the sound of any invalidating statements such as this one. Grieving doesn't have much room for you-should statements like this.

She wasn't the only human I loved and respected who said things like this, who tried to "lead me to the cross" or point me in the right direction or remind me how I should feel or think. Many people in our life responded to us with an array of cliché statements:

"He doesn't give you more than you can handle." (I reject this—He allows more than we can handle; we are then driven to Him for comfort and grace).

"It was God's plan." (Loss is never His plan).

"Clearly there was something wrong with your baby, maybe it wasn't healthy, and God wanted to prevent you from that." (What?)

"It wasn't God's time for you to be pregnant."

"He is in control." (But what about free will and brokenness due to our choices in the Garden?)

"Find joy in your trials." (This often takes time).

"At least you can get pregnant." (This doesn't help).

"He gives and takes away life."

"Don't be mad at God. Don't blame God."

"It could be worse: think about Job," said to me the day after I miscarried.

The oxymoron of "he gives and takes away life" and "don't blame God" are ridiculous to me. I get it, though. I had thrown those statements around in other peoples' times of trial and suffering. I didn't know how to respond to pain and assumed those words would help. *Or did I? Was it for them or for me that I used those clichés in people's true times of suffering? Was it to make me feel better like I had somehow spiritually pointed them towards God in their grief?* I have learned to stop myself from saying much. I try to ask myself what the point is in whatever response I have loaded to release: is it to see their pain and validate or is it to show them I know where they should be emotionally? I don't think we can ever really tell people where they should be.

We sat on a rough, rocky ledge together with our legs and feet dangling high above the sand. Our eyes focused on the ocean's vastness. I pondered these things and wondered why Christians felt the need to make such statements. I pondered why, even I felt the need to attempt salve with stinging salt to raw wounds of the heart. Why was there so much shame in just allowing ourselves to feel whatever demanded to be felt? To breathe in the reality of pain, grief, and sorrow? We give people the requisite day or two (or however long we feel is appropriate) to feel the sting of loss and then expect everyone to be "fine" and move on as though nothing was lost. Why is there so much judgement when we choose honesty through grief and grief takes time? Why are we shocked when someone is still sad about a loss years later?

I decided again, there on that ledge, to continue to be honest. I would continue to find Him in the honesty even if it appeared ugly and "ungodly." It was on that rock, staring out over the sand and the sea, I realized to the depths of me how different everyone is. People grieve, process, and heal differently. Which also means loving one person looks different than loving the next: we aren't all the same. Our Christian (and quite possibly our culture's) textbook liked to lay out a "10 Ways To Respond To Someone Who's Grieving" manual—but I was discovering maybe everyone is different. Maybe there isn't a manual or a specific way to love people in grief: maybe the only way we can communally love people is by giving them permission to just *be*.

I may not find permission from society to grieve and acknowledge our loss, but I am finding it in Him. I am finding a freedom in Him I had never experienced. The freedom of gut-wrenching, pain-filled, ugly honesty.

[27]

June 22, 2015

A friend from Boise contacted me via email, letting me know she worked with an adoption attorney; she said an expectant mama had walked into their office earlier that day, asking about making an adoption plan. My heart leapt as I read through the email.

We had announced less than a month earlier our adoption journey. We were finishing up our training hours and scheduling our home study, had yet to make our family profile book. Eagerly, I responded asking if we could present to her.

She gave us 24 hours to create a family profile book and expedite it to her; Loren and I stayed up until 4 am pulling pictures from every corner of our internet and hard drives. We wrote sentences and captions, hoping to look awesome. We wanted her to see this book and find comfort: we were stable, we had a lot of love to give a child, we also hoped to include her in our life. On the last page, we wrote a little note, letting her know we truly did see her as an extension of family, if she were to choose us to parent her child. This transition of our heart is not lost on me: how we went from fearing communication with our future child's birth family to hoping for it is an act of grace. I was unaware how freeing it would be to read and discover how beneficial openness in adoption really is for everyone involved.

The day finally arrived and she was a state away looking over our profile book. It was between us and another family who owned a dairy farm.

There were so many emotions mixed up inside of me. We had known about this mama for weeks, waiting for her to return to the attorney's office. We'd been praying over her situation and her baby, wondering if her baby would one day be our baby too. Many well-meaning people warned us against becoming too attached too early; but it was impossible not to. How could I not attach my heart to someone I was genuinely praying for? How could I not love someone who may be carrying the baby who will join our family? How could I not love a mama who continues to choose life for her little one, despite the sacrifice it is to her? I shouldn't have been surprised at these warnings; our society is uncomfortable with risking hearts. We are wary to choose love, especially when it means we are likely to get hurt.

At this point, presenting our family profile book for the first time, I was hope filled. I was joy filled. I was in awe of the journey we were on, though I am pain filled. So many things. Maybe after ten presentations and ten rejections our hearts would become more guarded, more closed off, less hopeful. But maybe not. Maybe He was using each situation to open our hearts wider than ever, making space with the pain of waiting and "no." Maybe if we continued to make this less about us finding "our baby" and more about being available for an expectant mother and her baby, then I wouldn't be crushed with every "no."

I laid in bed, refreshing my email every two minutes, waiting to see the attorney's email in my inbox. Finally, the email was there, my stomach churned and my fingers were quick: this could be the day our life is changed forever. This could be the day an expectant mama chooses us to parent her baby.

Natalie,

I just wanted to let you know that M chose two local couples to interview to parent her baby. I am sorry she did not choose you. Good luck.

She did not choose us. We were bummed but we were at peace. The peace shocked me. I expected to crash if she said "no." But the praying heart I had wrapped up in Him was wrapped up in His peace. He was showing me adoption is not about the [potential] adoptive family. God used her to open our hearts wider for love, for His people, for expectant and birth families.

I realized in those moments, laying on our white comforter, hope is never wasted. Even if what I hoped for did not come to fruition as I had imagined, *as I had hoped.* Hope is placing the beautifully vulnerable parts of ourselves, our raw selves, into His hands. Hope is letting Him know our desires and trusting Him with them.

I believe hope moves His heart; but hope also moves us into healing spaces, it moves our hearts into His hands.

[28]

July 2015

A village was forming right before my eyes. It was amazing, you know? Breathtaking. My blood rushed as people I knew well and barely knew at all poured their belongings and treasures into my friend's garage as we prepared for a big yard sale. My friend, Jesse, was expecting her first baby to be born in August. It was a hot July week when we decided to sell everything we could. Rough timing. Adoption fundraisers united our village in ways nothing else ever had.

People from near and far were donating items big and small to our sale so we could make as much as possible: cars, boats, work out machines, clothes, cookies and lemonade. We woke up early, categorized the lawn of items into women's clothes, men's clothes, kid's and babies' clothes. We had a table of knick knacks, dishes, toys, and lamps. Picture frames and furniture. Cookies sold by little red-headed boys, lemonade sold by my pregnant friend, my sister brought a kiddie pool filled with puppies, and a jar available to donate extra cash towards our adoption.

We had lost our biological baby only months earlier and were still grieving as the waves hit, but we were also on our path to becoming a family for another. Soon after signing our papers with our adoption consultant, we realized adoption wasn't about finding a baby for us, but more about being a family for vulnerable children. We were now an available family with two different adoption attorneys we had connections with, waiting to be a resource and a forever home, for a baby or two or three. *Triplets?* We were in for whatever and we were eager.

I found myself perpetually raising my eyebrows, jaw dropping, amazed at the village forming. We hadn't been matched with an expectant mama making an adoption plan yet, but had people pouring out their hand-me-downs of baby items. Our little nursery was becoming organized. I found Him there in the nursery time and time again, as I rocked in the wooden chair, praying for our future baby via adoption while simultaneously grieving the brokenness in my body. It was a room filled with big, opposing emotions, the air thickened with both sorrow and anticipation. I would find myself crying out about the betrayal of my body one moment only to be rejoicing in hope as tears streamed down my face at the complexities of adoption. Adoption is redemption but adoption is born out of tragedy.

Time and time again, rocking in the wooden chair or kneeling on the plush rug of the nursery, I found myself revisiting the words of Isaiah. Chapter 61 verses 1b-3 says, "He has sent me to comfort the brokenhearted and to announce that captives will be released and prisoners will be freed. He has sent me to tell those who mourn that the time of the Lord's favor has come...To all who mourn in Israel, He will give beauty for ashes, joy instead of mourning, praise instead of despair. For the Lord has planted them like strong and graceful oaks for his own glory." I banked on His promises. His people, our village, was being created and it was beautiful. Though I still mourned the loss of our first biological baby, I knew He was giving beauty for ashes. Praise rang on my lips for the goodness of community.

Our village was forming and among them were people in our city and community, including those online and across oceans. Some of our village had walked through loss, others were in the process of adoption, and still others were simply people who loved us. The diversity of our village did not escape me, and I was perpetually blown away by how our one family's journey could rally so many others. Emails flooded my inbox with inquiries of both miscarriage and adoption, of ministry and family life, of people pledging to help and support us in every single way they could.

Our village was forming and it was a beautiful picture of all the brokenness, all the fragments of this world, coming together in unity for one purpose: to make a family out of love. Love grows families.

[29]

July 2015

"Your pride is ugly." Matthew's eyes bore into mine, unwavering, as he tried to hand me the $20 bill out his car window. I was trying to be polite in denying the offer; we didn't need his $20 desperately—we still had some cash left until payday. His words pierced me, though, and I stared right back at him with my mouth slacking. I was in a tired daze as I moved my hand up to his and grabbed the $20.

"Thank you." The words fell out my mouth like an automated response. It wasn't the first time the pride-label was thrown at me, slapping me with humiliation. It was quite possibly the thirty-millionth time. Maybe the gazillionth. I wasn't sure but I was put in my place by Matthew once again, reminded how prideful I was.

We walked inside our small apartment, the sky dark.

"I think it's time to start considering leaving this city. Maybe find a new church to be on staff with." Loren's voice was careful, steady, hesitant even. To uproot our life during an adoption seemed irresponsible, but I had been desperate to leave for over a year. My heart was weary.

"You know how I feel about that, love." I steadied my voice, attempting to ignore the quickening of my heart inside my chest, trying to wipe the smile inevitably creeping into my face.

"I just..." he rubbed his forehead as he struggled to find the right words, as he so often did, "I just think that for a time it was okay for us to be under this stress and anxiety, on this leadership team, and help plant this church.." he sat at our table, fidgeting with his square wallet, eyes staring through the leather, "but if we are going to adopt and bring a baby into our family...it may be time to find a more stable and healthy space to live. You know? Less tension." His knee was bouncing as he rubbed his hands up and down his thighs. "But it's hard thinking about leaving the students."

I knew. I knew it for over a year we were done here, but was waiting for him to meet me in that painful admission. It is hard changing the things we hope for, you know? It is hard deciphering between loving criticism and harsh manipulation and even spiritual abuse. It is hard to uproot all you know when your entire marriage has been built around a community, a ministry built from scratch with your own money and tears. It was so much more than a job.

The vacillating realities of anticipating what could be next and remorse from losing our community hit me. My limbs were tingly but I felt right in my soul. It felt right to talk about this with each other, to think there may be something else for us, something a bit safer for our hearts so we were able to serve others better, able to become a family in a healthy environment.

We found ourselves in Bill and Bella's home once again, sitting crisscross applesauce on their living room floor. They were our safe people, our wise people, our counsel. "We think it's time to go, but how do you know when it's time? How do you know you're not just fleeing because it's hard? How do you know you're not just being selfish? How do you know if it's the right thing to do?" The questions we had about the "right" thing to do were falling out of our mouths, we were talking in circles, covering every angle, *stumped*. We wanted someone to just tell us what to do.

The whole notion of pursuing "God's will" for our life was much less about practicalities of where to go to school, what church to be on staff with, when to start trying to have a baby, etcetera. And more about our hearts being in line with His. God's will for us wasn't to be found in *when* to leave this church, but rather *how* we went about it. How would we care for His people as we pursued a transition out? Our fears piled high, too many to count, and we continued to narrow our focus on our most desired aspect of this: to transition well, to transition with integrity.

Bill and Bella let us lay all our insecurities, fear, and frustrations out onto their floor. They let us be ugly and honest, as we navigated all the ways we hurt inside and all of the fears we had about moving on. Did we do everything we could to fix what was broken? Is it even possible to mend what has been shattered? We shared our selfish desires and our not-so-selfish desires, our vulnerable feelings. They never shamed us.

How do we simply "move on" from a community we built our life and marriage around? How will anyone understand, without disclosing the intimate details? The details weren't pretty. They were also complex. It wasn't all bad; we had so many beautiful memories too. At best, our relationship with Matthew was difficult to process and explain.

We had grown some contempt in our hearts towards Matthew. Our relationship once seemed wonderful but slowly transformed into something more than uncomfortable, *unhealthy,* maybe even abusive. Bill and Bella validated this.

We had attempted to have honest conversations many times with Matthew, but they always ended in frustration and being misunderstood. They often ended with him telling us: "The reason this is happening is because you don't know my heart. You would know my heart if you spent more time with me."

It was here in the spaces of Bill and Bella's living room we felt, for the first time, a freedom to hope for something different. We began imagining a ministry and leadership team we could serve with without fear. It was time to start planning our transition.

[30]

July 19, 2015

I walked out of the room we used as the sanctuary, climbed the stairs, found a hidden room, and balled my eyes out.

It was an abnormal Sunday to begin with, but that had become our normal: never knowing what to expect. Some church planters from Washington were visiting our church. This was pretty normal being part of a church plant: brand new church starts coming for prayer, thanking us for support, our church taking up a financial offering for them, and giving encouragement.

It wasn't the first time I had to leave the theater-sanctuary. After my miscarriage, I often wouldn't even enter the room. But this Sunday, I had. I entered and I decided to sit in service because it had been months since I had done so. I had been avoiding people, the people I love and cherish, because I needed to protect my heart. Grieving demands protecting our hearts. Sometimes people, out of their uncertainty with suffering and other's pain, say things that perpetuate the pain. Sometimes, well-meaning and loving people dismiss pain and loss and suffering because they don't know how to engage in the brokenness. Suffering is uncomfortable for everyone who comes into contact with the sufferer. I needed a break from that. I needed a space to protect my heart and that space became the light booth for months on end.

But this particular Sunday, I chose to sit in the sanctuary.

It didn't dawn on me how insanely ignorant we are as humans, until we lost our baby. Now I see it everywhere; I notice the way we keep a distance from entering pain, how we don't *really* care how our words may impact someone. I secretly scoffed at people, too, the "super sensitive" people asking others to work on becoming a bit more "politically correct" in the way they speak. But I now realized it was so much more than being "politically correct" in our language: *it was about really caring about the hearts of humans.*

I was fumbling through the pages of my bible, restless in the red, velvet, theater seat, when I heard Matthew invite the other church planters up to the stage—our "future daughter church." I felt unnaturally quiet as I watched them unfold shirts for our pastor and his wife. The giant words "I'M EXPECTING" was printed on them, everyone laughing, my pulse pounding like a hammer to a nail.

This "expecting" joke used to fly right over my head, felt normal and permissive, funny even. Until we finally conceived a baby only to have our expectation ripped out of our hearts and my body unfairly. It is a pure-hearted joke, intentions were never to hurt anyone, but it felt unseemingly cruel to someone like me. Someone infertile and broken, whose body rejects expectation.

They started using the analogy of "miscarriages" in relation to losing staff members; I felt so entirely uncared for. These trigger words should not be used in front of a mass of people who are living stories we don't fully know; *and what about me? They know we just lost a baby.* To talk about miscarriage as if they knew the grief when they didn't. To compare someone leaving our church to someone losing their baby. I looked down at my chest to see my skin mottling. Stress seeps through my skin.

Avoiding notice, I quickly stood up to escape the sanctuary. My body tingled from the tips of my fingers to the tips of my toes, the air attempting to escape my lungs was thick like molasses and I couldn't breathe correctly. I fixated on withholding my tears, my sorrow from bleeding through my eyes, and sat hidden in the actors changing room. The stench of alcohol invaded my senses and my eyes burned as I finally let the tears fall. My body shivered, trembling as the lies of shame forced their way into my head: *you are pitiful, you are prideful, they weren't trying to hurt you, you baby.* I shook my head and whispered, "No, I have permission to cry. I have permission to grieve, to feel real feelings."

I catch every tear, Natalie. I record your sorrows, Jesus whispered.

My chest ached. It seemed to always be aching and tight. My eyelids were hot and gummy, I was sure my face was puffy and flushed. Church was long over and I still had to tear down the hospitality set up. I had stalled as long as I could, hiding away and reluctant to move from my secret space. I glanced around the filthy small room, empty glass beer bottles and ripped carpet, lips pressed together, I gathered enough strength to walk down the stairwell. I was shaking and wanted nothing more than to be invisible.

I was hoping I had avoided most people, evaded any conversations—church was over a while ago and people had gone home. I walked back into the theater we call our sanctuary, the space that now has held more hurt than healing for me.

I continued to struggle with hating who I had become: the one who was easily hurt, a cut perpetuating, running deeper than any other wound I had previously. They run straight through me, my wounds, holes of harrowing agony all over my body like bullet holes shot straight through. I am embarrassed these things sting like vinegar and salt, I am humiliated I am this sensitive. That the mere thought of expectancy or pregnancy or miscarriage or people trying to conceive breaks me. *Isn't sensitivity weakness?*

Something significant in me snapped when our baby died; that something hadn't *un*snapped yet. It hadn't been put back together and I was afraid it never would. I knew God was with me, I knew He was with me in the mess making up who I was, but my stomach throbbed and my heart jolted and my insides twirled around threatening to take me down from the inside out. I knew He was with me, giving me permission to *be* in the broken parts of my story, but what I felt I needed was permission from the bulk of humanity. From Christians. I felt like I needed their approval to grieve, to feel, to be honest.

[31]

2015

I wanted to love deeper than I ever had.

It would be so much easier to avoid all the things and people that could potentially bring me hurt, deepen the cavernous wounds. But if I lived that way, I would not have friends, I would never use social media, I would quit my photography business, I couldn't grocery shop or go to church or do anything involving other humans. I would have to live in isolation from humanity. If any of us wanted to truly avoid pain, we would need to live alone and never see another human.

I continued to enter situations that caused pain, I chose friendship, I chose church over complete isolation. Community is important and I decided to keep on living because hiding from life is not living at all, but merely surviving. It felt like a perpetual sacrifice, entering relationships and choosing to risk my heart. I felt like it was a hidden sacrifice. Mostly, I felt like an ugly-fragile-mess of feelings making life suck for all others in a ten-minute radius. But once in a while I would pull myself out of that thinking and see how Jesus was transforming me. He was teaching me to see more clearly, to listen instead of fix.

The hurt I carried around with me, the harrowing of my heart, made room for sorrow to permanently reside inside of me. With that came a sacrificial and selfless love often difficult for me to see in myself, but I know now it was there. It was a love saying, "I will risk being hurt repeatedly, as long as I get to continue knowing you. As long as I get to love you and your babies and your story and be a part of your life."

In my pursuit of honest grief and honest community, I knew my heart would continue to be run over with windrowers of words, phrases, and images. But I realized in risking that, in risking my heart, I was choosing to love deeper than I ever had.

Isn't that what I wanted? Didn't I pray for this, acknowledging love as a risk, but believing love was worth it?

[32]

August 2015

Matthew asked me to pray over the babies and the children at a Wednesday night service. I was no longer officially on staff. I wasn't the children's pastor. I didn't even volunteer in the children's classes anymore. I wasn't married to the children's pastor. I wasn't even married to him, the head pastor, Matthew. But I was married to the youth pastor. I would pray over the youth in a heartbeat and without layers of grief surfacing.

I felt my mouth slack, unsure how to respond, caught off guard and not ready for this kind of request. "You want me to go up and pray over the babies and kids and their parents?" I repeated the question, slowly, verbalizing what he was asking of me. I was at a loss for words of response because my heart ached in its depths. My chest tightened, squeezing the air out of me. I wanted to scream *no*.

"Yes." Matthew said, nodding with his eyes locking into mine.

"But, why me?" It was the first time I had not done something on the spot for this church. It was the first time I outwardly challenged Matthew's requests or demands in a moment of spontaneity—we had a lot of spontaneity around this church plant. It was the first time I felt brave enough to stand up like this for my weakened heart, trying to find space to grieve the loss of our baby as we also pursued adoption. I didn't want to be taught a passive lesson; I wasn't a tool to make someone else feel like they are the wisest teacher. I was on a journey of giving other's worth, but I was also learning to give myself worth and dignity too.

"I just think you're sensitive to these things. I think you need to do it." Matthew's words were sure, knowing, and determined. I stored up rocks in my stomach and my breathing continued restricted. *Is he trying to be my Holy Spirit and teach me a lesson?* I wondered. I stared at his chest, avoiding his eyes, fumbling through a response, "I don't think…" My chest tingled. "I'm not ready for that."

I perpetually felt like I was being taught lessons, being told how prideful I was when I was unable to do something. Pride is the very opposite of Jesus and His word and His heart. So, if I was being prideful, I was the opposite of Him. The One I wanted to emulate. The prayer service ended sooner than Matthew was ready for and people began leaving; I wasn't going to pray over the babies in front of everyone, but this cut the opportunity altogether.

I sat in the back of the room dimly lit by candles, hands folded in my lap, exhausted. This was exhausting, this grieving thing. It was exhausting to be honest with my emotions, heart, and feelings. It was exhausting being honest with a man I highly revere, when it meant I said no to him, disappointed him.

I continued to find myself saying "no" to Matthew. I had stepped down from staff to give myself space, but it didn't feel as though he was giving me space. It felt as though my need for space only confirmed to him how deeply prideful I was; those were the thoughts I fought often.

Was it prideful and selfish to give myself space to grieve? Was it selfish to not be on staff?

I was invited to another planning meeting with the staff. I wanted to say no, but couldn't. My boundaries were worse than I thought. I realized boundaries (or lack of) directly correlate to my self-value.

"Why are you guys here? If no one wants to lead any teams or events, what's the point of being on this staff and leadership team?" Matthew's blood pressure appeared to be rising as he threw his hands in the air. I bit my lip as his lips pinched together. I didn't want to come to this meeting, but was invited and still haven't mastered the fancy technique of "no." Plus, I *was* on staff months ago. Which means I was still secretly on staff, just without the title and $200/month I had fundraised.

"Well? No one is going to lead this celebration, outreach event?" He responded to our blank stares.

"I will see what I can do, but I only have so much time with two littles at home with me all day," Bella said quietly while staring at the table. She is one of the most honest and gentle people I've ever known.

Though I was scared to be fully honest about how little I could do for this event, I was in a place where I felt somewhat confident to protect my time with this event. But it was hard, and painful. I felt Matthew's approval of me shrink; his face growing red. He rubbed his scruffy cheeks with his entire palm, covered his eyes, and placed his elbows on the table. I could see the stiffness in his jaw trickling down to his neck muscles tightening with tension.

Frustrated, hurt, annoyed, exhausted, and insecure emotions twirled in me. This man's approval of me is what has defined me for too long; it was clear we were all lacking it right now. We were all tired. We had been leading multiple groups with multiple people by organizing multiple things in the church. But someone needed to plan the fourth-year celebration: the church's birthday.

We finally distributed the responsibilities between us all, but his frustration didn't leave my mind. I was sure he just wanted what was best for the church. He wanted to celebrate how many years we had made it together as a community. I thought maybe all the pressure of building this fraction of The Bride weighed heavy on him, making his heart and head tired.

You know how you reveal a bit more of yourself to your family, like all the ugly parts? You know how you sort of just let loose with them when you're upset and tired and the world feels like it's too much, but the people you live with are the ones who aren't supposed to leave? I think that was us to him. We were the closest to him, so he felt safe to let loose, even when it was uncomfortable to us. Or harmful. Looking back, abuse was written all over our relationship. I would have scoffed if you warned me years prior.

The fabricating lie I bought into was that it was okay to continue in this relationship. It was okay to stay put, keep my mouth shut, and not talk about how Matthew's reactions to us continually affected or hurt. I believed telling him his words cut into me was too much for him to handle—he had enough happening as the pastor. *I was probably too sensitive anyway, I was probably making it up in my head.* I felt crazy.

So, we went on, smiling and pretending no cuts were made in our heart. Honesty hurts too many people.

Matthew invited Loren and I to his place before a leadership meeting. We were gearing up for fall and he knew we all needed to get on the same page. We were all afraid to say it out loud, except in the confines of our homes, but our church and staff were falling apart. We were a mess. Church is a mess. The Church is a mess. But I continue to believe in it.

Matthew invited us to meet with him to prepare for the big meeting. We had decided it was time to start looking into removing ourselves from his staff and this church. It was distressing but a necessary boundary needing to take place as we pursued the growth of our family. We constantly battled whether or not to tell him, unsure how he would react. We prayed out loud as we drove to his house, both anxious about our sit down with him.

We parked and prayed. We walked up the stairs and sat at the round table on his back deck. My stomach twirled into knots, braids of pretzels. I wanted to disappear; this had become an all too familiar desire of mine. Doing my best to not appear anxious, I folded my hands in my lap, sat up straight and threw a slight smile onto my face. I wasn't sure it reached my eyes, but I was tired.

Matthew started the conversation, "I need to know you guys are *here*. I need to know you are with me, you have my back. You've been pulling away since the beginning of the year and I can't have that. We've got to figure out what is going on between us."

A lump of coal lodged itself into my throat. My mouth felt like cotton was stuck inside. I am usually the assertive, know-what-to-say responsive one of the two of us. But I looked to Loren. I didn't want to lie. But I didn't want to be honest. Honesty hurts. The truth would wreck the night.

Loren nodded slowly, choosing his words carefully, "And we want *to want* to be here. But it's hard. We are really struggling with that."

Matthew's response felt like a quick kick to the pressure points, "Multiple men have left this church and my staff. If you guys leave too, I will be ruined."

"That's a whole lot of pressure." I said, slightly mad. Annoyed. Frustrated.

"I know it is. And I'm sorry. Somewhere along the lines I began to idolize our relationship and how you guys feel towards me. I'm sorry. We need to figure out what's going on with us and we need to fix it. I need you guys to have my back, to be on board. You are my main staff." His voice was pained, desperate.

We nodded, said we would be present tonight, and lead our group.

We all felt broken at the table. None of us was winning. We were all grieving various things, all pained. We were a mess at best.

[33]

I parked my car outside of Jesse's duplex and waited for the thoughts of sadness to hit me. I wanted to let them run their course in my car, while parked in her driveway, so when I entered her house I could be fully present with her. I gave my heart space to grieve, to feel sorrow, to *be*.

But they didn't come. The grief didn't hit. The sadness didn't shake me up.

I stared at my steering wheel, waiting.

Peace.

It was the first time since my miscarriage I wasn't gripped with grief before walking into a pregnant friend's presence. I had been training myself to allow space in my life before events or meet-ups that may be taxing on my heart; it helped. But as I waited for the waves to wash over me, nothing came and instead a smile crept onto my face. I felt nothing but pure joy for her: she was a few weeks away from the big due date. She had invited me to attend her birth, and I was nothing but excited in these moments.

He whispered to me a promise He has spoken over me time and time again. It is from Zephaniah, chapter three verse seventeen: "For the Lord your God is living among you. He is a mighty savior. He will take delight in you with gladness. With His love, He will calm all your fears. He will rejoice over you with joyful songs." Slowly but surely, all my fears were being calmed with His love. I was finding Him to be steadfast and faithful.

Grabbing my purse and keys, I walked up to her door and let myself in. Her big white, furry firstborn greeted me with too much tongue, but that was sort of his thing. Jesse was sitting in her rocking chair, gliding back and forth next to the bright, white crib. Their nursery was almost ready to welcome their little love.

As she rocked, I shared with her everything I was learning about adoption. We talked about the stupid things people ask like, "What if you get a troublemaker, messed up kid? What if he grows up and does drugs? You just never know what you're going to get. What if he doesn't look like you? What if his real mom is on drugs? What if the real mom tries to kidnap your baby?"

"People really say these things?" Her eyebrows raised as the question rolled off her tongue. I launched into that morning's story about how I was laying in the dental chair with the bib draped over me. I see this woman, my dental hygienist, two times a year and yet it feels like I have known her for years: I know about her marriages, daughters, political thoughts, and whatnot. We share significant words as I try to ignore the cold utensils tearing apart the vulnerable parts of my gums.

Our conversation that morning ranged from backpacking to ticks to adoption to gay marriage to sex changes. She knows I love Jesus and sometimes I wonder if she is testing me to get a reaction. I don't give it to her; I find pride in perpetually shocking her with a smile and reminder that I am not the moral police.

"Are you still working as a doula?" My dental hygienist asked as she scraped away scum.

I shook my head no, my mouth wide open, drooling out the corners.

"You should write a book," she says with a shrug of her shoulders as the silver cold-jabbers clanked around the ivory in my face. I updated her, sharing I hoped to, but first I wanted to focus on our adoption.

"You're adopting?" she pulled the cold tools out of my mouth, both hands suspended over my face with the light beaming down into my eyes.

"Yes." I smiled.

Immediately she tells me horror stories from Oprah, about two adoptive families who "couldn't return their kids and didn't know what to do, because they were wreaking havoc and trying to burn down the house. I mean, you just never know what you're going to get and what their genetics are and what have you...what if they try to kill you?"

My stomach plummeted, stones piling inside to weigh it down. The words "couldn't return" never sit well with me. I swallowed as best as I could with my mouth pried open as she shared story after story about her friends' marriages crumbling, ending in divorce, certainly because of the children they adopted; they "couldn't have children of their own so they had to resort to adoption and it ruined them."

While the words were spewed carelessly, my heart was beating fast and I tried to remember the opportunity this moment was. She clearly doesn't understand the reality of adoption; her preconceived notions are that these children are less-than, they are messed up because of the broken parts of their story, the tragic loss they endure at such young ages.

I adopted a sadness into me that these are real thoughts, for more than just her. This idea of our children being returnable if we don't like them, if they are troublesome, if they don't serve us well or fit into the box of perfection we hoped for. Like shampoo. Our children aren't bottles of shampoo to return when they're not as we wished.

"Jesse, it hit me in that dental chair people will place these preconceived thoughts on my baby like it's acceptable. Like...they will wonder 'how he or she will turn out' and if it's because of their being adopted. It hit me that more than one person views kids who were adopted as...less than and not actually *mine*."

It was there in Jesse's nursery I began processing the loss of what was to come. The loss for my future children. The loss accompanying their identity. People not connected to adoption would most likely hold views of my child so wrapped up in their being adopted, the lens placed over them would be skewed. Everything would be blamed on their being adopted. They couldn't just be a kid, they had to be an adopted kid.

Subconscious beliefs and stigmas sprouted from the very language used surrounding adoption. I had never noticed it, but now it seemed to pop up everywhere. Choosing the adoption story grew more and more costly; not just costly regarding our bank account, but to our and our future children's emotions and hearts.

These opportunities to share about adoption and confront stigmas presented themselves nearly daily. People were constantly asking me how much adoption was going to cost, *what a scam*, who is getting all this money? I felt it was my duty to begin tearing down the stigmas and misconceptions now; this was part of becoming a parent by adoption.

Derek Loux said, "My friends. Adoption is redemption. It's costly, exhausting, expensive, and outrageous. Buying back lives cost so much. When God set out to redeem us, it killed Him."

I saw this quote and it sat right with me. People are always commenting about how expensive adoption is, about how ridiculous the cost is, but I continued to come back to how costly life is. How worth any cost it will be to become a stable family for a vulnerable child.

We finished the pounds of paperwork, hours of classes, and updating of our home in June. We were prepared for our home study and waiting for it to be scheduled; it was difficult to not be impatient and frustrated with our social worker. She was taking what felt like years to return our emails and calls, to set up our in-home study. We couldn't apply to agencies until she conducted these visits; if we weren't active with agencies, we weren't getting great exposure with expectant moms making adoption plans; if we weren't getting any exposure, we wouldn't be discovered! We weren't available to be a family. My emotions were constantly spent on the cascade of things needing done. Urgency was an understatement.

Vacillating between impatience and hopeful anticipation, I found myself writing down dreams about our little one. Our budget was tighter than ever, so instead of purchasing a sweet and perfect journal to write letters to whoever he or she would be, I found a plain gray one in the box of notebooks to be discarded. On the long and hard days of waiting, the days where I could not seem to get the thought of our little one growing in another mama's womb out of my head, I wrote. I wrote letters to him or her in anticipation, hoping and praying. I prayed for our little love's first family, wondering if they will want to continue contact with us.

The urgency felt thick because I knew we were not sticking around Corvallis for much longer; I knew if we moved soon, we would have to virtually start all over with a new home study and rewrite all the applications to agencies. The idea of this reality exhausted me. I wanted to be agency active, meet our baby and his family, and move.

The last summer days were filled with coffee-dates, scheming up fundraising ideas, and youth group activities. We hunt for bugs, we play frisbee, I circle up with the girls and giggle about me becoming a mama and them loving our baby. We talk about Jesus and how sweet He is, how trustworthy and good He is.

These girls hold so much of my heart and I fear I will have to say goodbye too soon. No time seems like a good time. I fear

Loren will get a job much sooner than summer of 2016. I fear we will move before we are matched or placed with our baby and these girls will not be in our little one's life. The life they dream with me about will be ripped from them.

Claire, 13 and the most tender soul I've ever known, has taught me so much about loving well. She listens to you with her whole self, she takes in the words said, she validates and smiles sweetly. She is always finding Jesus in all the pieces. I ask her often about her parents; I can only hope my children will grow to be as humble, loving, selfless, and Jesus-chasing as her. I had always envisioned my little ones being around her, but with everything up in the air about us moving, my heart experienced the tension of the unknown.

As Claire shares with our youth group about her sponsor child, my eyes well with tears knowing she is going to love big. She already is. Her whole life will be a radiant picture of His grace. Like mine, her strong faith is a gift from Him. Her faith in His goodness is easy, natural, ever-present. She, like me, is confident He will bring all the funds for our adoption together when they are demanded. She, like me, has a faith so big that He can and will move mountains.

Even when the mountains appear immovable.

[34]

September 2015

It's our second summer camping in yurts with The Sands; they were the head of the elders-in-training at our small church. They invited us to spend a week with them at Sunset Bay in yurts and we don't decline. They are in their 70's, maybe, I'm not sure exactly. We haven't asked.

She's from England and her accent lets you know. We love listening to her talk. Sometimes Loren asks her questions just to hear her talk and share stories. Her husband, Kevin, loves Jesus a lot. They've been married for 35 years and found Jesus somewhere along the way.

The week spent yurting was also spent laughing and crying through Jen Hatmaker's *For the Love*. I was filling out more piles of adoption agency and grant applications. There was zero phone service which was an undeniable gift.

Both years we rotated providing dinners, eating together, and spending the evening roasting marshmallows or playing scrabble. We talk about Jesus and the Bible and our church.

Carefully Kevin asks, "So how do you think Matthew is handling the finances of our church? I fear we are heading downhill. Do you think our church is going to last another year? Then what will happen with you guys, do you have a back-up plan?" He asks with care.

Loren and I exchanged glances and knew we wanted to be careful. Kevin and Matthew often have breakfast together to pray and talk church-stuff. Very few people knew we were heavily considering what it would mean to transition out of this church leadership and community.

"We have been thinking about what could be next for us, yes. But we have no plans." Loren answered simply. It was true. Entirely.

"Sometimes I wonder if Matthew needs a sabbatical. He's had a lot of really big life changes this year and I think he needs to regain health. He invites me to offer my thoughts but then doesn't want to hear what I have to say." Kevin shares, inviting us into an honest and necessary conversation as the elder of our church.

"Yes, we have found that too." Loren responded, shortly.

We talk about what we see ourselves doing in our future. Kevin asks us if we see ourselves at a big mega church, leading a giant youth group. We do not. We really like this small church stuff. We really like being able to know more than just the kids' names: we love knowing their stories intimately, offering space on our couches as necessary, being a safe space for them.

"But we do see ourselves in church ministry for quite some time. Then maybe eventually Loren will go back to school for a master's degree in divinity or something." I shared.

Our conversation continued, all of us delicately dancing around the reality of how broken our staff and leadership had become. We were each so careful, doing our best not to be gossipy, but also have an honest conversation. Loren and I felt nervous Kevin might go home and tell Matthew anything we said; we had to be ready for the backlash that could come. We kept details to a minimum, didn't tell Kevin much of anything except we feel tired. But still, the anxiety spun itself with fear in my stomach.

We were trying to remain cool, calm, collected. We wanted to focus on the really, beautiful parts of our story: our adoption. We didn't foresee us moving in the next few months, *maybe* by next summer. It was a scary idea, but exciting too. The week was spent on the sandy beach of Sunset Bay, exploring the beautiful gardens of Shore Acres, and roasting marshmallows over the campfire.

Our conversations were spoken in some sort of code, all of us careful and not sure what was appropriate. I mean, he was the elder-in-training, so shouldn't we be able to talk to him? It was all confusing and we just wanted to do the right thing.

[35]

September 2015

Our first marathon was approaching. This marathon held so much meaning to me, meant so many things, was so important. My grandparents sponsored us to run the Portland Marathon. I was stoked. I had already run a few half marathons and a 17-mile trail run; I was ready to conquer this.

With the chaos of pursuing adoption and preparing for our home study, agency applications, grant applications, and all of the things ministry entailed, training had sort of been...well, yeah. Spotty at best.

We'd been in the official process of pursuing domestic infant adoption for five months as the marathon approached. Our home study planned to be finalized by the end of September; our last visit fast approaching on the 16th of September. Our marathon was Sunday October 4th. I was giddy and antsy about conquering this feat; it was so much more than a run to me.

My body has failed me in so many ways. It has failed to conceive, conceiving with treatment only to miscarry. I have endometriosis which I am certain is a sliver of a glimpse into hell: I am in constant and perpetual pain. Surgery was scheduled for two weeks after the marathon, to remove it again. Then my blood clotting issues.

This marathon was significant. As I trained and spent hours running, pushing my body further than it's ever been pushed, I reminded myself of its beauty. My body is beautiful and not *entirely* broken. I tear up just imagining running through the finish line, dominating the victory of 26.2 miles. My body will do me right. I will run this race and I will celebrate the victory with immense joy. And then I'll lay on the couch crying in pain for the rest of the week. Seems awesome.

It was a big training day. We made it to 20 miles without stopping. Our small town doesn't offer a lot of variation in our routes, but we do what we can. We have tested our gear, tried different power snacks, and have camelbacks to sip water from. My body aches but it is worth it: I can do this. I am not entirely broken.

I talk with God a whole lot while training for the run; He meets me in the hills and stretches of difficulty. Our conversations went like this: "God, if my body can't hold a baby inside of it, then let's show it what it can do: it can run. It can defy normality. Running 26.2 miles is like running your body down and then hitting it with a train. That's almost like giving birth, right? (*Go ahead and laugh, or cry, I cried a lot*). Let's be proud of my body— God, help me be proud of this body you created for me. I want to run this marathon and complete it. Because, really, I should be seven months pregnant right now. And since I am not, let's run this marathon."

We were approaching the finalization of our home study and our biggest run. Two incredibly meaningful marathons: the marathon of the heart and the marathon of the body. Our home study finalization would be just the beginning, really. It would be the pistol firing to start the run and meet the next multitude of milestones in the adoption process.

Wednesday the 16th of September 2015 arrived quickly. This was our last home study visit with our social worker. We finished our long twenty-mile training run and showered. I swept up the crumbs spilled from the fresh cookies I baked. I chopped cheese, meats, and set out some crackers. Tea and coffee were ready. Our tiny home was spotless and ready to be picked apart as needed. It was a Wednesday I won't forget.

Loren finished up a lunch meeting with a student while I was interviewed by Cathy, our social worker, about my childhood. Loren walked through the door making it his turn for an interview. I walked the short distance to our precious gray and yellow nursery to spend time praying for whoever our future child's biological parents were. I sat in the wooden rocking chair recently gifted to us.

It was cycle day twenty-nine for me. Usually I would have tested a day earlier, cycle day twenty-eight, checking as early as possible for those two pink lines. But one month earlier I had felt this beautiful freedom in not testing for pregnancy. I also secretly knew if I had indeed seen two lines that morning, my head would not be clear for our important home study interview. I didn't want that. I wanted to be fully present.

I was working so hard to wrap my heart's hope around Jesus; not my body, not adoption, not humans or babies, but Jesus. Solely Jesus. I knew putting my hope in my body, in our family growing, in expectant moms making adoption plans, in two lines, in babies, adoption matches, and placement and processes and *anything* but Jesus was only setting myself up for disappointment.

I knew this to my core but sometimes it is hard.

Our home study interview finished quicker and with much less stress than I anticipated. Our social worker loves Jesus a whole lot and gifted us with the confidence of receiving an approved home study within two weeks. She ducked out and headed home.

Wednesday passed into Thursday, cycle day thirty. Sometimes my cycle was twenty-eight days and sometimes it was thirty-three days. It was better than the cycles I used to have, varying between fourteen and forty-four days. As cycle day thirty turned into cycle day thirty-one, Thursday into Friday, I worked on our nursery, nesting. I met with ladies I adore. I prepared my heart for Aunt Flow to arrive. As I boxed up junk we no longer needed to hold space for, I boxed up the hope I had been placing in my body, and placed it into His hands.

I wanted a fast match. I wanted an expectant mama to see our profile book and know immediately we were her child's family. I wanted there to be no doubt. I talked with Him about it, asking Him to continue growing our adoption fund, knowing I would put every penny right into it. Trusting anything He provided for us was for our adoption. Adoption is costly.

Tomorrow was Saturday, and we had our longest training run yet: twenty-two miles. Tomorrow I would press my entire self harder into running, deeper into impossibilities. Tomorrow I would see that my body was stronger than I was giving it credit. Tomorrow would be a day of victory. I was ready for that victory.

[36]

September 19, 2015

The sun woke me up at 7:30 a.m. *Happy Saturday, let's do this run.* I let Loren sleep a little longer. I brushed my teeth and think, *Okay, but if I AM pregnant, I probably shouldn't run 22 miles, right?*

Disgruntled and slightly annoyed with myself for giving in, I reached under the sink to pull out a small litmus pregnancy test I had purchased in bulk from Amazon. Growing more embarrassed by the second, I look around the tiny bathroom as though there were people watching: no one was there. I knew it would be a One Liner, but for peace of mind, I wanted to cancel out the idea of there being a baby inside of my tender, broken, weak womb.

You are so stupid, I hear my voice saying. *You fool.*

I had become so good at peeing into a plastic cup. I stick the test in it, open the lower cabinet door to set it inside so Loren doesn't see. In the off chance two lines did appear, I wanted to tell Loren in a happy memorable way again; like last time. I wanted it to be a sweet story, the kind you tell your kids so they feel loved and cherished and wanted. You know?

The second line started appearing before I even set the test down. I heard a voice seeming to be outside of myself saying, "Oh no, no, no, no. I can't, I can't, no, I can't." and all went fuzzy as darkness started tugging at the corners of my vision. I was looking through a tunnel.

"What? Is there a spider?" I hear Loren ask from the bedroom.

I blacked out slightly, slumping against the hall wall.

He heard the thump of my fall and the next thing I know he is racing towards me. I hold up the tiny thin strip of litmus paper; all I could muster through a shaky voice met with tears was, "It's positive. I can't do this again. I can't lose another."

I noted the tears in his eyes. He grinned while he held me; I sobbed.

"Are you sure? Can you take another one?" He wanted to see for himself.

I grabbed the big fancy digital test. The expensive one. The word "pregnant" appeared quickly. There was no denying I was pregnant again. As the reality of the positive test settled in next to the fear of being pregnant, I decided I should take a bunch of pictures to document this moment. In the case we had to say goodbye too soon, I wanted something to show for our little one.

"You're still on board with adopting, right?" It was one of my first thoughts. I felt my brows furrow, fearful he would suddenly go back on our agreement to continue our adoption process if I fell pregnant. We needed to be on the same page.

"Of course. I wouldn't think to do anything else but pursue both of these babies as much as we can. This isn't a back up plan; it's the plan." His words reminded me how amazing he is. I married a good one.

Earlier in 2015, I had watched the second line turn pink, parallel to the control line. This was the culmination of months-turned-to-years of trying to conceive a biological baby in my womb, the culmination of doctor's appointments and fertility medications and cycle-tracking and finally making the decision to become parents through adoption earlier rather than later. I watched the second line show up, not on just one test but a second and then a third and then a fourth and a fifth.

The whole pregnancy after loss fear was more real and more intense than I had anticipated. I never would have guessed the crippling fear to take ahold of my entire self like a giant prickly hug from a thorn bush. It was so unexpected. I had read stories and blogs about pregnancy after loss, but a lot of those stories were after still-born losses. And ours was lost very quickly after discovering the little life; though the loss ran deep, I feel a stillbirth may have wrecked me in an entirely different way.

Our midwife Julia was amazing and met me that afternoon to check my hormone levels. She ordered me some progesterone cream which helped my body have enough of what it needed to keep baby inside. She ordered an ultrasound for week 6, just a week and a half away. She encouraged me to set up my maternal fetal medicine doctor to immediately get on blood thinners. No need to wait.

Our pace for the adoption of a baby, growing our family, was steady and certain. But more unexpected fears surfaced: Will I have to say goodbye again? Will our adoption journey be interrupted? What if we lose our adoption journey AND this baby? How will I get through another loss? How will I keep breathing? Will people validate this biological baby more than our adopted baby? Will our adopted baby feel less-than or less wanted in people's eyes? Will people think we got pregnant because we were adopting?

Despite what felt like unending fears surrounding our biological baby and the baby we had yet to meet via adoption, I was determined to celebrate the life created in my womb. I was determined to find ways to see grace and goodness in the dailyness of pregnancy, to remember the statement made during grief support group: Today, I am pregnant; I can celebrate that today.

[37]

"I told Matthew it was time to transition out."

"WHAT?!" I responded to Loren. I nearly dropped the pot I was scrubbing. My mouth fell open. I tried to keep calm, but the wave of nausea was all too consuming. We had agreed time and time again we weren't ready to tell him; his reaction was too unpredictable. He went out for a Thursday breakfast with Matthew and returned with this news. After consulting with some leaders and a youth pastor who were mentors to us, we all deemed it best to wait until another job was secured. I was sure he wouldn't, but our mentors warned he might stop our income if he knew.

"Our breakfast meeting was good. He brought it up; I was pretty surprised. He said when you and I thought it was time to transition out, to let him know and he would help us do it smoothly. So, I told him I wanted to start talking about what that looked like. It seemed good."

"Well, wow. Okay then. Now what?" I asked.

A jolt coursed through my body sending a flutter into my belly. This transition seemed much less painful than it could be. It could be smooth, healthy, and worth celebrating. Although pain is inevitable, this transition could be as painless as possible. No matter what, there is such a loss to come in losing this sweet community.

The only people who knew about our hope to transition out in the next year were Bill and Bella, an older couple who were elders, our out-of-state youth pastor mentors, and Loren's parents. This was a very quiet thing. We had done our best to avoid gossip and were terrified to do it all wrong. But we also wanted to counsel.

"I'm not exactly sure what is next or what the timeline is. I am assuming next summer sometime, after we have our youth ministry really set up and thriving with the leaders. He said he needed to talk to his management team to see what they suggest." Loren's statements were matter of fact. This was the beginning of the next chapter and we wanted to take extra care of all hearts involved. We wanted to honor Him and every community member who has impacted us.

I knew our moving out of this church and city was going to inflict heartache upon many people. I wanted to soften the blow as much as possible by sharing with wisdom and intention, through prayer. It didn't help we were now physically pregnant and hoping to adopt; many of these people had walked with us through the throes of loss and waiting. Everyone in this community supported us so intimately; it felt far past time for us to move on but so unfair to say goodbye.

Yet here we were: Matthew knew it was coming, making it more official than it was yesterday. The transition out was coming and we hoped for a beautiful, smooth as possible, goodbye.

[38]

October 4, 2015

They don't know I'm not running the marathon. My grandparents, dad and his wife came to cheer us on in our great feat of 26.2 miles. We had been training for months. I created small, little pregnancy-announcement cards for them. The nausea hit. The tenderness too. I am certainly pregnant. "Why are you not running? Are you okay?" My dad's eyes are round and wide, his concern loud as he approaches me from across the street. I try not to smile too big and hand him an envelope. "What's this? Why aren't you running?" He persists.

I point to the envelope, "Open it."

His eyes scan it and stare at the tiny sesame seed I had taped inside, demonstrating the size of one of his future grandchildren. Tears begin to swell up, "You're pregnant?"

I nod and my dad and I embrace each other to share this long-awaited moment.

The national anthem starts and the downtown Portland blocks are saturated with bodies, hands over hearts, voices singing in unison the song of our nation. I tear up, thinking about how beautiful this moment is, this moment of unified voices singing our anthem.

The trigger is pulled and the fast marathoners pass by at a pace I would never have been able to keep. We eventually spot Loren waving. I am bummed I'm not running with him. It's confusing; I was running it in part to prove to myself my body isn't indeed broken. I was still pregnant, revealing it was working this time so far. I had trained so hard for this run and wasn't sure the next opportunity I would have to run a marathon.

It's bittersweet, missing out on this run. More sweet, of course: I have a baby in my womb. I didn't want to chance depleting my body and creating an unwelcome habitat for our newest little one. If I decided to run it only to miscarry, I would have blamed myself for selfishly running 26.2 miles to prove a point. So I chose not to run. Maybe one day we'll have two babies in a jogging stroller and I'll run a marathon with them.

Loren disappears in the crowd of runners and we find a place for breakfast. My mind is stuck in the middle of chaos: adopting with a high risk pregnancy, looking forward to moving but no one really knows, *where will we even go?*, feeling the urgency to tell everyone about our pregnancy in case we lose it, feeling the pressure to not announce online in case adoption agencies tell us to pause our adoption and then we miscarry. Fears of losing our community and hurting hearts, losing our pregnancy and adoption. It all weighed heavy on my hopeful, weary heart as we walked the blocks of Portland in search of some eggs and bacon.

[39]

Tuesday, October 6, 2015

It was an average Tuesday: Loren packed up his work bag and went to the church office. Tuesdays were office days, spent preparing for the upcoming nights of youth group and ministry meetings. Matthew also spent Tuesdays in the office, along with two precious women who spent their time and resources as our administration team.

I stayed home, still getting used to not being on staff officially. I had spent years of Tuesdays in that office; it felt weird not going with Loren. Instead I showered, knowing soon enough showers would be even more scarce. I spent time in my bible and journal, quiet in the stillness of our empty home.

A year and a half earlier I was at our annual women's retreat and Jesus led me to Jeremiah 33:3: "Ask me and I will tell you some remarkable secrets about what is going to happen here.'" He whispered this as a promise when we were in the trench of waiting and wondering if my body might fail us to procreate and host a baby. Inviting me back to these words and His promise, He reminded me of His great authorship. "I take broken things and make beauty," He whispered. "I don't cause the brokenness, but I will use it. I will work through it if you let Me. Keep calling to Me, especially when everything is chaos and broken. Keep calling to Me and know I will show you remarkable things you do not yet know. Trust in My bigness."

I sat with my hair wet and hanging down over my shoulders,

a bowl sharing the couch with me, ready in case my nausea acted out. The room was quiet and still, His presence as though the room was steeped with His grace.

When I heard our front door open, I was surprised to see Loren home so early. As he rounded the corner, I noticed his jaw was tight and he seemed to be grinding his teeth; it was something I've only seen him do once.

"What's going on, honey?" I asked, a bit taken back. It takes quite a bit to fluster him.

He looked at me long and hard before answering: "Matthew gave us a deadline. Which isn't even the most frustrating part."

I stared at him before filling the silence with questions, "A deadline? Like, to leave? How soon? Will we get the money we fundraised? What if we can't find a job? Please tell me every detail." My mind scattered, but I knew He was with us.

Loren shared with me the conversation with Matthew, step by step: "Well, we were just sitting and working in the office like normal when he looked up with a steady, lower pitched voice and said, 'You need to be gone by December first.' I was shocked, but also understood where he was coming from on one hand. So, I just said, 'Yeah, wow, okay.' He then told me he talked with the management team; they want us gone by November first. He said he bargained for us and tried for January so they settled on December first."

I felt my jaw drop. This was completely unexpected. Loren went on, "He said we would be paid until then. So that's good. It makes sense, I mean, who wants a guy around who is planning to leave? It just feels abrupt and unexpected."

"So, if that's not the worst part, what is?" I asked. Loren said they returned to working on their computers as though nothing happened: Matthew dropped a deadline of less than two months left of income and a job, and Loren's expected to just keep working as though it's an average Tuesday.

"The admin team came in," he continued while rubbing his

forehead, "began working in the tiny space of our office. My brain felt fuzzy as I thought about the impending end of our paycheck and community. How was I going to tell the youth kids? I thought it would be another year before we left. Anyways, then Matthew starts packing up his bag to go. He stands up, holding his motorcycle gear and work bag, and says, 'So does the admin team know you're leaving?' The ladies were sitting *right there*, Nat. They started panicking and Martha's hand flew to her chest as she gasped, 'But what about the youth group?' I was so mad, Nat. This is not how people are supposed to find out. Matthew grabbed his helmet like it was no big deal and says, 'Well payroll will change soon. I've got a meeting to get to,' and ducked out."

He continues: "I was left with unending questions from our admin team. Questions I didn't even have a chance to ask because I just found out too. I finally packed my things and came home. I have never felt so betrayed." My husband's voice cracks as the last sentence left his mouth.

My mouth was dry. Listening to his experience left me feeling less gracious than he. I spewed frustration in the form of "How dare he" and "How could he?" and "Why would we have trusted him? I never would have expected him to do this to us."

"I mean it makes sense. I wouldn't want a guy hanging around if I knew his heart was already ready to transition out. I had just envisioned having more time to set up leadership for the youth, you know? What I'm really upset about is how he handled it with the admin team."

My jaw clenched and now I was grinding my teeth. Bitterness began rising and bubbling inside me. My pulse quickened. I felt panicky, and I wanted to scream. "Can you at least send him a text telling him not to tell anyone else? It's not fair. We should be the ones telling people. This is how people's feelings get hurt: when they hear from someone else in an off-handed situation. We need to do this right and he needs to let us."

So he types up the simplest text: *Hey, can we not let what happened in the office today happen with anyone else? Nat and I would like to be the ones to tell certain people. People we deeply care about.*

It didn't take long for his concise response to appear: "*I'm sorry you're choosing to be offended.*"

Livid. I felt my throat closing and I pointed at his phone with my index finger. The words were not coming. Now, I'm extremely focused on solving this seemingly, uncontrollable problem. We called Bill and Bella; we give them a play by play, ask them if it is out of place for us to set up a few meetings with the few families and friends we want to tell. They encourage us it is perfectly normal for people to hear from our mouths we are leaving in less than two months. "What about our youth kids? Can we at least tell the core five teens who have been with us since the beginning?"

Bill and Bella felt this was perfectly understandable. We texted the five kids who had worked their way into our hearts years ago. The ones with whom we had spent countless hours living life with and loving. Two of them were Matthew's kids. I sent a quick text to their mom, Helen, letting her know we planned to tell the five of our leaving by December first. She agreed it was a good idea.

That evening's youth group was fast approaching and everything was out of place. I felt sicker than sick. They still didn't know I was pregnant. I had been throwing up for weeks, eating popcorn and peanut butter toast, applying for adoption grants and praying through expectant mom situations. I was not ready for this. This was not supposed to happen for months. I felt knocked down. Everything was so out of our control.

He whispered to me His promise of showing me great and remarkable things, secrets. I felt soul tired, but nodded at Jesus's sweet voice. He affirmed this was out of control, this was broken, but He was with me in the mess. Jesus affirmed He would be with me as we tell our beloved students we were leaving, but He would also be with them. They will feel the unexpected shock, and be knocked down, too. This was the worst. I had nothing left in me but to open my hands and ask Him to guide our words.

[40]

Tuesday night, October 6, 2015

We had a small amount of kids for youth group that night as it was. When 8:00 P.M. came and passed, we said goodbye for the night to some students, then invited the five core teens into the prayer room. At the last moment, we decided to snag Danny, a committed youth leader and elder-in-training, to be present. He had no idea what this private gathering was for, but we thought having another adult was wise. We were not ready for this. I wanted to vomit.

We sat in front of everyone, twelve beautiful eyeballs all focused on us. Loren and I were quiet, too quiet, and the atmosphere was somber. We didn't know how to start or where to start or what to say exactly. How do you prepare to puncture wounds into the people you love most?

We look at each other, Loren and I, unsure who should begin. I nod.

"So, we haven't told anyone this. You guys are the very first to know. We hope you see it for what it is: love for you. We want you to hear from us, to be the first to know. You guys mean *so much* to us. My family doesn't even know." The words carefully came out my mouth and I shivered slightly. I looked into each of them, trying to speak to their souls, deeply wanting them to know how much they mean to us.

By now, I am fully aware of the goosebumps covering my body in this freezing room despite my heavily, dressed layers. I suck in another breath, steal a glance at Loren, and continue. "We have known for quite some time we wouldn't be in Corvallis very long. When we were first married, we thought we would be here for maybe five years at most. Anyway, over the course of the last year," I spoke slowly, trembling, knowing none of them were ready for this. I wasn't ready for this, "...it became apparent to us it was time to prepare for our leaving. We had been putting it off, for months, because we love you guys. You mean so much to us. It hurts just thinking about it. We shared with our management team we felt it was time to start transitioning out. They responded by giving us a deadline much sooner than we expected."

My tears began to fall. I wiped my face with the cuff of my sleeve. My top teeth bit my bottom lip. My feet were bouncing, my body trembling, nausea twisted my insides into knots. Loren picked up in a hushed tone, "Yeah. It was very, very unexpected." He said lowering his chin to his chest, avoiding eye contact. I picked at my fingers, looking around only to see every jaw dropped, tears threatening to fall. I immediately thought we were spending too much time on the unexpected decision our management made. My heart picked up speed.

Puffy eyes companioned forced smiles, and tears were wiped as sadness met an unwanted acceptance. The students tried to hide their pain from us, but they were visibly breaking into pieces. Their hidden sorrow couldn't protect us as they hoped it would.

"We are very excited to see where God takes us, though." I quickly lie; I am unsure I am believable. I am trying to add hope. It was a partial lie because in those moments I felt nothing but brokenness. I felt an overwhelming sadness join despair, betrayal, and anger. Yet, I *was* hopeful for a new and healthy place. But hope held little space in this current moment.

"Where are you going?" Matthew's son asked, his voice cracking halfway through.

Loren and I look at each other unsure how to answer. "We don't know."

"But why are you leaving so soon?" He pressed further.

"We didn't expect that either. But man, do we love you guys. We trust Jesus a whole lot." Loren responded, clearly unsure how to handle the questions.

Our loyal youth leader, Danny, was leaning against a table. He stood up and said, "Let's circle up, lay hands on the Brenners, and pray over them."

I dug for tissues as my whole body quaked and shivered. They laid hands on us. Teenage fingers and adult hands entwined as tears rained onto the carpet. There was not one dry eye. *This is not how it was supposed to go*, I thought. *Our leaving was not supposed to be clothed in sorrow.*

Her name popped up into my phone's screen around 10:30 p.m. and my stomach lurched. Helen, was calling. Nothing in me wanted to answer, sure we did something wrong again. It felt we were always messing up in their eyes. But I knew if I didn't answer now I wouldn't sleep and would still have to talk to her tomorrow. Or worse, him. It felt like needles stabbing me as I picked up.

"Hello?" I answered.

"Hi Natalie, just wanting to talk through what our kids told us was said this evening."

Helen explained calmly but clearly frustrated and hurt that her kids heard it as us blaming the entire ordeal on Matthew. That we were angry and we bad mouthed them. That we were slanderous. Matthew and Helen were told we shared specific names—Matthew's name—telling our precious students he fired

Loren. Which we didn't. A deadline and firing are different and we knew that.

As I listened to her recap what her kids heard, my jaw hung open. This was not what we had shared. This was a shaken-up soda can of miscommunication ready to explode. I felt entirely anxious, wanting nothing but to do this right. It was already messed up, now this?

I quickly reassured her of the exact terminology we used. I shared with her our heart, how we were doing our best to do this well. I told her about what had happened in the office earlier that day, revealing to us the absolute urgency to tell the people our hearts needed to tell before Matthew did out of a reaction to hurt.

She asked me if I wanted to talk to him. No. I did not. My heart was hard and hurt, bitter and broken. Helen asked us to cancel any more meetings with people until Loren and Matthew met Thursday. *Don't tell anyone else until a plan is in place.* So, Loren and I complied. We wanted to do things right.

I was watching a show and attempting to eat peanut butter toast. Loren was working on his resume. The depression hangover from the last night's youth group was pulling me into its heaviness. Stress was eating away at my already nauseated stomach. I had no appetite and even if I did, I'd throw it back up. I injected the soft flesh of my stomach with blood thinners, thankful for medicine, but entirely exhausted emotionally.

The show was supposed to distract me from how wrong the last week continued to unfold. While our job was up in the air as a jumbled mess, I remembered not everything was wrong: I was still pregnant. I was carrying a life, *expectation* inside of my body. Our adoption was moving along and we were learning so much about positive adoption language and adoptees. These were realities to see glory in.

We had texted the five youth kids last night after my phone call, recapping to them: we weren't fired but were optimistic for what was next. We loved them. Those who responded said, "Yes we know, thank you," confirming they didn't think we were fired. Our youth leader who was present also confirmed we did not say those words or name names. Danny thought we did well. But I just felt sick. This felt entirely dysfunctional and maybe a bit hopeless.

[41]

Thursday, October 8, 2015

Loren's Thursday mornings are often spent with Matthew eating breakfast and talking about the week's ministry. The Thursday prior they held what we considered to be an open and honest conversation about us transitioning out of this church and community. We thought it went well, hopeful for a smooth transition, but then Tuesday were given an unexpected deadline to leave in less than two months. Immediately after given the deadline, Matthew reacted by sharing, without warning, with the two admin team ladies who were dear to us. When confronted about this, Matthew responded with "I'm sorry you chose to be offended."

After this fiasco, we prayed and discerned it was far more important to be the ones telling specific people with care. We weighed the pros and cons of setting up meetings with select students, the elders-in-training we were close to, our youth leaders, and of course a few close friends: the pros far outweighed the cons. Unsure how Matthew would conduct himself with the hurt we were causing him, we set up meetings. We started with the five students who'd been with us since the start of this church. Matthew and Helen heard the recap of this meeting and felt we went about it all wrong; unfortunately, the recap they heard was twisted with big emotions and hurt hearts. Helen then asked us to cancel any other meetings we had until Loren and Matthew meet Thursday morning. The eighth of October.

Loren attended this breakfast meeting with Matthew, prepared to plan our transition and how we were to go about it. Still nervous, he was ready to get this going since our deadline was fast approaching. When Loren returned from breakfast far too early and told me he was not only fired but also banned, my world spun and shook. Everything we thought we knew was once again ripped out of our control and we wondered where we messed up to deserve this. Did he really feel we deserved to be banned from our community? Did he really believe we were toxic and even detrimental to our beloved community?

Loren told me the last statement Matthew said to him as he left Starbucks was, "I'm no longer your pastor, your boss, your mentor, or your friend." The only other time I've seen my husband so hurt was when I miscarried.

We sat on our bed together, suspended in the shock of loss once again. Loren was furious, betrayal lacerating his heart sure to scar forever. My heart slumped and strained, experiencing both anguish and betrayal. An email from Matthew popped into Loren's inbox; attached was his termination letter. We read his written words with our mouths gaping, the shock furthering with each false accusation:

Dear Loren,

Per our conversation on Thursday 10/08/2015 your employment in the role of Youth Pastor has been terminated effective immediately. The reason for termination is that there is a lack of trust between you and the Lead Pastor. That resulted in the follow:

Actions and attitudes detrimental to the unity and health of the Church:

Those actions include:

- *Unwillingness for open, honest communication with supervisor rather choosing gossip and slander, resulting in a lack of unity and contributing to division among your peers.*

- *Violation of agreement to collaborate before sharing your already planned departure in a unified manner in order to protect the church and your family. This showed an unwillingness to manage your exit in a way that put the church before yourself.*

  - *This represents a huge risk to the health of the church and is the primary grounds for termination earlier than the original Dec 1 date.*

- *You've consistently shown an unwillingness to communicate peaceably and respectfully with the lead pastor.*

Requirements of you:

- *Make every effort to end ties to the Church and youth ministry peaceably.*

- *Refuse to gossip or speak poorly of the Church or its leadership.*

- *Meet with Church Leadership for final exit interview.*

The message we will send the church that I believe is accurate and fair is this: "Loren is feeling called to pursue a career in ministry that is going a different direction than that of the Church. There is agreement that the Brenners would use their gifts to serve God better in a different environment."

This Church will continue to pay your current salary

157

until December 1st on the condition that you meet the requirements and spirit as expressed in this letter to make every effort to peaceable depart in a manner that protects the future and unity of this Church.

It is with deep regret that your employment with the Church ends so abruptly, however on the advisement of management team members and key church leaders, I am submitting to their recommendation to protect the organization of the Church.

I trembled reading his words. Through and through, my heart's desire was always to honor Jesus and have integrity. Never in the history of our unhealthy relationship with Matthew did I ever see this coming. Never would I have attempted to destroy him the way it felt he was trying to destroy us. My dignity was shed with my tears, imagining people reading this and our reputation being varnished with falsities.

With our day's plans to prepare for middle school youth group being suddenly dismissed, we needed friends. Finding ourselves in the trenches of a brand new, irrevocable loss, we needed safe people. Bill and Bella were unavailable so we called my friend Jesse who was home with her newborn. Packing up our anger, hurt, betrayal, and wounded hearts, we headed to her house to tell her we would be saying goodbye soon. We needed people who knew without needing told about the dysfunction of our leadership, but also who could be trusted: we didn't want our severance pay stripped from us.

I pulled down the visor-mirror in the car to check my face. It was speckled pink and my eyes had a tint of red, but I've looked worse. We hadn't told them I was pregnant, yet. Jesse had just birthed their first baby not even two months ago. She was one of my best friends.

I sat on their couch. Loren and Jesse's husband were in the nursery swooning over their little girl. Jesse sat in her white glider, glass of water next to her, unknowing what was coming. No idea where to start, I pulled out my phone and pulled up a picture I had taken almost a month earlier to show her 3 positive pregnancy tests. I couldn't help but smile.

She looked at the screen, mouth in a wide and long smile, looked at me, "Are these yours? Are you pregnant?"

I nodded quickly, smiling. "Yes."

We oogle and we oggle over the little lives we had created. We talk about adoption and how we are still moving forward, currently waiting to hear back from an expectant mama.

The conversation starts to lull a bit and the fiery anger is burning my chest, so I finally spit it out: "Matthew fired us."

Incredulous, her eyes widened and she set her water down. "What? On what grounds?"

"For being toxic, unhealthy, and detrimental to the church. You want to read his termination letter? You can't tell anyone. We need the paycheck we fundraised." I am angry. Unhealthily angry? Maybe. Maybe not. I was not about to pretend I was okay. I was not about to pretend I thought this was "God's plan." I knew better by now, I knew His plan is never for pain and sorrow, for broken relationships and bodies, for brokenness.

We recap our week, Loren sharing and I interjecting, so many words and sentences jumbling together from our frustration and hurt. My phone rings. It is the elder, Kevin, whom we adore, respect, and sort of talked with briefly over the summer while yurting about the mess we found ourselves in.

"Hello?" I attempted to keep my voice cool and calm. He

may be clueless or he may have some weird rendition of what happened today.

"Hey Natalie. Just checking in, how are you guys doing?"

Still entirely unsure if he has a clue of our day or not, I speak slowly and carefully, "We are...okay...been better." I decide to ask in a roundabout way: "Do you know what our life is right now?"

"Well, Matthew called me and told me a story. I am trying to fix things. Just know we support you. We love you. We are on everyone's team. We are trying to screw heads back on straight."

Relief washed over me: we didn't even have to defend ourselves, we didn't have to explain anything, he knew. He knew the chaos of our circumstance. I thanked him and told him we loved them.

Maybe people knew us better than we believed they did. Maybe we didn't need to walk around defending ourselves, explaining our hearts away, fearing falsities spoken over and about us.

[42]

I checked my inbox every hour, waiting to see emails from our adoption agency about expectant moms and parents making an adoption plan. It was a nice distraction from our traumatizing church situation. We received about four each week; some weeks as many as seven and other weeks as few as none. These emails were sent to multiple potential adoptive families working with said agency. Included are invasive details about expectant mothers' (and sometimes fathers') medical history. Often times we would read about their jobs, favorite music and foods, weight and height and race, whether or not they are married. Sometimes pictures were included. We had the opportunity to take each situation and decide whether or not to present our family profile book. Presenting incited so much anticipation. When we chose to present to an expectant mom making an adoption plan, this meant she could choose us to parent her child and our family would grow an entire extension.

We were presenting to expectant parents of twins, due in February. Twins! We were unsure if this expectant mom making an adoption plan would even look at us, since we had the sticker on our profile reading, "This couple is also pregnant, but still hoping to be a family for a baby." To us, it was always worth presenting; what if we were meant to raise virtual triplets?

"I just wanted to let you know the expectant mother narrowed down her choices to two adoptive families, and you were not chosen." This email had come many times, along with this one: "The expectant mother has decided to parent her baby and is no longer making an adoption plan." At this point, neither email made me cry. I trusted the best decision was made.

We had said "yes" to four different potential adoption situations. Four yeses only to receive four "noes" by November of 2015. In the grand scheme, this is very few; it was a wild emotional toll, though. We continuously did our best to breathe in and out, trusting Jesus had the adoption story in His palm. He was writing the story, and we needed not worry.

Yet, saying "yes" to a situation was much more than a verbal agreement, or typing words into an email. Saying "yes" was allowing our hearts to be at stake—open and vulnerable—loving strangers we had never met face to face.

We were not only saying "yes" to potentially parenting each baby or set of babies, but we were saying "yes" to all the unknowns; the hidden baggage and tragedy inevitably accompanying adoption. We were saying "yes" to a history we had no information about.

We may have said "yes" to staying in the NICU for weeks to months, watching our baby be weaned off cocaine or meth. We may have said "yes" to risking transferring Hepatitis C from mama to baby. We may have said "yes" to an unknown father. We could have said "yes" to any unknown medical or substance histories; someone for whom we could only trust Jesus with. The fees due for any adoption would be thousands of dollars we didn't have, but we remained confident He would provide for us perfectly.

Hearing "no" wasn't the end of the world, or our adoption journey. I found myself confident, *this is the one,* situation after situation. I imagined meeting expectant mamas and how in the world I would walk the tension of grief and joy.

We received such invasive details about expectant mothers

making adoption plans; my heart cracked wide open to love deeper than ever before.

In crying out to Him and praying for these parents with unplanned pregnancies, I was reminded over and over this isn't about us. For every no we received, it meant someone else receiving the blessing of a baby; whether that be expectant mom choosing to parent or another hopeful adoptive family. We continued saying yes to presenting, holding our hands open and clinging to His closeness in all the uncertainty.

We were not chosen to parent this precious set of twins, due in January/February. Though we were not chosen to parent those twins, due in the next three months, we hoped our "yes" would one day be responded to with another "yes." We trusted whoever that expectant mama chose to parent her twins was exactly who her twins needed. That family will be very, very blessed to grow by 4 feet. In this truth, I rejoice and move forward. Rejoicing comes easy when I make the journey less about me and more about Him.

2015 was scraping me thin and punching me in the gut. Loren experienced it too. We were growing soul tired. And though we were soul tired, weary and thinner than thin, adoption was forcing me to lean into Jesus in a different way than anything else ever had. During a time of complete unrest and chaos (jobless and without our community, a high-risk pregnancy), we had been given an amazing opportunity to pray for expectant families and in-utero babies. Knowing such intensely intimate details about these expectant mamas and families made praying for them an immensely powerful journey.

Despite the continual "noes," we continued waiting and praying. We knew we were meant to become a family with the birth of a baby. We continued saying "yes," even at the risk of what felt like rejection. Adoption isn't about us.

[43]

The Friday after we were fired, an emergency meeting was held at church to address the fallout. It was only a day later, but the group gathered to discuss the successes and weaknesses within the leadership team and our parting. We were not invited to share on our behalf.

We received a phone call afterward to update us on the meeting's conversation. We were told people showed up for us to remind the leadership we were not dragging them through mud. We were told what was said and asked about us: *The Brenners have integrity, what do you think will happen? Why are they suddenly not allowed to talk to anyone from our church community, the one they helped plant and grow?*

With that, our termination letter was rewritten and hand delivered by Danny, our youth leader. It was now titled as a separation letter. I still felt like vomiting as I read the words, but the gag order was lifted. We would have our severance pay until December 1 no matter what. A slight sigh of relief came.

The first Sunday without a "home church" was approaching fast and we knew we needed to attend a church service for our own hearts. We found a church that was about eight years old, and although it was bigger than our previous community we sat in the back. As we walked into the historic building for their Sunday service, we spotted one of our youth kids. He was a pastor's son at another local church, but he was only sitting with his mom; his parents were currently walking through a rough divorce. We found them to be home away from home and sat next to them.

It was weird. Loren and I—youth pastors—kicked out of our community sitting with people we adored: a pastor's wife and son at another church, who also felt unwelcome and out of place in the church they called home. It was ironic and sad. I felt numb.

With the new letter of separation, the leadership gave us permission to say goodbye to our youth group. My husband and I decided to carefully craft a letter to them, using Jen Hatmaker's letter to her children in her book *For the Love* as a guide. With the laptop open, Loren and I sat on our bed in Corvallis. This may be the last time we see many of these kids. We wanted it to count.

We talked about the important legacies we wanted to leave our youth group. What last words do we want them to hear from us? What message did we give to them over time in our precious, shared moments?

The thirteenth arrived faster than we were prepared. How was it already Tuesday? It fell into the category of events you wanted to quickly arrive, but once it did you preferred not experiencing. Like, let's just hurry up and get passed this, but do we have to actually walk through it? Can we just skip and jump over it entirely?

Some of the kids in our youth group knew what was coming. Most did not. No one knew we were cutting off our time at the church cold turkey. This was entirely difficult. They still didn't know we were pregnant. My nausea was in high gear standing next to Loren on stage.

With our printed letter in trembling hands, Loren began reading the first half and I jumped in somewhere near the middle to end it.

Dear students:

Loren and I love you ever so much. You could not possibly have any concept of how often we think about you. We probably just seem like bossy youth leaders, I'm sure. One day you may understand when you are youth leaders and mentors. This letter has been adapted by one of my favorite authors and we hope you listen to it with hearts and ears to hear.

These are our hopes for you:

Kindness. We deeply want you to be tender toward people. Empathizing is key to a wholehearted life. We pray for your kindness more than your success, because the latter without the former is a tragedy. God measures our entire existence by two things: how we love Him and how we love people. Get this right, you can get a million other things wrong.

Some kindness requires more serious courage. I'm not being dramatic: you can save hearts and lives with grace. Have courage in being exactly who you are. It takes courage to march to your own drumbeat.

Learn to be true here and now, you will bypass the devastating "undoing" so many endure later.

Finally, let's talk about God. I know we haven't perfected even half of this youth leader thing, but we hope however imperfectly we have done it, we have given you God. He is the only Thing we're sure of. If you are ever unsure what to do, remember how Jesus loved people. He was the best at it.

Anywhere He asks you to go, He's been there too. This is not an easy path. Jesus went to hard places, did hard things; He loved folks everyone hated or despised. If you trust us at all, believe us: this is the life you want, this Jesus life.

Be kind.

Be you.

Love Jesus.

We continued reading the letter to the students, telling them to embrace who they are, to not allow others to be bullied, and be compassionate. We expressed our hearts and love for them with encouraging words. It was such a remorsefully beautiful moment. Bitter-sweet, but beyond precious; for one of the first few times, I watched my husband cry.

[44]

Our Sunday-goodbye was maybe one of the most awkward and ingenuine moments of my life.I didn't want to arrive to church early. I sat in the car until the very last minute. Every moment felt like it was pricking me, each second ticking felt like needles poking me in my tender parts. When we walked through the theater doors, the sanctuary was dark, the lights dimmed, and I found some safe seats in the back of the sanctuary. I shimmied my way past a few people who were there solely in support of us.

I couldn't help but glance around; this was my last Sunday ever in this theater space used as a sanctuary. My lips were pursed into a tightly, thin line as I clenched my jaw. I felt like I was inhaling molasses the air was so thick. I was sweating. Still, Loren stood beside me holding my hand. My mind was focused on saying goodbye and getting out. I needed fresh air.

I saw Matthew up front and tears instantly stung my eyes. I was furious. Hate burned inside me. I hated hate, but I wasn't going to deny the experience just because it was ugly and ungodly; I was pursuing honesty. Although its process was far from my mind, I knew healing would only start by being honest. I felt disgusted. I couldn't help but think about how much of a façade I thought was being worn. How could he go on with the church service as if nothing was wrong? The hate and bitterness, and the scorn building inside me was not something I was proud of. Would I ever be able to think of this man and not burn with rage? Would I ever be able to forgive him?

A few songs were sung, prayers prayed, and announcements were made. I was freezing and sweating, unsure of what my body was experiencing as we were called to the stage. It was time for our final farewell. Again, most people did not expect this. We were part of the backbone of this church and I am sure we shocked many. Matthew spent a quick moment thanking us for being with them since the beginning. He backed up into the stage's corner while we walked up to stand in its center. Loren unfolded the piece of paper with words typed onto it. It was vague. Pointless really. It didn't carry any information and felt shameful.

He read how we have loved the church before it even existed. We mentioned the many laughs and memories shared; Loren read on about the community groups God created through us and how we loved our time with them. He acknowledged we have known for some time this was not our place forever, and that the time to say goodbye has come. We will love them continuously. There was no good reason for leaving; there was no ministry calling us; we had nothing set up. Just: we love you, goodbye.

Service ended and I refilled my coffee. A few people snagged us to ask why the sudden departure, and where we were going. They expressed the usual "we'll miss you." Loren and I quickly left. Never again would we return to this beloved community who changed our lives; the people who were embedded into us; those who had created a piece of heaven in our hearts. The community who launched us into our adoption, and who supported us in more ways than we could count; we already missed them deeply.

Why did the goodbye have to be so harsh, so abrupt, and pain-filled? Will we be proud about the way we conducted ourselves in later years, as we left this community? This is what I hope for: to look back years later and be proud of the way we handled ourselves. I've asked myself these questions over months into years. I turned them all back to God. Why, Jesus? Why is this so painful?

[45]

September-November 2015

The first trimester of our pregnancy was hard. I struggled a lot. When we were first married, I imagined our pregnancies being beautiful and shared week-by-week with the internet world of my blog. I envisioned weekly updates on how I was feeling, my cravings, how the baby was doing, throwing up, exercising and eating. I pictured this as a lovely time for our friends and family to watch my body grow. Who doesn't love to know about vomiting and tender boobs?

But then 2015 happened. It threw me off, changed me, and altered everything. The fear of hurting those trying to conceive, or dealing with loss kept me from posting too much on social media. I also had inner battles. I feared taking the precious gift of our little one for granted, when all I wanted was to cherish every heart beat within my womb. I craved to share with the world how grateful I was for our baby, and if we did lose him, I would be grateful for the time we shared. I was determined to give pregnancy my best shot, and tried living life with arms extended in surrender. But it was hard. I was weak, exhausted, nauseous, and stressed out. I had bronchitis. Twice a day I was giving myself blood thinning injections to prevent blood clots. It was dreadful, but each time I'd remind myself how grateful I was for them. It meant a baby lived inside me, and I counted it a blessing to *survive* pregnancy together.

Having this baby inside me was exciting, but I still

struggled with my previous losses. The pain hit slyly: pregnancy announcements still hurt, jokes about the ease of conceiving was difficult hearing, and I hated hearing the joke, "at least I kept my child alive today." The idea of not knowing if the pain from the wait would ever subside annoyed me. What I didn't know about pregnancy after loss was how I'd need time to process this pregnancy. A positive test result is gripping. It felt like a giant hand had grabbed ahold of my torso. It squeezed all the air out of me.

I didn't know fear and anxiety would consume me, or that each day I would constantly wonder if I would have to say goodbye to this new baby too. I expected to be just as optimistic and confident and excited. I expected to jump into every pregnancy with gladness while cherishing all its moments. But I didn't feel this. I felt guilty for being pregnant when so many others weren't able. Guilty for celebrating a life after recently losing one. Guilty for being afraid and fearful instead of purely excited. The guilt covered me like butter on bread everywhere I went. I didn't know whether to celebrate and share the news of our newly, discovered baby or to withhold it; I didn't want to trigger someone's ache and pain of desiring pregnancy. This new baby taught me people refrain from talking about your loss once you're pregnant again too. Like somehow, with the addition of this life, the previous life lost never even existed. It made me feel the need to quiet myself about my forever unborn baby. But, I wasn't ready to stop acknowledging the loss of this precious life simply because I was pregnant again and adopting. Loss is loss, and forever loss. Isn't it?

On the adoption side, worry increased about not being chosen by an expectant mama. I was always concerned about not having a mama choose us, especially since we were pregnant now. I felt guilty for how badly I wanted to be chosen, and before our biological baby arrived. I knew wanting to be chosen was completely self-centered.

The journey of becoming like Him didn't end when I became pregnant. It was proving to be so much more than conceiving and carrying. The process helped me learn how to see beauty in the small and minute, finding pieces of Heaven when most things seemed broken and everything unclear. It was me learning to live with hands open, palms up, in surrender. Learning to cherish the life He has given me, even if it is a life on earth infused with brokenness and loss. Perhaps the greatest perseverance built is in learning to somehow cherish all the moments, this life journey and the story, *even when* it's not what I expected.

[46]

November 2015

The boxes had been packed for over a month. We were just trying to figure out where to go, what to do, and who we were. I was pregnant still with our miracle life in my womb. It was a sprout of hope. We had been emailing with our adoption consultant fearing she would suggest we pause our adoption process until we were settled and had our stuff together. But we didn't feel that was right: the pausing and halting. We felt we were to keep pressing in, there was no time to lose in our adoption process.

We had job offers on the table for a youth pastor position at an established church, a pastoral position in Washington, and a job in the administration office of Boise Bible College. None of them seemed right. We pressed into believing God's will for us was much more about our hearts and how we loved others, less about literal jobs and locations to live.

There was a tug for us to move to Portland; though still the whitest urban city in America, it was the most diverse in Oregon. We never really thought much about race in Corvallis and were taught racism pretty much died when MLK was assassinated; upon reading *Inside Transracial Adoption*, we realized the importance of being in a diverse community if we adopted transracially. Since we were in a place of changing up our lives entirely, we pursued this decision. We started studying and reading about how important it is to acknowledge race, and how color blindness is detrimental and hurtful. We wanted to be the best, healthiest, and most loving parents we could be for our children. We recognized this meant being listeners, hearers, and seers especially if we adopted outside our white race.

Oregon was where our hearts resided. We had already paid for our home study to be approved here. We wanted to be in the best place in the state in case our family became transracial. So, we decided on Portland. We had spent days on end driving two hours north searching for housing there. Loren applied to various youth shelter facilities. There was a residential treatment facility he had worked for part time previously in Corvallis, but he was wary to return to the company. If needed, it was a last option. The position was a 32-40 hour a week at Trillium, and started on December 14. Eventually he gave in and accepted the position hoping it would be different than his previous experience We were running out of time and money. Not to mention, our lease for our apartment was up on November 31. We needed to land somewhere.

On a Friday in November we finally found a small apartment for less than $1,000 per month. It was a tiny, one-bedroom on the top floor. It had a washer and dryer, so *that* was something. We were signing the renter's application and filling out a check for the application fee when my sister-in-law called me.

"There's a small, two-bedroom duplex like a mile from you! It just popped up on the rental site. You should call them!"

She sent me the link to the duplex, and it looked perfect. It even had a yard. I had been asking Jesus for a yard. I called the property manager who gave us the keypad password, and we were on our way to go view the duplex half. As we pulled in, I knew it was the place I would become a mama. There was a fenced in yard, small and covered in sticks and weeds, but it had potential. The front window was giant. When we opened the door, I instantly envisioned a birthing tub in the center of the room and my home birth unfolding right here in this space. *This was it.* The bedrooms were tiny, the kitchen even smaller, the bathroom a shoe box. It was less than $1,000 per month; it was a duplex and not an apartment, had a yard, and *two* bedrooms. I was going to birth our biological child in this 650-square-foot home. I couldn't get the thought out my head. I called the property management back. We told them we wanted it and they unlisted it for us.

Life just sort of felt heavy. Our drive home was a bit more eager now that we found a place to call ours. A place where we would deliver our biological baby and hopefully welcome another one via adoption. I knew where our couch would go. I envisioned a DIY mug rack in the dining room; I was ready to set up two, white mini cribs and our babies' dresser. I was ready to be my introvert self, not knowing anyone around me, not having access to nearby friends. Craving alone time with no pressure of doing anything sounded like a slice of perfection.

We were moving to Portland. Loren had a job. Things were coming together. There were things to grab onto, even if our hearts were in total broken disarray.

[47]

No one understood my social media pregnancy announcement. Well, that's not entirely true but a good portion of people messaged me very confused. When we first began the adoption journey earlier that year, we had agreed if we were licensed to adopt and became pregnant, we would keep going. No question about it.

But so many things happened at once. We weren't sure if we should make one, big bang announcement, or spread the news out? How do you tell everyone that you are moving out of the city you spent years cultivating life in, not returning to vocational ministry—which you thought you were made for—oh, and you're pregnant, and still adopting? It felt like a lot.

We decided to announce our pregnancy in what we thought was a creatively, clever way: the three of us wearing "waiting for you" shirts. "You" being our baby via adoption. Loren and I wearing shirts holding a onesie. But as life usually rolls, it did not go smoothly. People were so confused. I thought we were clever.

As Facebook messages, texts, and emails came in we explained: yes, we are pregnant and yes, we are still adopting and no, we did not get pregnant because we adopted. The urgency to adopt only grew stronger as the baby in my womb grew bigger. I could not stop thinking about and praying for all those involved through this adoption journey. I was antsy to meet our future child's birth family and learn about them. I wanted to etch the details into our baby book. Anxious excitement overcame me to get settled: setting up two cribs, becoming a mama to two, to meet our heart grown miracle and our home-grown miracle.

People kept saying, "Oh yeah, that happens to everyone who adopts. They get pregnant." This notion bothered me deeply. It was uncomfortable and never sat well. I usually shook my head replying with, "That isn't how it works." I did some digging in my heart analyzing why it felt icky when well-meaning and loving people threw this statement around like some sort of fact.

Adoption is not a means to pregnancy. There is no formula to pregnancy except sperm and egg. Even still, there are a list of factors that need to take place. Sometimes pregnancy occurs the first time a couple has sex, which I find mind-blowing. If not the first time, within several months of trying; but those who struggle for six months or more to conceive are placed into the category of infertile.

When in the thick of wanting our family to grow we decided to pursue adoption sooner rather than later. We were nearly confident we would conceive and successfully carry a baby, eventually. The two were not dependent on one another. The plan to adopt was not contingent upon whether I could birth a child. Becoming pregnant was not our goal. During this time, people who loved us shared stories about adoption and pregnancy following. The stories implied adoption having something to do with the wife suddenly being able to become pregnant. It almost always sounded like this, "I have these friends who couldn't get pregnant so they adopted, then they got pregnant! Have you guys thought about trying to adopt?"

One thing I am more confident of than most things is this: adoption is not what impregnated me. My husband is. Adoption and pregnancy were both means to children and family growth. But not for a second did adopting make a child any less ours than a biological baby; not for a second was pregnancy and biological kids our ultimate goal.

Maybe these people did have good intentions, but were unaware that their formulas to fix infertility furthered my pain. I'm sure people didn't mean these statements in malicious ways, but more as a branch of hope. Regardless of intentions, it always seems impact will have its way. Especially for deep thinkers and word lovers like myself. From this I've learned be a better listener and value what others share has hurt them.

I reflected on why these statements were painful. I wanted to know the purpose they served in this season of life, and came up with a list of explanations:

- *Pregnancy after adoption: the "because you relaxed" statement. The saying goes, "Because this [infertile] couple adopted, they relaxed and were able to conceive." Adoption is neither relaxing nor stress free. It doesn't void the desire to experience pregnancy and childbirth either. Aside from that, infertility is a diagnosable disease and I have not heard of any other diseases being cured due to relaxing. Yes, relaxing is great, but I have a feeling it won't cure my endometriosis, my blood clotting disorder, or reverse the obscene amounts of radiation that has fried my ovaries.*

- *Pregnancy after adoption: a reward. There is often a subtle, or not so subtle, implication that pregnancy after adoption is some sort of reward. This implies that pregnancy and biological children are superior to those adopted. What does this implication say to adopted children? That they are second best? That their siblings are a reward for them? Let me go vomit a little bit.*

- *The formula: adoption equals pregnancy. Instead of making the free choice to love outside of our bloodline, this formula is implicitly implying the only reason we would adopt is to have biological children one day.*

- *Adoption is a means to pregnancy: not all people who adopt are infertile. I have many friends who have chosen adoption before trying to conceive, or instead of trying at all. I have many friends who know they are able to have biological children but don't feel the need to procreate. This statement proposing adoption as a means to pregnancy assumes it to be "plan B," the alternative for those who cannot conceive.*

I was determined to be sure everyone knew this. My love as a mama was fierce for my biological and adopted children. I was ready to educate others on their word choice to make sure my children and other adoptees knew they were just as valuable as the next kid. The baby in my tummy was not a reward, or any more loved or hoped for than the baby we would bring home via adoption.

[48]

December 2015

It was one day past two months since our world exploded and our hearts crushed. With my belly growing rounder, I sat at Starbucks weekly drinking from decorative, crimson cups. I couldn't believe there was a precious, tiny human inside of my broken body. I stared out the window and saw a piece of the window-pane covering part of an "r" in a sign, reading "Spanky's Pizza". But I think it was supposed to say Sparky's Pizza. All I could think about was a pig being spanked because my brain and heart still hurt.

Our gender reveal ultrasound and party were scheduled. We lived two hours north of our community, but still wanted to celebrate with them, so we set up the party in the middle at my mom's house. On one hand, I had never felt so free to *just exist* as I had since moving out of that small town and leadership team. On the other hand, loneliness was threatening to settle in; all I wanted to do was process everything that had recently happened. I wanted to process it all through writing it out on my blog with brutal honesty. I wanted to etch into the internet all the ugliness I was walking through; there's a message in revealing our rawest, "ugliest" states. Even still, in our great big mess, God is with us.

The problem with sharing it all on my blog was that it would shed light on people I loved. Even those I never wanted to see again. People like, well, Matthew. I seethed with an anger too close to hatred, but I also still felt the responsibility to protect his family.

I kept asking Jesus questions: *what happens when being honest is ugly and filled with uncomfortable truth? A reality people don't want to face because it hurts? The stories that don't make us feel happy, or bursts our bubble? What happens when being extremely honest means coming to grips with the fact that we all hold great capacity to wound others deeply? Even pastors? Even mentors? Even best friends? Even me? What if I expose how messed up The Church is?*

He gently reminded me it's a public truth how imperfect His Bride was, but He still loved Her and worked in and through Her.

I wondered if we then put up our guards, not allowing anyone near our hearts. Do we withhold love out of protection of ourselves? Do we safeguard ourselves to remain whole, or continue risking being burned to learn what authentic love is? Was I able to be truly repentant and see clearly where I had hurt others, or would I find ways to justify my imperfections?

I wasn't sure if these questions mattered or would make a world of a difference. I grappled with God, searching for Him, wanting to know how to love like Him even when my world was chaotic. I hungered to see Him and move past my hurt all while wanting my feelings of betrayal validated.

Is this possible? To hunger for God and love like Him while grieving the loss of relationships, a career, and a community? The fear of false stories being told about us gripped me; would people believe the twisted stories? Fear of being pregnant and losing the tiny human our bodies created overtook me. I feared mourning another loss. I feared not being chosen by an expectant mom making an adoption plan; fear of agencies suspending our adoption; fear of the words, "You got pregnant after adopting? It happens all the time." Fear tried to consume me.

I sipped my warm drink as I typed, asking aloud, "Where did we go wrong?" The first week of October replayed itself in my head. I wondered if God would be our defender as He promised and noted all the ways He already had. I questioned if we were horrible and faithless. If we were weak people because we chose to not pursue vocational ministry. What were we if we weren't youth pastors and church staff?

Who was I if I was no longer infertile? I was now in an odd population, one in which we tried to conceive for two years. We endured the fertility treatments and a miscarriage; decided to begin our adoption journey, and not as a Plan B. I walked the road of infertility for a short, few years that felt like forever. During this time, I joined the adoptive parent community, and was now sixteen weeks pregnant. I wondered if my body would hold the life it had helped create. What category did I belong in, who were my people? Pregnancy after loss? Pregnant while adopting?

My infertile friends were saddened by me. Many friends had never endured miscarriage. Yet others believed pregnancy was the worst thing ever and assumed I would join their thinking. I didn't understand where I belonged. I didn't identify in the infertility group, the easy-fertility group or accidental pregnancy crew. I wasn't even a candidate for the Pastors' Wives group. My spirit was a mixture of crushed and whole. I was a mess of joy and grief, fear and hope, hungering and thirsty for God through each of life's layers.

[49]

December 20, 2015

The days leading up to this monumental Sunday were infused with anxiety: going to church in our new city. The thought of sitting among people in different stages of their faith walk seemed scary. Loren and I attended service in an elementary school; it was our friend's church. Even with time passing, ever since being fired abruptly, I haven't felt comfortable during Sunday services.

Loren's hand laced into mine as a security blanket as we walked through the school doors. We were greeted by people with the dreaded question, "What brought you to Portland?"

Instead of word dumping, we stated simple and less complex things like, "A job," or "work." I found myself breaking eye contact and wanting to shout, "We are with Will and Annie, don't worry about us! We love Jesus! No need to ask us questions! Move along, move along!" But I stood in the corner instead, talking and awkwardly answering questions.

I never realized simple questions could invite so much stomach turmoil. "Church" has always been my first nature. "Church" was the life I was planning to live. "Church" was where my children were going to be raised, but now it was weird and uncomfortable. It was scary looking for a community to accept us as we were with all the fragments and feelings that made us up. We weren't mad or bitter at The Church or Jesus. We hadn't given up on The Church or negate its necessity. We were just in a weird, unfamiliar space when it came to Church.

As we navigated service and new people, I was thankful when the worship music started and it was time to sit down. I was thankful to not be what felt like the center of attention. My mind wandered to all the sadness I was carrying around as a piece of me. I was afraid if I locked up the sorrow that asked for space, if I shoved it deep inside and ignored it, one day it would explode on the people I love most: my kids and my husband. I tried letting myself process pain, knowing by giving myself permission to feel brokenness—and the aches it caused—I would somehow find wholeness. There is a completeness found in allowing yourself to grow in and through sorrow.

I pondered all this as the pastor spoke of Jesus and His birth. Shortly after, we stood and sang Christmas carols. I felt Him so close to me, reminding me that Christmas is about Him. It was His way of nudging me toward the cross, quieting my heart, reminding me that The Church is meant for good even when life gets messy. "Do not give up on My Church. My Bride needs your heart in all its brokenness." I heard Him whisper. Tears silently streamed down my face as my lips whispered the lyrics:

> "O holy night the stars are brightly shining. It is the night of our dear Savior's birth. Long lay the world in sin and error pining. 'Till He appeared and the soul felt its worth. A thrill of hope the weary world rejoices. For yonder breaks a new glorious morn. Fall on your knees, O hear the angels' voices. O night divine."

I was reminded how precious this time of year is no matter what: regardless of how uncertain my life was, the dysfunctionality of our families, the brokenness we feel. Despite who is missing (I should be sitting here snuggling and cradling a one month baby), or emotionally exhausting trips to visit family because of divorce, Christmas is precious.

I want to remember what Christmas is about. It claims that

though we are depraved, He came. We are a real hot mess, humanity, but He came. He squeezed Himself into flesh and a tiny sized body. He arrived in the form of the most vulnerable and defenseless state a human exists in: a baby.

My heart longed to meet the baby growing in our hearts and another mama's womb. I looked forward to making ornaments with our baby's messy hand print to give as a Christmas gift to his birth mother. Adoption has dug its roots inside my heart. More than that, I long for Jesus fiercely. I long to keep Him close. I want to grow more into who He has created me to be.

I am also learning to rest in who He has me as today, *even with* bitterness in my heart and big wounds to be healed, because He is so much bigger. I am learning to find simple delight in His presence here and now, amidst all the unknowns, celebrating the moments I find Him in unexpected places.

We were certainly in an awkward limbo: resettling and relearning our new life in Portland. Surrendering with hands open and palms up is a freeing posture and was an invitation I accepted. We sang about hope for the weary world, rejoicing, falling on our knees in humble surrender. Which was exactly where I was at during service: humble surrender. In my humble surrender among people I did not know, I experienced His gentle, unending love.

[50]

January 2016

The leaf has finally turned from 2015 to 2016. What a relief. I find it intriguing how our brains can compartmentalize time. We box up adventures and experiences, stick the joys and trials of twelve months into a filing cabinet of memories and move into a new year with fresh hope, goals, and bright ideas. Yet, as we box them up and close the drawer to one year, the loss and hopes remain. They still phase us, scar us, boost us, and help make us who we are.

We look toward a new year with anticipation: a ball being dropped, the whistle blown, lips kissing, and then, something special happens. Hope arrives. For us, 2016 is looking a hell of a lot better than 2015. Too many moments strung themselves into days, or weeks long. They dragged on forever and made me crave a hope only a new year could mentally bring. I did not enjoy 2015. It was ugly, painful, wound-inducing, and heart breaking.

I suppose it had its highlights too though. Yes, we lost our first baby, but we also experienced a positive pregnancy test unaccompanied by fear and loss. We also had the most joyful of moments infused with laughter and dreams, name games, and dancing. We planned our nursery, and dreamed of Christmas snuggles.

Travel adventures weren't scarce in 2015 either. Loren and I explored five countries in three weeks. We sipped wine in Paris, ate frites in Germany and the Netherlands. We climbed the Eiffel

Tower, prayed precious prayers in ancient churches and rode trains through Austria. Countless hours were spent with the best of youth, and memories were made with them that will last a lifetime. Our family began its growing process too. We began our incredible journey toward adopting a baby using hashtags like #bringhomebabybrenner. The thought of when it would change to #broughthomebabybrenner made me giddy. We discovered another baby in my tummy. We moved to a new city and discovered a mutual love for good ice cream with Seth and Lacey.

As we turned our faces toward the new year of 2016, I didn't want to completely spit on 2015. I spent many days and nights on my knees crying prayers into carpet fibers, but it was in those moments I knew more than ever God was with me. It was in the carpet fiber crying I found His grace unravel and wrap itself around me. His presence gave me permission to exist in the grief and sorrow.

Facing 2016 with anticipation, I reflected on 2015 and found more grace in the broken pieces than in the wholesome and pretty pieces of it. Instead of burying the ugly I wore throughout the year and pretending it didn't happen, I craved to remember how messy fragments often serve as avenues to grace.

Amidst the dirt in this world, I still chose to clothe myself with dignity; yet, in my most vulnerable moments, when I found myself at the pit's bottom with nothing left to experience, I found God. His tender grace and presence met me. It was there that Jesus and I met. He was most present in the splinters of life.

New Year's Eve brought unexpected fullness and hope to my heart. Hope budded beautifully and created a joy more profound than I had ever known. Hope is most radiant when birthed out of darkness.

[51]

Our baby via adoption was coming. I mean, I thought he was. I felt it in my heart. How could my heart be wrong? I checked the agency website at 8:00 a.m. and saw a baby was born that morning, a boy who was only a few states over. "URGENT" was highlighted near his situation. He had an adoptive family who fell through. I looked over the few notes their website had and looked at the agency fees; we had a quarter of the fees due and this didn't include travel and lodging, food, an attorney, and all else needed. Tens of thousands of dollars would be needed within twenty-four hours. It was impossible.

Discouraged, I picked out a floral dress. The day marked twenty weeks of pregnancy with our sweet, little tummy baby. I constantly felt urgent in raising funds and being ready for The Call. We had decided our budget would be No Spending January; we wanted to save every extra penny we had and throw it into our adoption fund. I had an interview on this Wednesday. The extra income would help store away funds for our adoption fees.

I threw on some make up, straightened my hair, and glanced over my resume. I was applying for a barista position at a retirement village. Swanky.

"Can you tell I'm pregnant?" I asked Loren, turning to the side, attempting to hide my growing bump from the interviewers.

"Is this a trick question?" He kissed my cheek, "You look great."

"Will you take my picture? I'm 20 weeks today! Did you see that a baby boy was born in Utah?"

"Yeah, did you see the fees?" With that, baby boy's situation was dismissed. I wasn't surprised, I was bummed.

We walked out the front door. I stood in the middle of our dead-end street, turned, pulled my dress tight against what I thought was a giant protruding belly, and smiled. In reality, it looked like I ate a few too many pancakes. I hadn't had a job interview in over five years, and here I was twenty weeks pregnant and adopting, all while trying to get a job.

The interview was smooth and easy. It felt natural. The guys who would be my bosses were kind and professional, but personable. I felt like I had the job in the bag.

When I walked through the door to our small home, Loren was at work, and I checked the agency website again. *Maybe that baby boy still needs a family*, I thought. As I logged on, the first little boy's situation had been removed and replaced with another baby boy who was to be due that day. The fees were substantially lower, and we had slightly over half of what would be due when he was born. This was possible. This had to be our future boy. I sent off an email to Emilie, the agency employee, letting her know we were interested in possibly presenting.

My stomach fluttered. Excitement swept over me, and I prepared sweet potato biscuits for the next morning's breakfast. When Loren got home I brought up the situation, and we sat down with a notebook and pen. We calculated the fees, what we had saved, and concluded we could present. Everything seemed perfect. Not to mention, this baby's expectant mama was planning a homebirth. We already had that in common.

My phone buzzed around 7:00 p.m. "Hello?"

"This is Emilie. Listen, this boy's mama is in labor now. Could you send me over a few pictures via text and a small blurb about yourself? I have one other family who is interested. I think she would definitely choose you; you're a lot younger."

I jumped up and down smiling. We went through my phone, picked two pictures that best displayed our shiny and bright, welcoming smiles, and sent a blurb about how awesome we were. We also wanted this laboring mama to know we were pregnant, so we included that.

As we waited for a response, my heart was racing. This was it. Our baby was coming. We were going to be parents. I texted my twenty closest friends and family explaining the situation, and asked them to pray for this baby's mother, the baby, and us. "This is it," I said confidently. I can feel it. I started pulling clothes out of my dresser, preparing to pack my bag when Loren stopped me: "Nat. She said there was another family. Can you wait? We don't know yet. This may not be it. She may also still decide to parent; we don't know."

I dropped what I was holding, my mouth fell open, tears stung my eyes. "What?" I was in disbelief, how could he not feel the weight of urgency and confidence?

"I know, it's hard. I want it to be our 'yes' too. But it may not be."

My phone buzzed again. The Utah number let me know it was Emilie; I leapt to grab it. "Hello?" Somehow, hours had passed. It was 11:00 p.m.

"Hey guys, so because of state laws, I went ahead and just presented the other family first. She went ahead and matched with them. I am sorry. I am sure she would have chosen you, but Oregon's laws weren't as easy."

My heart sank. Tears welled in my eyes. How could this be? How could this not have been our baby? Why did my heart feel so certain?

I attempted to sound calm and collected, "Okay. Okay. Thank you, Emilie."

"Did you see that another baby was born today? He still needs a family and—"

Disheartened, I cut her off. "Yes, I saw. The fees are too high.

We have nowhere near that amount. I'm sorry. I want to. I so want to, but we can't."

"Okay. Are you sure?" She pushed.

I took a moment to answer. I turned and looked at Loren. His hands in the air, shoulders shrugged; he had no idea what Emilie was asking.

"Would there be any way you could extend the due date of the fees?"

There was a pause. Tension through the phone lines had never felt so life altering. "Like, how long?"

"I don't know...three, maybe four weeks? Even that feels impossible." I closed my eyes, rubbed them with my right hand. We were closing in on midnight.

"I don't know," She said slowly with care. "We have never allowed an extension. I can ask."

"Okay. I will call all the grants we applied to and family members to see if I can pull some strings in the morning."

The phone call ended. The weight of the day was crushing me. I laid on my side, facing Loren, watching him sleep. I felt tummy baby moving around, wiggling inside, letting me know he was doing well.

How could they have presented that other family first? What if that baby's mama would have just seen our family? Why was this nagging at me so intensely?

[52]

Thursday, January 7, 2016

Tired and fragile is how I woke up. I slept about three hours and was feeling somber. The weight of other people's lives felt like it was resting on me. It was 7:00 a.m. and my phone read three missed calls. All were from Emilie. Her voicemails were asking me if we had found stashes of cash or grants or *anything* to make it possible to present to the other situation from yesterday. I had pretty much written this situation off in my heart, knowing it was impossible. I knew God was big, but *this* big?

Everything felt unreal. My heart was weary. I felt entirely lonely. I sat and ate my freshly, hot sweet potato biscuits. Tears fell into them and the coffee I had poured. Then, I heard God whisper to me, "I am with you in this uncertain mess. I am with you in the joy, hoping, and chaos. I am with you, holding you close to my heart. I know this pain far more than I can tell you. Do not fear. We are in this together."

I finished my buttered biscuit and began doing everything I could to find extra money. I sifted through all the grant applications, emailed and phoned each of them, inquiring if there was any way they could decide today and now.

I drove Loren to work, heavy-hearted and with a saddened soul. As he opened the door, my heart spilled from my mouth, "Honey, I need you with me out here in the water. It's scary and lonely. I need you out here."

He closed the door partially, leaned towards me, "What?"

"What if this is our baby? The baby born yesterday? What if we need to trust that He will provide all the funds?"

"Oh Nat…" he looked through the window, his voice trailing. I always felt like the crazy one asking him to join me in wild and ridiculous things. To enter into illogical, irresponsible living. I was the one who encouraged him to quit his part-time job and live fully off fundraised income. I was the one who was sure we would find jobs up in Portland if we just relocated. It was always me always asking him to jump into deep, shaky waters with me.

"Listen. I know this seems impossible. I know it may actually be impossible. I also know this may not be our baby. But what if he is? What if he is our baby and we are missing the opportunity to be his family, to let him bless us? I need to do everything I can to be sure. One of my spiritual gifts is faith. I know it is hard to meet me in these crazy and unrealistic, illogical places, but I need you to really ask Him to bring you here with me. I need you to wander out into the deep, turbulent, crazy waters. We may be fully let down, but it is worth the risk. I need my husband—more than anyone—to know it is worth the risk."

I stared at him teary-eyed and vulnerable. He stared into my eyes, with a still and expressionless face. He nodded, "Okay. I'll try. I've got to go to work. I love you."

My sister-in-law Emily and I had a date at her aunt's that morning, so I cleaned my messy face up and prayed my way there. They welcomed me into her home and my tears immediately started falling.

"How could that baby not have been ours? Why do I feel he is ready and waiting for us? Why aren't our funds bigger? Who can lend me tens of thousands of dollars so we can say yes to this situation?" I sent a text to Emilie, the agency employee: "Has mama found a family yet?"

Emilie quickly responded with, "Can I call you?"

I stepped into the other room, being a real hot mess.

I answered and listened to Emilie cut right to the chase: "She has looked at more than five different adoptive family profiles and is feeling quite hopeless. She isn't connecting with any of them. Are you sure you can't present? I really think she would connect with your family."

My stomach twisted into knots. I hated this. I hated that I couldn't say yes with ease. I hated that the cost of adoption was so high, but also understood we were dealing with human being's lives; this is costly.

"I just...I just don't think so," I said.

"Okay, I have three more families to show her. I'll go ahead and do that." Emilie ended the conversation and I hoped to hear back from her soon.

My heart was crumbling beneath the weight of saying no. I couldn't stop thinking about this baby, his mama, and how terribly hard all this was. The baby in my womb was kicking me, moving around in my belly. I placed my hand on my stomach letting him know I noticed him. My sister-in-law, Emily, invited me over to her house. I was unsure what else to do, so I went. This waiting game was entirely lonely. No one in our circle quite understood the pain it involved. Even I barely understood it. It's always in the suspense of waiting I learn what it really means to trust.

I sobbed all over her dining room table. I called friends and family members, asking them if they had any extra cash they could lend or give. I was desperate. Emily encouraged me there was no shame in not presenting. No one would think less of us. I tried explaining that I feared the opposite: what would people think of us presenting without funds? I feared we were being so full of faith, even unwise, that we become irresponsible. Where was the line? What was the balance between great faith and irresponsible, and was there such a thing?

I said to her, "What if this mama chose us, wanted to place her precious son into our family, and God let us down? What if He didn't provide the funds? What kind of heartbreak would that be?"

[53]

January 7, 2016

Emilie had called me as I was walking out Emily's door to the truck. I had a shed to pick up at Sears. We could empty the storage out of the second bedroom and make it our nursery.

"Hello? Hi. Did she find a family?" I asked, my words smooshed together.

"Yes, but it didn't work out. The state laws don't work together. If we gave you three weeks, could you come up with the funds? She really wants a young family and I really feel like you guys are it."

I swallowed hard. "I know this is a big no-no, but this situation seems so unique. Could you present us to her saying, 'This family isn't sure they can come up with the funds, but if they can, would you choose them?' If you feel that is too hard on mama's heart, don't. I am just struggling over here with knowing what to do."

"Yes, I will do that." Her voice quickened, "So I can present you?" Emily spoke in a high-pitched tone. She was ready for this.

"Be sure she knows I'm pregnant." I clicked the "end" button on my glass screen and stared at it. Once again, I found tears falling out my eyes and it started raining. It was almost as if God was telling me He felt the weight I was carrying. I felt His soft and gentle voice was whispering, "You have to trust me. I won't fail you." *Jesus, don't let her like us if we aren't this boy's family.* It was more of a begging demand, my heart on its knees, fearful and scared, wide-eyed before my King.

I clenched my jaw as my mind raced. My knuckles white as tears of fear fell into my lap. On the drive through traffic to pick up our shed, the sky turned dark blue, nearing black. I pulled in and parked, looked in the mirror, and wiped off what was left of my mascara. My skin was spotty. My nose dripping. I wiped it with my sleeve, opened the truck door, and hopped out.

The shed was packaged so small I feared for my husband. This was not going to be an easy assembling task. It may take years to put this shed together. I pulled the, "I'm twenty weeks pregnant, can you lift this?" string and two men loaded it into the truck. I turned the ignition on when Emilie's name popped onto my screen for what felt like the millionth time in the last twenty-four hours.

Quickly, I swiped to answer with a quivering, "Hi. Yes, tell me."

"Natalie, I showed her your pictures. The moment she saw you, I noticed a change in her demeanor and she said, 'Yes, those are my son's parents.'" She paused. I waited for Emilie to continue, "Then I told her you were pregnant and expecting a baby boy in May…" I felt my whole life waiting in the cold January air, "and she said that solidified it and made it even better. She wants her son to have a sibling close in age."

I stared at the steering wheel shaking my head. I was in disbelief. I needed her to tell me again, I needed to hear the words clear as day. "Wait so…"

"You have a son waiting for you in Utah. Can you get here tonight? We can give you a few weeks extension for the fees; we've never done this, but we recognize how unique this is."

My hand clapped over my mouth. Tears began bursting the seams of my eyelids. I hung up and called Loren three times. My whole world was rocked. I was overcome with disbelief, shock, joy, and an utter fear that He would fail us.

I sent Loren a text reading, "Call me it's an emergency," hoping it would get his attention. While I waited, I called Loren's parents. They were the only people I hadn't yet reached out to for financial help. His dad answered and I struggled to get the words out. I told him the story through disbelieving tears. He told me he would talk to his wife and get back to me.

On the drive back, I kept wishing Loren would be home when I arrived. Just when I thought I'd need to show up at his work, he called.

"Is everything okay?" he asked.

I wasn't quite sure how to share this news to him. He had been working all day. The last thing we talked about was how I needed him to join me in the craziness of faith, in the illogical spaces of trusting that God really is bigger than we believe.

"Honey, we have a son waiting for us in Utah."

His voice broke into a softness I had never heard, "What?"

"I need you to come home. Can we fly out tonight?" I begged.

"Please tell me every detail. I am going to come home now." Loren later told me he went into his boss's office and said, "I think my son was born yesterday." His boss dropped the sandwich and his mouth hung open before he smiled widely and said, "Go! Go home now! What are you doing here?"

I sent Loren the tiny pixilated picture Emilie had texted me of our soon-to-be son. His little lips turned up into a smile and Emilie's caption read, "He knows you love him." Later Loren told me the moment he saw that picture, his world stopped. Any leftover fear of not being able to love a child not born to us diminished immediately. All fears of there being a barrier were shattered with that small 1.6-megapixel image; he doesn't have a Smart Phone. "I am a dad," he said. "I finally have a face to love and connect with. A face not looking anything like mine, but a face giving my heart the jump it ached for."

When Loren got home it was around ten pm. By this time, I would normally be sleepily waiting up for him; but not tonight. My adrenaline was surging, hormones wild, and mind running. I recapped the afternoon, I cried, Loren teared up. He continually stopped mid-packing to hug me.

"Nat, I can't believe it. This is wild and scary and we have a son." He repeated these words countless times that night. We were matched. We had a son waiting for us. It was time to make travel plans to meet our son.

[54]

January 7-8, 2016

We weren't prepared for this gift. We had not yet had a baby shower. Our nursery was filled with boxes, bikes, and random items. We didn't have a car seat, blankets, swaddles, or clothes; all we had was a Moby wrap. I quickly wrote a blog post titled "WE'RE MATCHED" asking for financial help. It went viral and the PayPal donation alerts flooded my phone so much I turned off the notifications.

It was hard not to constantly check my email and social media updates when we should have been packing. The world's excitement for our growing family blew my mind.

My brother called late that night and offered to purchase our airfare and rental car. The agency's social worker told us about a house that is often rented out to adoptive families. It was located directly across from the hospital.

My friend Emily (I have a plethora of Emilys in my life) brought over an infant-carrier car seat they no longer needed, tiny newborn onesies, swaddle and receiving blankets. She arrived around 10:30 p.m. and stayed until after midnight talking about attachment and important baby things that I hadn't spent much time researching. Things like umbilical stumps and baths and swaddles. All my time up to this point was spent on paperwork: home study applications and agency applications and grant applications; reading about attachment and transracial adoption. I had forgotten I would need to know basic baby care things like the rainbow of poop to come and how to clip their tiny little fingernails.

Emails from the agency were waiting in my inbox. There were financial agreements to be signed, piles of paperwork that was scanned and returned, and a loan application awaiting our information and signature. Around 1:00 a.m. I decided to take a long, hot shower. This was my last shower as a childless mama. I was going to enjoy it.

Hot tears blended in with the shower dripping down my face and body, my protruding, tummy. The baby kicked. "You have got to come through, I don't want us made to be fools of faith," I prayed through gritted teeth. "Oh Jesus, is this real?"

It wasn't until around 2:35 a.m. that I closed my computer, threw my wet hair into a bun, and laid my head onto my pillow. With my eyes closed, I attempted to sleep, but all I could think about was how we were here and our son was there and we had already missed so much of his small life.

Our alarm rang too loudly for three in the morning. I smiled realizing the last two nights were just a small glimpse into what was to come as sleeplessness. The time was here: I was becoming a mama. I was stepping into the skin I had longed for and waited on all this time. This was the skin I wanted to keep; this was the skin that felt right.

My brother drove us to the airport before 4:00 a.m. He snapped a sleepy photo of us, prayed sweet prayers, and sent us off to meet our son. Both of us were nervous wrecks. I couldn't eat, my adrenaline high; Loren spent a lot of time in the bathroom, and neither of us had spoken a lot.

What if his first mama didn't like us? What if we are too young in her eyes? What if we say hurtful things? What if we say ignorant things? What if we are too excited? What if we don't show enough excitement?

I was suddenly aware of all the ways I was clueless. Soon enough we found ourselves in a rental car in Utah, ordering a beautiful bouquet of flowers, and attempting to write in a card. What do you say to a woman you are meeting for the first time, who is giving you the gift of being a mama? How can you find words to share with someone who is surrendering the most precious thing to her while you are simultaneously receiving this precious baby as yours? Are there adequate words?

The weight of the tragedy was suddenly more real than it had yet been. This woman loved her son so much that she sacrificed the comfort of her body for eight months; she knew he was a blessing, and she recognized she was not in the space to parent him the way she desired. For none but him, she was choosing adoption. She had made an adoption plan months ago. She had made the decision to place him into another family, at the expense of her own heart.

Our social worker snagged my camera as we rounded the corners of the hospital. That hospital smell lingered in the air. Loren and I felt our stomach twist into knots and our emotions vacillated from joy to grief.

"Focus on how beautiful your son is. Tell her how good she did. Empower her with how proud you are of her and how perfect he is. Ask her questions about herself. You'll do great. I can already tell." Our social worker attempted to calm us. As we turned into the room, I wasn't sure what to expect. It was hard to grasp this was happening. We all smiled nervously at each other as she held her son. He was swaddled up in a white, hospital blanket with a blue and pink stripe.

I walked over to the bed, and sat down. His mama placed our tiny, new son into my arms. My eyes glazed over with tears as my heart slowed its pace. My soul whispered: "Oh, there you are."

I looked up at his first mama with tears in my eyes and a smile. She was smiling so big, and tears flowed from her eyes too.

We get to be his? My eyes were asking her. She nodded with a grin with tears streaming down her face.

[55]

Friday, January 8, 2016

The weight of love was overwhelming. Witnessing with our eyes and feeling with our souls we experienced the weight of sacrificial love. The room's air bled tragic love.

How could someone's tragic loss be our unfathomable gain? How would I ever fully understand this paradox?

This is the boy for whom we had been praying eight long months and for whom we had done countless fundraisers. He was the child our village rallied to support. We waited so long for this moment. The long days and long nights, the endless rejection. Suddenly, it was all worth it.

My heart wrapped itself around his mother and her child. Nothing in this world could undo my fierce love for them. How could I not embrace and cherish the one who chose life for our son? How could I love my son, but not the people who gave him life, and placed him in our family? My great and unexplainable joy was intrinsically encased with her indescribable loss. My understanding of adoption deepened. Our world is so broken and often, so backwards too.

Weakness in my legs forced me to remain sitting on her hospital bed, as I sifted through the realization of how much she loved this boy. As I witnessed her watching him, tending and caring for this baby, I saw how she observed us alongside her child. I wanted to always have open communication with her. How could we deny her knowing him? Why would we deny him the opportunity to know her, his birth mom? I knew she chose us, after saying no to countless others, but I had no feelings of entitlement to him; I loved him upon meeting him. Seeded into my heart was assurance to be his. Simultaneously, I had peace acknowledging she still had the opportunity to parent, to not sign relinquishment papers.

Feelings of love and humility ran over me. I was not mama. I was *potentially mama*. I clung to the unexpected calm accompanying this reality.

I sensed the sacredness in these hospital moments. I did my best to be fully present, to take note of every single detail. I wanted to store these moments in my mind as memories forever and ever, accessing them as needed, sharing them with our son when he asked.

I didn't want to say goodbye to her. I wanted to spend hours, maybe days, together. I wanted to learn everything there was to know about her to share with our shared child. What kind of work had she done? What were her dreams? What was her favorite color, type of music and food? What did she crave while she was pregnant? What was her story? But it was time to give her some space with her son. We returned to the waiting room after thanking her for everything. She picked up a pen, placed it upon the paperwork, and selflessly signed away her rights to her son. She placed him into our family forever.

Deep inside, I knew she had brought forth her child with unconditional love. Then, made the painful decision of placing her child into another woman's arms. I became mama because she wanted what was best for her son.

Then and there, in the sacred space of a hospital room in Utah, our shared son became a mark of His goodness and grace. God's faithfulness to our barrenness, the waiting, and longing. This baby was the answer to so many prayers and served as a reminder of another mama's strength. Our son was a gift we would learn to celebrate and unravel for the rest of our lives. His story proves adoption can truly be beautiful.

But with tears in my eyes as I write, I must acknowledge that though his adoption embodies goodness and graciousness, it is also a reminder this world is not as it should be. Brokenness permeates our world. Sure, beauty is born from ashes, but the ashes don't just magically disappear. Suffering and all that is wrong in this world still exists. This side of heaven, tragedy remains and the moments of her son becoming ours is a representation of joy and suffering deeply intertwined. Our son, the living proof that love *is* what makes a family, reminds us that adoption is born out of undeniable loss. Irrevocable loss of wholeness, of what was meant to be.

To only acknowledge the beauty without giving voice to the tragedy, is to detract from adoption. In diminishing the tragedy of adoption, I decrease my son's story, along with others a part of the adoption circle. I would be choosing to ignore a massive portion of who he is. Ignoring pieces of my son's identity unintentionally will drive him to feeling shame. Pretending tragedy doesn't exist in his story implicitly shouts that part of who he is is shameful, embarrassing, and isn't worth talking about. Ignoring something speaks that it should remain hidden.

Anytime we pretend tragedy doesn't exist, we implicitly believe it is not worth a voice. Then, I think of Jesus. He set aside His comfort, desires, and physical body. He accepted the crucifixion, denied life, so we instead could have it. Until He endured the depths of Hell, the depravity of this world, we were not given an opportunity to truly live. Our son's birth mother resembles Jesus. Withholding her from our son is to suppress a necessary picture of Jesus from him. That is a tragedy on many levels.

[56]

January 15, 2016

I realized what the terms "primal wound" and infant trauma meant. About a week into being Sage's mama and daddy we found some sort of almost rhythm. Our swaddling techniques improved quickly. I was learning to assemble the miles of fabric made into a Moby wrap. Still in Utah, we downloaded a white noise app. We memorized "Brahms' Lullaby" touched with sounds of oceans and wind. We spent our days snuggling and bonding, skin to skin with mama and daddy, singing songs and praying sweetness. Attempting to be fully present with Sage, we also raised funds online to pay for the adoption fees.

Our online adoption auction raised nearly $2,000. We sold *Live Out Love* adult t-shirts, onesies, and toddler tees. I booked as many photography sessions as possible, asking clients to pay up front. I was offered the barista position I interviewed for days prior; those twenty hours a week would be put straight toward the loan we took out. It was the perfect position: my work schedule would be Sunday evenings, Mondays, and Tuesdays. Loren could continue working Wednesday-Saturday evenings. The time with all three of us together would be slim, but our top priority was having Sage with at least one of us.

Nearly every day in Utah we visited a doctor, or attended an adoption related appointment. Aside from appointments, we spent our days focusing on our little Sage, doing our best to let him know we were his. We weren't going anywhere. Being his mama seemed my most natural experience. I sung and whispered sweet truths to him, and prayed bold and brave prayers over his life. Loren told him about Santa and the tooth fairy and all the things he would too soon discover.

January 15, 2016 has forever marked itself in our memory. We stood before the judge nodding and saying "yes." It is with both with great joy and deep sadness we stood before the judge: we celebrate for us, and grieve for Sage and Mama R.

After reading all sorts of lines, our judge looked us straight in the eyes and said, "Sage I. Brenner is yours as though you birthed him. Do you understand this and agree to this?" With tears stinging our eyes, we confidently said "yes." He wasn't born to us and we wouldn't let this very important part of him slip into the cracks of his story. We will always talk about his birth mother, Mama R. We will continually welcome conversation and questions without shame. We already love him as though he was born to us. We love him something fierce.

Sage's first week with us flew by. Immediately following our court hearing, we planned lunch with his birth mama, R. Anxiety ate at me. My heart hurt. I figured seeing us only perpetuates her wounds. I hate being the cause of pain. Then again, it wasn't like she isn't already thinking about him.

We head to the store to find a gift for R. Our hearts wanted to pick out the perfect gift for our son's first mama. Strolling countless aisles, stores, malls and corridors, I sweat with stress over my ignorance. Picking out a gift for the woman who trusts you with her child is not easy or simple. We search through necklaces, bracelets, frames, and albums. What are you supposed to gift the woman who is handing you her child, with great hope and confidence you can offer him something she cannot?

We find ourselves on a bench, Sage tucked near my heart, tears welling in my eyes. "What in the world are we supposed to get her?" I look at Loren through wet eyes at a loss.

"I don't know, Nat. This is hard." Staring at the wall, we hope the answer appears. It doesn't. We end up in Target. I hopelessly pick through dozens of necklaces and find an eternity necklace. An eternity necklace signifying, no matter how far she is from us, our love withstands distance. I hold onto it.

Photography is one of my passions. I document life to cherish moments forever. I print out over 50 images taken since meeting Mama R and Sage. I print two copies of each image, find matching photo albums, and write little notes inside of hers. One album for Sage, one for R. We walk towards the checkout when sweet stuffed animals pop into view: *perfect.* We grab Sage and R matching stuffed animals.

I package up this little gift and imagine handing it to her. My conflicting emotions are vast: I hate that we are the ones walking away with part of her heart, but I am beyond grateful to be his mama. I hope this small gift can serve as some sort of representation of our gratitude. In purchasing matching items, I hope she knows she will never be forgotten by her son or us.

We pull into the Chili's parking lot. Sage is sound asleep, nestled tightly in his infant's car seat. It is much too big for him. He is a whopping five pounds and eight ounces. Swimming in the newborn onesie we carefully picked out for this lunch date, I unclip his car seat buckles and assemble the Moby wrap on me.

He's ready to be snuggled close to my heart. I carefully move him from his carrier, tucking in his little limbs, as he remains fast asleep. I rub the back of my neck. My throat is dry, my lips chapped, a ball forms in the tight muscles surrounding my heart. Loren and I look at one another and pray together that our time will be honoring and loving. We grab our gift basket and walk into Chili's hand in hand.

My eyes meet Mama R's and I smile. I work hard not to let my threatening tears fall. Breathing deeply, I bite my lip and pat Sage's bum which sits perfectly on top of his brother's belly bump. We hug, find our seat, and stare at the menus. The waitress pours water into glasses, our social workers help our conversation along, and I suddenly find my legs standing me up. I start pulling Sage out of the wrap to pass to Mama R.

"Would you like to hold him?" I ask, assuming to know the answer. She nods yes with a beautiful smile. I carefully take his tiny body out the Moby wrap, his limbs all coming together at his midsection. He's like a little, squishy ball. I kiss his brown forehead and pass him to her. I sit back down to look at the pieces of wobbly plastic with words plastered to them. *This is the menu,* I tell myself. I wonder how in the world I am to process the words before me. *What is this? What is a burger? Fries? I think I like fries?* My brain is mushy.

We all order food, but only our social workers are able to stomach anything. I take some photos of Sage and R as they spend precious moments together. I want to forever imprint these into my memory. She rocks him and stares at our shared baby, then feeds him when he awakes. Tears fall from her eyes and run over her smile. Her love radiates over him and into my heart, forever marking me with a grief-stricken joy. I see brokenness in her eyes, brokenness meeting a deeper love than most can dare to muster.

Mama R is doing the very best she can with what she has. Watching her with Sage, once again, makes me feel deeply motivated to be the best mom possible. Witnessing her loving her son brought into my mind what a shame it would be to allow mama-exhaustion to turn me weary and bitter. In the depths of who I am, as I watch her cradling her tiny premature son for the last time, I commit to serving him to the best of my ability. Even at the expense of my comfort and pride and ego.

Goodbye comes all too soon. We stand up from the table to head to our cars. I walk side by side with the mama who made me mama. We trail in the back of the group, as if walking slower could somehow extend time, delaying our goodbye. I want so much more: I want to know her, for her to be available to our son, to find funds to fly her and visit Sage yearly; I want to share so many words of love. I feared overwhelming her, and instead offer a long embrace, ensuring she knows how grateful we were. We exchange email addresses. I tell her I'll wait for her to email me first. I didn't want to overwhelm or bombard her.

"If you ever make your way to Oregon, please let me know. We would love to see you again." I stare into her eyes as I say it, meaning every single syllable. Our communication was originally categorized as "semi-open, through the agency," but we crave openness; I want it for our son but also for us and for her. She nods. I think she believes me. She hands Sage back. My sweet, firstborn son. Hers has now been made mine. We hug again, but it doesn't feel long enough. I don't think anyone can prepare for moments like this. These moments aren't *meant-to-be* moments. None of this is the original plan; this separation was not in God's hope for our world. If we were in the Garden, in the perfection of the world's beginning before the fall of man, Sage wouldn't be my son. Adoption wouldn't be necessary.

We wave until we are out of sight. I tuck our sweet son into his car seat and he comes undone like never before. His siren-like screams pierce my heart in ways I didn't know it was capable of being pierced. In an infant-type way, he is manic. His bony fingers pull at his hair, he restlessly shakes his head back-and-forth, and his legs flail around. Sage screams with every part of himself. It's as though his soul screams for the mama he knows. A longing for the mama who carried him all those months, with a familiar heartbeat, whose scent was known. The mama he left is the one who feels right to him.

Tears sting my eyes. I hold him close in the backseat of our rental car. Loren and I stare at each other through the rearview mirror, wide-eyed with streaming tears. My jaw clenches, my stomach is knots, I worry if the whole world can feel his anguish. I worry his first mama can hear his wails, knowing he wanted *her*. I am scared she might see us as unfit.

I close my eyes as tears press their way through and streak down my face. Rocking back and forth, I sing "You Are My Sunshine." I beg Jesus to help Sage feel safe, loved, and at peace: "Jesus help my son know he is safe with me; help him to know me as mama."

He tremors himself to sleep and I tuck his tiny body back into his big, infant car seat. My heart fissures for him in ways that won't easily heal because his story begins in the throes of tragedy and loss.

[57]

If I hadn't miscarried, I wouldn't have my son. Of this, I am nearly certain. When we found out we were pregnant the first time, our due date was November 2015 and we were planning to pick the adoption process back up August 2015 to "spread the babies out." But who knows if we would have actually done that? Who knows if we would have said, "Yes, let's pursue adoption while we are pregnant." I would love to say we would have, but knowing my husband, we wouldn't. He is a "take life slow and think about more kids in ten years" type of guy.

As I transitioned into motherhood, I was confident I had activated my mother's heart from long ago. The desire to be mama burned in my soul. I often read it was impossible to understand the love a mama feels for her child. The only way to understand it is to live it. I knew what meant. A mother's love is stronger than anything anyone will ever experience, but when I read about those statements it felt entirely unfair.

While waiting, my heart yearned and burned to be mama; I did every little thing in my power to prepare. I was nice to my body, eating all the right things and exercising. Yet, the perpetual twinge my heart felt with the absence of the title "mother" felt like the love those other mamas spoke of. A mama's love is fierce, sacrificial.

I thought I understood their love before I held a baby in my arms. The burning love I carried around was waiting to be birthed and placed in my arms.

When our son's birth mother placed him into our arms, he fully activated the mama-love I had been carrying around. He was the undeserved gift I get to unleash and pour this bottled up mama-love into.

Details aren't lost on me: we started our adoption process right around the time Sage grew a heartbeat in his first mother's womb. I believe He writes our stories, but I push back against the notion Sage was created by God *for* us. I don't believe God intended for adoption when He set out to create the world. But then we broke the earth and adoption became an integral part of humanity. If the world were moving and flowing as He originally planned it to, Sage would not be in our family. Selfishly, I hate this reality. But it's one I don't want to twist for my comfort. God didn't put Sage in the wrong womb; but God did work in the intimate details when his first mama knew her best decision for him was adoption.

Life on earth is a mess. Our world is often one, but if we had not walked through the loss of our biological baby we would not have been sitting in Utah with our firstborn son. If humanity didn't choose brokenness in the Garden of Eden, we wouldn't have waded through the trenches of infertility and miscarriage, and the heaps of pain it brought. We wouldn't have our son, Sage.

For the first time, I was thankful for our miscarriage. Sitting in someone else's home in Utah at their long wooden table, our less than six-pound infant snuggled up close against my chest. I looked into my baby's eyes smiling tearfully. Loren and I looked at each other smiling in awe. "I've never been so thankful for brokenness." I whispered to him.

We were living out of a suitcase in a stranger's home out-of-state, pregnancy sickness overtook me that morning with vomiting. We were unsure when we were heading home to

Oregon, yet I had never felt more like who I was meant to be. I had never felt so sure of my story, of His faithfulness.

Their dining room windows held a view of the most giant and snowcapped mountains I had ever seen. I thought on God's perfect love. When we found leaves to cover our nakedness, to mask the vulnerable parts we thought were shameful, He called out to us. God never shames; He invites us to be bare before Him, even in brokenness.

The crucifixion was what made our adoption to God possible. But our adoption to Him wouldn't exist without the loss of wholeness. We cannot acknowledge our adoption into His family, His Kingdom, and not give voice to the suffering endured. In ignoring the violent death He endured, we detract from the value of being a part of His family. In not talking about the depravity of man that crushed Him, in only seeing the good from being His, we miss out on the opportunity for immense wholeness. We miss out on the opportunity to experience a depth of joy only accessible by acknowledging the depth of darkness.

It was in the moments of uncovering this truth I found closure in the loss of our first biological baby, the baby we had miscarried nearly a year ago. I unpacked what I thought about "His Plan," and uncovered grace and joy in brokenness. Then I swore to myself to never utter the words, "It must be God's plan" in response to someone's suffering.

[58]

Motherhood comes natural to me. I was asked countless times how my transition into motherhood was; every time it caught me off guard because it didn't feel like one. Transitions always accompany a loss of some sort, or discomfort. Moving out of vocational ministry was uncomfortable and difficult; the transition out of childlessness and into motherhood was smooth and unnoticeable. It was like I was finally living in the space I had been craving. Transitioning into motherhood was simply becoming more of me.

Being well into my second trimester, I was used to sleepless nights. Whose pregnancy isn't filled with constant trips to the bathroom? The baby in my belly had a knack for kicking me in my bladder constantly from ten at night to six in the morning.

Our newborn son was the unhappy one of the bunch; he screamed inconsolably for hours on end, especially through the night. The first few days and nights of having him, we were in Utah awaiting state clearance (also known as ICPC). I recall countless failed attempts at swaddling his little, jittery body as his arms swayed around with tiny fists protesting in the air. His little lamb-like cry broke my heart in many ways, but it was an answer to years of prayers.

From the beginning of being his mama, he tried and tested me in ways I had never been tried. He invited me into being sanctified in ways only he could. As he fought with every part of himself to keep from sleeping, I was invited into a space of patience. Early on I discovered the delicate reality that it was not only my responsibility, but my privilege, to teach this little man about Jesus. I began to share God with him using words spoken, actions taken, and my attitude given. Every single moment with this little man was an opportunity to point him to God. It was in this that I found motivation to remain calm and gentle. So much of his screaming stemmed from early trauma, and that was not his fault.

While he couldn't comprehend what I was saying with my words, I believe he could experience the love and attitude they carried toward him. It became easy to see my tiny son as a baby and to not expect him to be consistently happy. It was easy to be his mama even with his desperate and constant screams. I knew of his trauma, validating his response; this made grace easy.

In Exodus 16, I read about God providing manna for His people, the Israelites, every single day during their journey into the wilderness. Morning after morning, His people awoke to His provision. I found that when I continued to return to Him moment after moment, He provided grace; there, within it, I found patience and an indescribable joy. My exhaustion was pretty intense. I was in my second trimester with a traumatized newborn, but I continued to ask Him for gentleness and grace and He continued to provide. It was in finding Him in all the smallest—and challenging—of moments that I grew into mama to our firstborn son.

[59]

February 2016

My son was referred to as a nigglet. The word split my heart right open through the small ear piece of my phone while driving. My comfortable world of whiteness shatters around me once again, and the high-pitched ringing won't stop. The skin on my knuckles turns transparent as I grip the steering wheel and stare ahead at a stop sign. Fiery hot anger bursts at my seams. We had only been back from Utah and settling into our home for two weeks.

I know racism exists. I believed in the oppression I read regarding people of color, but I wasn't ready for this. Who is? The word apparently fell out of a man's mouth like a joke, as if it was no big deal, but it burrows itself deeply into my heart, puncturing a wound that may never go away. This small wound is nothing compared to the wounds people of color have poked in and through them for generations.

My understanding of my own ignorance moves to an entirely new level, one which I have been blind to because why would I need to *really* see it? Systematic racism and oppression hadn't directly affected me. In Corvallis, I didn't have close friends of color; therefore, I hadn't heard the experiences first hand. I hadn't seen it as clearly as I do now because, embarrassingly, I didn't realize it was needed. You only know what you know, right? You don't know what you don't know—until you learn, or perhaps—until you *must* know. I was unaware of how very real racial injustice is, and how deeply racist our system still is. Our system is designed for the success of the white man and very few others.

What a privilege, right, to be unaware of how so many people and communities are suffering every single day because of their skin color. This privilege accompanies my white skin. I realize in these moments how incredibly important it is to acknowledge my whiteness, my privilege, and use it if I want to live and love like Him. For me, it's always about living and loving well like God. It always involves us asking ourselves questions: how would He love well in said situation or circumstance? How would Jesus respond to giant communities crying out, begging to be seen and truly heard?

My mama blood boils and my mind races. I unclick the car seat belt protecting my three-week-old son. It's late. Darkness covered the sky and now, my heart too. We were just getting home from visiting friends while Loren was finishing up his swing shift and then *this*. *This*! Someone telling this story thinking it is humorous. Someone saying these things to begin with. Not just about *my son*, but communities of real people with real stories and real hurts. Making jokes with a term so dirty, so foul, so unloving and unkind.

My instincts are to throw real daggers to the assaulter, making him hurt more than I, but physical pain will never match the agony those words bring to the heart. A joke or not, the term is not funny and there is no justification in using it. I am ready to lay down the rules of this family, to make sure everyone knows stereotypes and racial slurs are not acceptable.

Snuggling Sage in the kitchen, I turn up the song "No Longer Slaves" and sing to him. I speak truthful words over him as I grieve on his behalf and mine. I commit this brisk January night to stand up for racial justice. I commit to learning and listening. I know I'll fail and make many mistakes, but I must try. In the darkness of tonight, in the depths of discomfort and hurt and frustration, I knew I had to take a seat as a listener when it came to living the black experience in America.

It's apparent to me I need to seek out, listen, and learn from communities of color, as well as other communities who have been deemed otherly. It's past time to do my part in speaking up about racism, stereotypes, and prejudice when white people are around. Even the people I love most. It means I have to get uncomfortable. God is inviting me to do what I committed in my heart when I watched Mama R selflessly love Sage over lunch: to serve him to the best of my ability. Yes, even at the expense of my comfort, pride, ego, and the loss of relationships.

I was further discovering what it meant to be an avid follower of Jesus. Uncovering more of Him led me to realize how important it is to fight racism and stereotyping, to stand up for the oppressed and be a *true* listener. This was many people's everyday lives: racial slurs, jokes, unearned disadvantages, feeling less than, constantly fighting a system that oppresses them simply because of their skin. Constantly trying to get others to see from their point-of-view, only to be dismissed as too sensitive, easily offended, and dramatic.

Dismissed. Invalidated. Unloved. Unseen. Oppressed. I saw for the first real time this is what we do to people of color when we deny, ignore, or say, "But I didn't mean it that way," as our response. This is entirely opposite of His heart. No matter the cost, I want to chase Jesus into a life of loving well.

Wearing the title "mama" is so much more than changing dirty diapers and soothing tears. Being mama is learning how to love my children, sacrificially. At the expense of losing comfort from disagreements and hard conversations. Being mama is *choosing* my kids and their identity over myself. It is choosing to quiet everything I thought I knew so I can attempt to truly see what it might be like to live inside their different-than-my-skin lives. Who am I to say I could ever know what it's like to live in this nation as a brown or black person when I walk around with skin so pale? Who am I to discredit stories told and experiences shared?

In the safety of my home, I grip my son close and shed fragile, white tears, music filling the small room of our kitchen. I dance and I pray. I promised Sage I will do my best to not let him down and disregard his black identity; I will celebrate it. I pledge to him that I see my mama duty clearly: to fight for justice on his community's behalf as a white accomplice. Whatever this looks like, I am ready to listen and advocate. I don't want to simply say I have faith or think I love like Him; I want to live it out and believe Jesus' words of coming to serve, not be served.

[60]

March 2016

Sage's pediatrician, Dr. Miller, is admitting us to the children's hospital. He's had multiple seizure-like episodes leading us to wonder if there is something going on inside his tiny body we should know about. He also hasn't gained much weight. At two months old, he is still six pounds eight ounces, wearing teeny tiny newborn onesies. Can't say I don't love how cute and teeny he is, but we're concerned.

Dr. Miller has been keeping a close eye on him since his arrival from Utah. Twice a week we drive south two cities for checks ups: noting his weight and vitals, wondering why he isn't gaining pounds. He eats constantly yet, no weight gain. Dr. Miller decides it's time to admit him to the children's hospital for a thorough exam. She doesn't want to miss something, especially with the multitude of unknowns regarding his genetic, medical makeup.

"I'm sorry, guys. I can't seem to figure out what is going on and I have a ton of tests I'd like done. If you're at the hospital, they can easily do them back to back. I don't want to miss something scary, something that can be treated." Dr. Miller spoke with caution. I assume to keep us calm. I sit in the plastic chair feeling cool as a clam, looking forward to finding some answers. My husband has a plethora of questions about what she thinks may be wrong, "Is he okay? How long will we be there? Should we be worried?"

I place my hand on his leg, attempting to pass some of my

peace to him. It doesn't really work, but I continue to adjust my face into a relaxed smile. There isn't anything to worry about until there is something to worry about and if something comes up, we will walk through it one moment at a time. There isn't much else to do. I am confident that freaking out and worrying about uncertain things only steals from our energy. I don't have energy to worry; my gratitude to be this boy's mama exceeds worry. Loren and I make a game plan: run home, pack our bags, head to the hospital. They have a room all ready for us, set up on the sixth floor overlooking the greatness of Portland. Tall city buildings, river rushing through, traffic lights and honking cars. Our room feels giant. We even have a personal bathroom. Too bad the shower doesn't have a curtain.

We settle in for the night, my rounding stomach rumbling as it often does, a reminder to eat. The uncomfortable couch unfolds into an even more uncomfortable bed. The three of us snuggle up together, gearing up for the every-four-hour vitals. Every diaper we change is to be set aside to weigh and count. Every ounce he drinks is counted and calculated. They tell us to rest, but it feels like every ten minutes a new specialist or nurse is in the room to poke and prod.

During our four-day stay at the children's hospital, diagnoses are thrown around in the air carefully, but seriously. Very intense and life altering diagnoses. Questions are asked about medical history and we answer to the best of our ability, but our knowledge is little. Nurses tell us we are their favorite family: cheery with the cutest patient *and* pregnant? They bring in all the nurses to show them our family. Their awe makes me feel like they see us as heroes which makes me sick; we are just normal people being average parents. I enjoy showing them there *is* such a thing as being in very, scary spaces while experiencing immense peace. Jesus writes the best stories. He gives peace unexplainable.

Many of my friends and family members are freaking out, asking if we are okay and how we are doing. I am exhausted and uncomfortable, but my gratitude remains genuine. At times, I wonder if it makes me a bad mom not freaking out over all of these possible diagnoses. But the truth of the matter is I feel no other option but to trust in His bigness. There are countless unknowns and I will drive myself insane if I travel down the multitudes of rabbit holes being presented to us.

I continue to find grace in the spaces of the unknown, in the waiting. I find myself relying on Him fully; the wait creates space to trust. Really, nothing feels certain. Day after day, doctors sit us down and tell us the next diagnoses they are taking into consideration. They explain the plethora of procedures, the practices they are about to put our tiny, preemie son through.

The last night we are there, I sit next to the large window showcasing the big city's beautiful lights. The clock ticked after midnight and I have not slept more than in one hour increments since being admitted. It had been four days. Hospital rules are no co-sleeping, but Sage has never done well sleeping alone. So, I find myself either standing next to the giant crib holding his binky in place so he can rest, or sitting up in the plastic, purple chair staring at the wall while my eyes slowly blink. I sit half awake, half asleep, ready to be alert the moment the nurses come in; I don't want to be caught "co-sleeping."

The baby in my tummy moves constantly, confused about when is time to sleep. He's already tasting the diagnosis of Younger Sibling Syndrome. I sit snuggling Sage, staring out the window at the lit streets and craving to write. It's what keeps me sane and holds me steady. Writing is how I process uncertainties and ultimately, where I find God. I don't know if it's our last night in the hospital, but they say it could be. I sit staring and thinking about how I have had zero freak-out moments during the intensity.

Whenever a doctor or specialist mentioned an extremely, and sometimes fatal diagnosis, Sage's sweet story rushed to the forefront of my mind. We have been constantly asked how we are doing, and if we are holding up by nurses, friends, and doctors. Watching our tiny six-pound son undergo immense testing, pokes, and prods is not for the faint of heart. Yet somehow, during a million uncertainties, I can nod and confidently say we are okay. We will make it no matter what.

I find this extreme comfort knowing God indeed placed Sage in our family. The intricate pattern of our son's story was woven too carefully to not have been woven on purpose and by Someone greater than us.

I know if He, the great quilter of life, had woven together this beautiful story out of such tragic fabric, He would be with us no matter what the tests said. I am so grateful to be Sage's mama. I see it a privilege to be the one to hold and comfort him when everything is up in the air.

Apparently, twenty-eight weeks pregnant is the third trimester. I experience some weird form of denial. I feel so incredibly lucky to grow a life within my womb. Now it's nearing closure, a "new season" they say. My daily injections give me bruises and I often can't find a spot on my stomach that doesn't already hurt to inject a new needle with life-saving medicine. My feet are falling apart, my hips burn, and I am incredibly tired.

"You have so much energy," everyone keeps saying. But really? I don't. I have zero, zilch, nada when it comes to energy. My eyes burn, my body aches, I fear if I fall into a true sleep and enter a REM cycle, I might not wake back up. It's joy people notice, not energy.

Sweet Sage sleeps on my chest and I rock us in the purple, plastic recliner. I rock the three of us into the morning, uncomfortable and all. I rock and remember our first biological baby, the one we lost a year ago to the day. That little baby paved the way for Sage and for the one in my tummy. That baby, the one we said goodbye to much too soon, pushed and challenged and deepened us. The baby we said goodbye to taught me to surrender to sorrow. It's okay to weep, and there is no need to freak out, but if I do, it's perfectly okay. Our miscarriage revealed to me there is no formula to walk through hard things.

I rock us through our last night at the children's hospital, unsure what is going on in my tiny son's body. I rock, unsure if I will have the privilege of meeting our second-born, but basking in peace that whatever happens, I will keep going. Covered in grace as a product of honesty. It's an odd thing: when I decided to be fully honest about whatever my heart undergoes, I found immense peace among the chaos of uncertainties. In my honesty and by acknowledging our big, big God, I found peace.

[61]

March 2016

"When your real son arrives." It was said so quickly I didn't catch it in time. Truth be told, it took the wind right out of me in complete shock. I don't even remember what we were talking about and the conversation ended abruptly. Her lunch break was over and she headed back to work.

My hand found my son, the one who I was holding; my other hand finding the other safely swelling me wide. What if he were old enough to hear those words? How did those words just happen? What just happened? How did I not correct her?

I sit on the couch, dizzy from the questions and my disbelief. I'm frustrated at myself for not saying anything. The shock of her statement hit me so hard I didn't know how to respond. *My real son.* The son due in a few months. The son who shared our DNA and our blood.

Words don't adequately articulate what a blessing Sage is to our family. Before we even knew of him, his adoption knit our family closer. Our journey of adopting him brought Loren and me more intimacy. Adoption led us to love bigger than we knew capable. We have wiped countless tears, soothed incalculable screams, changed a legion of diapers. We spent more than a week in the hospital with him, days on end fighting for insurance, resources spent to provide the best feeding system for him. And somehow, he isn't considered our real son? What are we if we aren't real? A fake family? Pretending? Acting until he is eighteen?

His little fingers wrap around mine, swooning my heart. I make eye contact with him. We do so much staring at one another, learning one another's faces and features, our scents and smells, becoming one another's favorite pals.

We aren't playing house. We aren't pretending to be a family, we *are* a family. I find myself praying out loud: "If or when he comes to a place where he wonders and doubts, and is asking hard and valid questions, Jesus help him to know he is our very real son. When people equate biology to 'realness' in the validity of a family, Jesus help him know families are so much more than blood. Help him identify even more with you, Jesus."

We pray together on the couch often. I know in my gut this isn't going to be the last time we hear this statement. Uneasiness settles in as my stomach twirls. He'll grow up so close to his brother who happens to share our DNA, perpetually being compared to and asked if he is our "real" son. *Are they "real" brothers?*

There isn't such a thing as illegitimate or fake families. All are equal, and no family is less than the next. Though his skin, hair, and eyes are different than ours, he will still resemble us: in character, in love, and in all the tiny seeds we are planting. Common roots create families, and Sage will forever be rooted in our hearts. This is not to discredit his first and biological roots, this is to validate his identity as our son.

I commit to him I would continue educating people. I will let people know with gentleness and grace how their word choice matters. More than anything, this is about not detracting value from real individuals in real families with real hearts. Not just our family, all adoptive families. I commit to him, and to every future child we have the honor of parenting, to do my part in bringing justice to this world. Justice and validity to families and people of all kinds. I cannot sit back and let life go on in ignorance, but I will be purposeful, learning to listen in the same manner I desire to be heard. I want to leave a legacy of loving well.

[62]

April 2016, thirty-two weeks pregnant

At most, ten weeks remain. My high-risk pregnancy is soon ending, and I can hardly believe it. How is time lived so quickly? The emotions surrounding this future birth are substantial. I am stoked to conquer birth. I will birth a human through my body, and he will be delivered straight into my arms. I've held that magical moment of meeting close to my heart for so long. I have been dreaming of labor and birth for years. Not just off and on, but consistently and frequently and possibly to a fault. I spent time mourning the loss of not being present for Sage's birth; I had big hopes of being present as a doula, or simply supporting our child's birth family in any way I could. His first mama and I both shared our sadness in that loss.

A home birth is something I'd always wanted, so this was the plan. Less than six months earlier when we first found our tiny, duplex home, the first thing I envisioned was a giant birthing tub in the small space of the living room, laboring and delivering our biological baby in the comfort of our home. It was going to be perfect for so many reasons, the first being not leaving Sage. Birth was coming, and I anticipated it with joy and excitement, not fear.

Due to the nature of my pregnancy, my body, my blood clotting disorders and the daily injections I was on to prevent blood clots, I knew there was a slim chance of having to be transferred to the hospital. My blood could clot too much, or not enough post-delivery. But this is highly unlikely, not causing me stress or fear. Worrying about these things demanded energy I didn't have. I am so ready to conquer this miraculous experience. I am ready to show the world of birth-fearers there is nothing to fear. You can mostly control the birth if you listen to your body. Having a natural birth doesn't need to be scary.

We assembled our birth team, wrote letters to each member, and etched out what soothes our little man. A list was made for who is telling who when I go into labor, where food will be located and what I'd like to eat. I dug up all the items my midwife, Julia, had given me to set aside to utilize when the time came. My friend Angie offered to be present with her camera. It is all being prepared perfectly.

But I'm not ready to be done with pregnancy. Our due date is May 25, but anytime anyone asks me, I am adamant it is mid-June. I embedded into myself the expectation of going overdue. And yet, mid-June is fast approaching and I am scared for so many reasons, though not of birth itself.

What if I don't love our second son as much, or as fiercely as Sage? This fear takes up so much space in my head. I cannot wrap my mind around having enough space in my heart to love another human as much as I love Sage. I confessed this concern with Loren and he shared it also. But people have tons of kids, so somehow, they must love them each as much as the previous, right? Do our hearts truly have the capacity to expand? Our hearts are already overflowing with love, there is no more space. It needs to grow.

Am I a horrible mom because I wonder these things? What if our son is stillborn? In the hospital or in the comfort of my own home, this is a possibility. With the blood disorders, along with my freak-accident history, it wouldn't be a huge surprise. Though it would rock my world, it is a possibility I need to think about and acknowledge.

I was told at the age of twelve I would most likely not conceive and carry life to term. If I did, the doctors said it was unlikely to be a breathing baby. The doctor shared this before he sent the first of many rounds of radiation x-rays through my lower back, unable to protect my ovaries. In high school, I suffered three major events that were incredibly packed with force on my body: a terrible car accident, an ATV accident, and a wave accident in Hawaii. These happened within six months of each other and the x-rays, CT scans, and MRIs were plenty. I couldn't walk and had a neck brace. They said I lost a one inch of my vertebrae, and were frying my ovaries with more radiation. They said my sacrum was stuck and forever crooked; unable to be straighten, it was said I would have chronic lower back pain. The medical professionals said I would not be able to produce healthy eggs and my uterus would not support a pregnancy. "I'm sorry," they all said dryly, "but there is always surrogacy and egg donors."

A month into my freshmen year of college, I had bilateral pulmonary embolisms, the fancy term for blood clots in my lungs, and was diagnosed with two blood clotting disorders. My OB at the time said getting pregnant would be incredibly stupid, and if I did, I and my baby would die (she was not a great doctor, because there are plenty of successful Factor V Leiden pregnancies. I just didn't know and sat in her office listening to her. She's not my doctor anymore).

Another year later, I was diagnosed with endometriosis, a painful autoimmune disease that inhibits fertility as well as makes life chronically painful.

I've wondered for years if their prediction of never conceiving and carrying to term was my reality, but part of me knew deep down it wasn't. Part of me knew I would one day carry a baby, deliver him, and kiss him. I have not made it to that point yet, but I am nearing it. It is planned to happen in ten weeks or less. Miracles.

I don't want people to use my story to make themselves feel better. I don't want people to use my story to *attempt* to bring hope to another woman who is in her shoes suffering from diagnoses and infertility. We like to pat ourselves on the back for sharing other people's stories to help them deal with their personal suffering. We do this instead of sitting and listening and validating; we rush to fix their pain with stories. Even if someone has endometriosis or blood clotting diseases, and their diagnosis matches mine, I do not want to become a random story used in an attempt to invalidate someone's deep anguish. I don't want to be used to hurt someone in the throes of infertility of miscarriage. I do not want to be used to offer false hope, or to be a reason someone continues to put hope in a baby or health or *whatever*. I want people to place their hope in a big, big God.

When in the pit of these spaces, these experiences, these losses, I never wanted to hear how everyone else could conceive and carry. I needed something bigger to hold onto. Something firm, secure, steady. Something supernatural. I needed Jesus.

Of course I wanted my story to bring other's hope, but not hope in babies or titles such as "mama." Nearing the delivery of a miracle—a biological baby—I craved to offer people hope in a Comforter and Healer and Friend. Maybe not Healer in the physical way yet, but Healer of broken hearts. Approaching the end of my pregnancy, I figure my story will be shared and told to many. I wanted to be sure every person who heard it, especially people who are walking through the loss of fertility and/or miscarriage, knew He isn't sitting up in the clouds causing all of their anguish and sorrow. He is instead sitting right next to us each, grieving and mourning with us.

And on this April day marking thirty-two weeks pregnant, I have no idea what our future holds. What I do know is I am pregnant. In these moments, that is enough and that is a gift. My pregnancy is high risk, my home-birth is perfectly planned, I am holding a hospital-transfer in open hands, and I am already a mama. If we lose tummy baby, I will be devastated. Words won't describe my devastation.

But part of me feels I need to somehow prepare for that, for the worst of the worst. And yet, how does one prepare for such tragedy? I don't. It feels entirely impossible to prepare for such an irrevocable loss. Instead, I continue the pregnancy-journey one day at a time. I know when delivery happens, regardless of the details, there will be so many emotions.

I crave more than anything for this nameless tummy baby to know we love him insurmountably, even if we have to say goodbye. I want to continue trusting Jesus with him, knowing Jesus loves this little life more than I ever could. Every moment with him is a gift. Ten weeks remain. The emotions are vast, the tears stemming from a place of fathomless appreciation. Appreciation and gratitude: it's an immense honor to love and care for souls. Human souls. I have the privilege of knowing their precious selves both in my womb and on my skin. This is something I'm not about to lose sight of.

With a high-risk pregnancy and fearing my heart won't grow to love more, I anticipated conquering birth; I would deliver our biological son. I couldn't wait and was antsy for Sage to meet his baby brother.

[63]

April/May 2016

I'm grateful to be me, which feels monumental. I'm that annoying mom nodding when older mamas-turned-grand-mamas say clichés like: "You'll miss these days, cherish it while it lasts, it flies right by." Because I know I will. I love these sleepless, poop-filled, and regurgitated-milk days because they mean I have a baby. They mean I am a mama.

Never have I felt more myself than I do at thirty-seven weeks pregnant, mama to Sage, wife to Loren. Though my due date is fast-approaching, it feels like I could be pregnant for another four months. I am only just beginning to meet Sage and I am soon to add a second? How can I possibly be mama to two infants? Is there enough me to go around? My heart wants to explode at the reality of doubled expectation in such a short time. My mind wonders how I will be able to physically care for the two of them. It's a grand adventure having virtual twins. A never-ending adventure with *two* little ones only months apart.

The reality astounds me. To think just one year prior, we were exploring Europe and grieving the loss of our first baby via miscarriage. I never doubted He would prove Himself faithful, but I wasn't happy with the pit of darkness I found myself in a year ago. I was not thankful for what had been handed to us: miscarriage after two years of infertility. In that season of loss, I attempted finding real reasons to give thanks but fought fakeness. I didn't want to pretend. I didn't want to put a band-aid on a broken bone. The reality of being a mama to two children—who are less than five months apart—blew my mind into boundless fields of gratitude.

Looking back over the previous twelve months, I'm in a place of confidence regarding some big things: I don't believe God causes miscarriages, or loss of any kind. However, I do believe He *allows* death and suffering, extending to us Himself in our pain. He offers Himself as space to mourn.

I cringe every time someone tells me "God only gives me what I can handle." He doesn't give us tragedy or loss, He doesn't create pain or brokenness. He allows it because we—humanity—chose it in the Garden. In allowing brokenness, God gives us Himself over and over again. When what is handed to us is too much to handle, which seems all too often, He hands us Himself.

In the words of Ann Voskamp, "Our fall was, has always been, and always will be, that we aren't satisfied in God and what He gives. We hunger for something more, something other." It was in the Garden, so perfectly planned and planned for perfection, we decided we weren't satisfied in what He gives. It was in the Garden we hungered for something more, something *other*. It was in the Garden, starting with the very roots of humanity, brokenness was formed and began. Not because of Him. Not by His choice or plan. God did not give us brokenness, tragedy, or trauma.

Miscarriage is too much for me. Losing our job in a traumatic way, our community, the identity of pastors, and the career of vocational ministry wrecked me. Acknowledging that my son will be asked questions like *who his real mom is* breaks me. Coming to grips with my white privilege, acknowledging systemic racism, is too much to wade through. My friend's home thickly infused in trauma and PTSD carried around by their four-year-old foster daughter, is too much to handle. *Brokenness is too much for me.*

God was and still is in the trenches of these losses, even when I am unable to fully acknowledge Him. He is with me in the thick of grief as it hits in waves even years later. When I have zero motivation, no strength, little dignity to call out to Him, His presence remains because He is faithful even when we are not. His mere presence is sweet.

Reclining in our blue, camping chair set up on the patio, my belly giant, I snuggle our sweet, sleeping son. Loren attempts to rake the mud pit we are supposed to call our yard. I stare at the miracle in my arms. Not even four months into being mama I can hardly breathe at how blessed I was. It may be the giant baby in my body (*there really is no telling*), but breathing through blessedness is difficult. I have many, tired and hard parenting years ahead. I foresee hair-pulling days and many mistakes. But today, with five weeks or less left before meeting our second-born son, I am overwhelmed with tears of gratitude. Life won't always be sweet as it is now, so I choose to bask in it.

I am thankful for the gift of dying to myself constantly, only to love deeper than I ever have. To love a soul so big, a human so small, a life so precious. Life is infused with sweetness, despite the losses we are still wading through. In the giving of thanks and acknowledging the very real honor of being Mama, I find immense beauty. In giving thanks, I can slow life down—even but for a moment—to discover an indescribable joy.

Because really, a lack of gratitude has always been our greatest downfall. It was the beginning of humanity's brokenness: wanting more than what God offered. On this late spring day, I sing thanks for the sleeplessness and the screaming sadness escaping my son's mouth. I sing thanks for all the things I could instead complain about because it is in that thanks I find joy and grace. It is in the thanks I am reminded of how deeply I longed for these hard, trying, and exhausting times. It is in this thanks where freedom is found, permission is gained to being the mama I desired to be. Gratitude is where I find more of God.

Perfecting motherhood is impossible, and perfection has never been my goal. I mess up daily and will continue to. Imperfection is a part of this world's brokenness, but it is in my mess-ups, in the moments I complain and forget gratitude, where I uncover His grace waiting for me. It's in the moments of not loving what is being handed to us, in acknowledging it is all too much, where He resides. It's sort of His business, covering us in scandalous grace, giving us the strength to find joy in chaos, and in being called Mama.

[64]

May 2016

Life is weird. It just is, you know? People are weird. People look at me and stare. I'm sporting a Target maternity dress, revealing my rounding body, wearing a tiny Sage against my chest in the Moby wrap. Grocery shopping in Costco is an invitation to comments and questions. It feels like every eye follows me around the produce section. As my body appears more and more pregnant, I guess people stop assuming my belly is leftover postpartum flesh and more pregnant flesh; people started staring. It makes me giggle, really. Loren and I smile and wave. *Take a picture, it lasts longer,* I want to sass.

I often wonder why people don't just ask, but then when people do they say the most hurtful things. I find my jaw drop a lot in shock. It seems to be a lose-lose for us all. I pick through the bell peppers, smiling, when a lady smiles at me and asks how old our son was.

"About 4 months," I say joyfully.

She responds to my smile with a smile of her own and asks, "And when are you due?" I want to hug her so hard.

"I am due in about three and a half weeks. So, five weeks?" I laugh, knowing full well I'll go past my due date.

"My daughter is due around that time too! So, did you adopt?" She asks gently with love. She cares. I can always tell when someone is kind and caring, and when they are not.

"Yes! We did. We were privileged to adopt this little one while

I was twenty weeks pregnant." I found the purest looking bell peppers and stuck them in the cart.

"My daughter and her husband tried for several years and endured many miscarriages. She is now in her last term and due in the next few weeks. I am happy for you. Two babies in one year, wow. What a blessing."

I nod with tears in my eyes. I feel seen and safe. I feel loved. It may be the only conversation with a stranger about having two so close in age that feels so safe. Usually, people raise their eyebrows and say, "You're going to be busy!" Or, "Oh yeah, pregnancy always follows adoption. People always get pregnant after they adopt." Or, "Are you crazy?" Or, "You are super woman!" They even ask, "So was his real mom on drugs?"

Some of these are true and some of them aren't. Yes, I am going to be and am busy; but what parent isn't? From the beginning of becoming Sage's mama, I told myself one baby was easy. I made myself believe caring for one baby was easy, and soon we would have two. *That* was going to be hard. Busy was an understatement, but we were busy when we were building a youth ministry. Busyness isn't reserved only for mamas of almost-twins.

People refer to me as Super Mom or Super Woman. But these titles are the furthest from the truth. I am just as much a wreck as any other mom. I am a hot mess and need Jesus just as much. I am unsure how to tear down the false beliefs that I somehow have it together more than the next mom. It is probably the same as tearing down every other false belief and stigma: by being honest.

And so I am. I remind mamas I cry a lot, constantly wondering if I am messing up my child's attachment forever. I *need* Jesus. Just like every other mama, I needed Jesus during our "waiting season," in discovering we were pregnant (both times), as we considered our son's situation, the moment we said "yes" and trusted He would provide, and when his birth mama chose us.

I need Jesus every single moment of every single day and I know when Sage's little brother arrives, I will need even more of Him.

Artificial or virtual twinning, whichever name society prefers, is certainly not for everyone, but it isn't set apart for super women either. Raising two babies less than five months apart, in two different developmental stages, is going to be hard. I know this. But I also know He is with me. He prepared me for this. He used the weighty wait to create a hunger in me to be broken and poured out into little humans. He was refining me to invest in these little souls; it was God showing me how to teach my boys what it meant to love and be loved well. If I teach these two how to love well, I will have done my job. It's easier said than done, and I'm not ready to think I know what I am doing. I simply agreed to take this beloved journey one day at a time, and be honest along the way.

There are so many reasons not to virtual twin and I agree with them. Before I knew I was pregnant again, I had an inkling we would live some beautiful, unique story. When our social worker told us we shouldn't be trying to also get pregnant while adopting, something in my gut said, "But what if we were made for this?"

As we approached nameless tummy baby's due date, I relished in our time with Sage as an only child. He will hold this spot briefly: five months if all goes well. He won't remember being an only child either. For us, this was unique and precious. We had a few months to be parent to one, before inviting our second treasure home. We will only experience being parents to one for a few, short months. This is unique and precious.

We don't know how the story will unfold, how parenting these two so close in age will work out, but we are thankful for the opportunity to do our best. I fully believe that doing my best means constantly stopping to ask questions, listening to others, hearing from adoptees, other virtual twins, and people of color. More than ever, I am learning that loving my boys well meant listening to others who had already lived a story similar to theirs.

I will continue to listen for the sake of my soon to be artificial twins.

[65]

May 2016

Constantly crying had become my new normal in preparing for my last few weeks of pregnancy. A basin was needed to catch the tears, but I guess my protruding belly did the job. Most women with my blood clotting disorders had planned inductions at thirty-nine weeks, but I opted out. I chose to go against the grain again. I wanted a home birth, and when the thirty-ninth week came and went, many friends said I was crazy to not be induced. Wasn't I *sick* of being pregnant?

Truth is, the complex emotions surrounding the birth of our second child were overwhelming. I was more than ready to conquer and defeat delivery, but less than ready to know how much I would fail as a mama to two boys under five months. If I wasn't already sleepless due to an inconsolable baby and having to pee every twenty minutes, I would have been from the anxiety and anticipation.

We found ourselves in Randall's Children's Hospital when a particular Wednesday, our thirty-nine week mark, passed into existence. Our son needed more tests done. Stationed there for twenty-four hours, I geared up for another night in the children's hospital. This place had become too familiar: sitting in the same purple chair snuggling our little, sweet man. Staring out the big, glass window overlooking the city, I thought about how I could have been induced *today*. Instead, I may be pregnant for another twenty-one days, and I am okay with that.

I mulled over the reality of declining an induction: on one hand, I was ready to be done squatting and grunting, picking up everything off the floor—why does everything I need fall to the floor? For crying out loud, I was a whale and my belly didn't bend or squish into myself. The constant everything-falling-to-the-floor debacle was annoying. Comical, but annoying. Also, the whole rolling out of bed and unable to sit up on my own fiasco? I was ready for the day I didn't need help from Loren getting out of bed. Then there was the strikes of lightning to my crotch. Holy hell, those hurt and I was ready for them to be done. My back was about to cave in at any moment and I was constantly peeing my pants. I was sure my joints were about to snap right off at any given moment. Throughout my entire pregnancy, I threw up off and on—not vomiting while holding a four month old sounded pleasant. And my boobs? Don't even get me started on those.

Even as I list the complaints and discomforts of the final weeks, the miracle of pregnancy astounded me. I was able to experience my body doubling in size, my uterus held and grew a baby, my body did not reject the life it helped to create...*what a miracle.*

I had been envisioning for months the melting-hearts moments of my boys meeting. I was eager to begin family of four walks together. Witnessing the miracle of Loren and I's DNA wrapped up and entangled into one human was enthralling. What would he look like? I expected a squished, alien-faced little human, bald and white, but cuter as the months rolled on when the pudginess set it. With those dreams of wonder I held the anticipation and excitement to be done with pregnancy.

But in the other larger and more complex hand, it felt as though this pregnancy had passed far too quickly. I loved pregnancy, despite all its flaws and discomforts, its aches and pains. The gift of a tiny human starting the size of a mustard seed, swelling me round, pushing my belly button inside out, made me forget about the ridiculous parts. The miracle caused me to forget all the discomfort and embrace the wonder of pregnancy. Feeling that little human bean wiggle and move around letting me know he was there baffled me. Every midwife appointment was met with anticipation. We sat with our eyes closed as we listened to his heart beat. It was the footsteps of stallions, pounding through the doppler. A perpetual challenge was found in the name game, dreaming and scheming the perfect names to fit with Sage's.

As I experienced spontaneous laughter at the reality of my pregnancy, I also enjoyed the preparation for labor and delivery. I had been dreaming of this event and experience for years. I wanted it to unfold beautifully, but knew birth was unpredictable. I knew my body was unique with its disorders and diseases. As I prepared for the end of pregnancy, I carried so many complex expectations of the event: what if this is my only labor and delivery? I wanted to wait as long as possible to soak in its anticipation. I also wanted to experience it as quickly as possible, finally understanding what victory felt like.

When I wasn't crying about being afraid of failing as a mom or giggling that I *was* a mom, I was dreaming about labor: breathing through contractions, pushing an actual human out of myself, feeling his swollen, bloody, messy flesh on mine. I imagined hearing his first screams, gasping for his first breath of oxygen. I thought of our first feed—nursing—naturally rooting in search of the wonders of breastmilk. I was grateful knowing we made it, baby and I, from the moment he was conceived until "now." I knew we would continue making it as best we can. As long as this broken world allowed it.

I often thought about these moments, sharing them with Sage, letting him know he and daddy will be close in case he felt lonely. I told him he would soon meet his brother, the one who he had been sitting on and snuggling for months.

Imagining these moments passing into existence, I welled with sadness and the world always began spinning out of control. Every time I thought of our upcoming labor, the world spun and slowed down simultaneously, creating a space for brokenness and blurred vision. In came rushing the thoughts of my son's birth mom laboring and delivering, meeting him for the first time, only to hand him over into another's arms. My arms. A keening pain enters my expectations, evoking the full spectrum of emotions I expected to encounter during labor and delivery. I was sure birthing a biological baby and experiencing the hormones and emotions accompanying it would help me understand Mama R's love. It would be painful, but necessary, to think about her too in those moments. It was a necessary pain I planned to choose as our second born is placed on my chest.

Sifting through the complexities birth would bring overwhelmed me. We were still in the children's hospital. I was waiting and trusting for the best for my already born child, and mentally preparing for the joys and pains of the one to come. I ache to show our boys what love is. Though Sage's story started in sorrow and loss, it also started in the selflessness of sacrifice. His first mama loved him more than she loved herself. I want to show these boys how to love like her. How to love like Jesus. How to love bigger: than ourselves, our safety, and our comfort. I crave to show them how freeing it is to truly love, even when it hurts us. Jesus loved so big it killed Him.

My eyes gazed over the city buildings, the river rushing through the big city, cutting the west side from the east side. Sage snores soundly on top of my round belly with wires stuck to his head in all sorts of places. My mind wouldn't let me rest in that purple, hospital chair; all I could think about was the upcoming event of becoming a mom to two less than five months apart. Preparing for labor and delivery was so much more than the act of childbirth: I was preparing to model a scandalous type of love to not only one set of watchful eyes, but two.

[66]

Tuesday May 31, 2016

My bathroom floor was filthy. I never liked our duplex's bathroom. It made me gag from the start. What does it say if your own home makes you gag? Before signing the lease for this small rental, I imagined a big, birthing tub smack dab in the center of the living room. "I am going to deliver our baby here," was my first thought when we viewed this place.

I sat on our filthy bathroom floor as the contractions, vomiting, and diarrhea kicked in full force. Everything suddenly wreaked sour. How had I gone so long without scrubbing every square inch of this space? Filthy. Leaning over the toilet I upchucked this morning's peanut butter toast.

Around 2:00 a.m. my uterus alerted me letting me know today was the day, but not enough alert to call my midwife, Julia. Six hours had passed by and my body flushed itself entirely. My uterus started contracting fast—and hard—by 8:00 a.m. These contractions were far different than my previous bouts of false labor.

I quickly downloaded a contraction-timer app unsure why I hadn't yet. Consistent contractions were my cue to call Julia. Loren didn't work on Tuesdays. "Good job, baby boy, you are timing this perfectly," I said. I looked at the timer as my contraction lightened; they averaged from three to five minutes apart, were sixty to ninety seconds long, and gripped my entire body. Where was my warm up? Why did labor jump to full-speed so quickly? Most of the births I served and supported as a doula started with a sort of warm up of contractions.

I snapped a few photos of our home: I wanted to remember every detail of this day. Loren folded mountains of laundry, scrubbed mounds of dishes, baked cookies, chopped fruits and veggies, prepared fresh juice. Sitting on our giant yoga ball I snuggled our four-and-a-half-month Sage, texting our midwife Julia. She lived over an hour away. Assuming my contractions remained regular, she planned to arrive this afternoon after picking her son up from school. If anything, she would check my cervix to ensure I was in active labor.

Those few hours passed quickly. I attempted to watch *Call the Midwife* and sip freshly squeezed juice. I was ready, in my element, and strong.

One of the only reasons I wanted to have a biological baby was to experience the conquering of birth. The other reason was experiencing the miracle of pregnancy, feeling life swirl around inside my own body and stretching me fat. My sister-in-law, Emily, arrived to care for Little Man Sage. It was beyond important to me to have Sage present while I labored: he brought me joy, he increased my oxytocin, and he was about to meet his little brother. Plus, we weren't ready to be separated from him. Having Sage with us was one of the main reasons we planned a home birth.

Loren's go-go-go switch was flipped on, he texted our family to let them know I was actively in labor: "We are hoping to meet our second born this evening. May 31, 2016. Tuesday. A good day to have a baby," he wrote.

Julia arrived around 3:00 p.m. My brutal contractions had double peaked. I breathed deeply through each one. Laying near my couch on the carpet, I stretched into child's pose position, belly down. Upon checking my cervix Julia noticed baby Ira was not in optimal position for delivery; she led me through the miles circuit, guiding my body to reposition him. It was uncomfortable, but worth it I told myself.

Loren obsessively watched the clock, offered me cookies, water, and fresh juice. He asked how he could help. He was a perfect mixture of helpful and quiet: leaning in to encourage me, crossing off items on our To Do Before Baby list. Loren supported me in ways I envisioned for years.

Contractions grabbed my body. My heart pounded. I breathed through each double-peak, my contractions seemingly months long but only seconds apart. Each contraction was too close to the next, unbelievably on top of the other.

Julia called her birth team to Portland. They set up the birthing tub. I was assigned lunges and squats, walking around the block, move this baby into optimal position. The birthing tub offered a sweet sort of relief. I imagined delivering my baby boy repeatedly.

Suddenly the sun set and Tuesday came to a close. We welcomed the night. I breathed deeply through each consuming contraction, envisioning the magical meeting moment, the time when my body would release him and we met flesh to flesh. I imagined him being placed on my bare chest after a long battle of labor. The meeting moment makes labor worth it, or so I was told.

We moved from the living room to my bed. I laid on my side set up for the long night ahead. The midwives and Loren rotated their service to me; compressing my hips together at the peak of each contraction, relieving as much discomfort as possible.

Frantically, I pulled out of my exhausted, breathing techniques. I felt helpless and hopeless. "Why am I still laboring?" I asked with teary eyes and a tremored voice. It was approaching almost twelve hours.

"Keep going, you're doing great, you are strong, you are made for this, you are doing this. Let your body open up," Julia repeated. My midwives and Loren prayed over me, read scriptures, soothed me, and guided my breathing. They continuously instilled confidence in me. I was strong. I was made to do this, and only needed to listen to my body and breathe. Envisioning the meeting-moment made me strong. I breathed and I moaned, I visualized the moments I waited years for. I recalled other mamas I served during labor to recount their strength. I imagined how hard they worked. I can do this. "If they did it, I can do it. I can do hard things," I told myself.

The long night's darkness shifted. The sun slowly sprang into the horizon, casting a sweet hue of pink and orange across the earth. Wednesday arrived hours ago, June 1 was upon us. The twelfth hour of active labor came to a close. My birth team agreed: the 1st of June was a great day to have a baby. A perfect birthday, easy to remember, and *foolproof.*

[67]

"I don't know guys; I may not deliver him today! What if I keep you here all week?" I ask Julia in between contractions, partly joking but also honest.

Julia smiled, "I already had my 50+ hour labor this year, don't worry. I only get one of those a year." Everyone laughed, June 1 was the day we would meet this little man.

Our night was long but I felt refreshed. We passed fifteen hours of active labor, but I felt I was made for this. "Do you have a name?" My friend Angie asked; she had my camera. "It's okay if you're not telling anyone." We knew this baby's name, but had yet to share it with the world. It's scary claiming names so definitively.

"Ira. Ira Anthony." I said smiling. Relief washed over me as I talked to Ira by name, asking him to keep my body working, telling him we were ready to greet him face to face, flesh to flesh.

My contractions slowed around 10:00 a.m. as a sign of transition: my body preparing to push and deliver Ira. The cascade of emotions geared up. Julia had me exit the birthing tub to walk around, eat a little snack, drink some water.

Too many hours passed with my contractions being irregular and unpredictable. I felt a loss of balance and control. This revealed to me how tired I was. Determined to deliver this baby at home, we checked his heart. My body was not in distress. My confidence about birthing this baby in our home remained, despite my lack of blood thinners. I imagined his birth here before we made the duplex ours. There was zero need or urgency to transfer to the hospital. Despite my exhaustion, I felt strong.

Ten in the morning turned into 11:00 a.m., then 12:00 p.m. Suddenly it was Wednesday afternoon and the irregularity of my contractions weren't correcting. My body was not doing what it should have been doing. It proved itself to be difficult and stubborn as always . But I am strong. I had all the confidence in the world that I can do this. I would have my victoriously glorious moment of meeting Ira, flesh to flesh after the fight of labor.

The sun fell abruptly. Wednesday, June 1 neared its close. I laid on my bed while my cervix was checked. My body wasn't opening further. Ira's swollen head challenged finding his position. Was he still asynclitic? Had my water broken? It was all a mystery. Loren danced around antsy.

Julia presented a few options to us: attempt to break my water with the chance of a prolapsed cord; leave my water unbroken and go to the hospital for pitocin to awaken my contractions; continue laboring at home with irregular contractions unsure when or if they will pick up, and making note it had been over two days since my last blood thinner injection.

Waiting at home was my first choice, but everyone else seemed to see my contractions were not becoming regular despite everything we attempted. I could tell Loren wanted to go to the hospital.

Transferring made me wary. Not yet. Our entire pregnancy I had held my expectations loosely in an open hand, knowing transferring was quite possible because of my blood disorders. But because my contractions are irregular? Because my body is being stubborn? Without any distress? These were not at all the reasons I foresaw a transfer necessary. The idea of transferring always surrounded clotting, placenta abruption, or me hemorrhaging.

Birthing Ira in the comfort of our home with Sage present and near me was my perfect birth. I hoped the birth of our family of four would happen together. I wanted the food I purchased, my bed and shower. I wanted to be home. I didn't want to leave Sage. Transferring was not in the attachment bonding options I gave us or planned.

Around 10:00 p.m. Wednesday we decided transferring was best with the hope of pitocin kicking my body back into gear. After accepting our reality through deep breathing, I clung to the piece of our birth story meaning the most to me: the magical meeting moment, flesh on flesh, swollen screaming baby on my bare skinned chest, and tears in everyone's eyes.

We wouldn't be at home in the birthing tub, but I would still conquer delivery: meeting Ira, experiencing the beauty of birth, and releasing my precious baby. It was a privileged gift. A few phone calls later, Grandma arrived to care for Sage. I cried as I kissed him goodbye. Breathing through contractions I pack our bags, unsure what to take, and load up for the fifteen minute drive.

Irregularly and painfully, I had contractions the entire drive to the hospital. We parked, and I slowly wobbled my way into the emergency entrance. In between steps, I paused, dealing with my contractions, and checking into the best hospital in the state of Oregon: Oregon Health & Science University Hospital [OHSU].

The hospital was out of wheelchairs. Assuming the nurse was joking when he said I'd need to walk up twelve flights of stairs to the labor and delivery floor, I laughed and looked around to see Loren, Julia, and the nurse staring at me. They are serious. I nodded. Okay then; here we go, I thought.

Waddling as fast as my body would allow, I was sure Loren, Julia, and the nurse were sprinting down the corridor. Then I see an elevator. *Oh right, an elevator.* I bend over and grab the railing as the contraction seizes my breath, knocking the wind out of me. *Come on, baby boy Ira.*

[68]

We checked into the already full labor and delivery unit. There was a room already prepared for us. At some point, the clock turned from Wednesday to Thursday and we all settled into our new space. I was so hopeful to finally meet Ira. The window in my room offered a view of our big city with speckles of skyscrapers and traffic lights. Though our world is frozen in the suspense of labor, the world lives on.

I ordered an epidural. My last blood thinning shot was Monday. This removed the danger of an immediate blood clot to my spine. More than anything, I was ready for rest. Multiple nurses came and attempted to insert my IV. Instead, I ended up with six bruises the size of golf balls. They adored my arms because of failed attempts.

Around 2:00 a.m., the anesthesiologist inserted a giant needle into my back to numb me from the waist down. I laid there as pitocin also attempted to kick in to bring my contractions into regularity. Half-awake, I look at Loren and Julia sleeping uncomfortably in the chairs near the big windows. Exhausted and tired, I was thankful for the steady heartbeat I heard through the monitor.

The sound of his heart beating steadily brought a certain calmness to me. Whoever knew that a beeping monitor would bring me a peace I didn't realize I was missing? Sleepiness was consuming me even more and my eyes were burning. The air conditioner blew loudly, I felt the oxygen moving through my mouth heavily, and the constant drumming of his heart pulsated throughout the air. Time stood still as I waited. God was meeting me in my moments of waiting again. He never fails me.

Hearing Ira's heartbeat helped heal the fear of him not surviving this long labor. The epidural wasn't working well and I continued to feel each blow from the contractions. I couldn't help but think about the chaos of labor and anticipated delivery I wanted to experience for years. Sometimes I feared it, the thought of delivering a baby without breath; it happens too often. Sometimes, I feared my body would fail me. I feared it would clot or bleed out, one of the two. At worst, I feared my son and I wouldn't make it because of a placenta abruption; it happens, especially with my blood clotting disorders.

Fear is so heavy and brings chaos. It deafened me, and drowned out my hope. Fear clenched like each contraction, but served in unhelpful, purposeless ways. It was the thing that prevented progress, forward movement, releasing, and gaining freedom. Fear-filled contractions tenses the body up, and hinders purposeful contractions to deliver a bundle of flesh. It holds your baby inside. Fear refrains us from relishing in a hopeful, deliverable promise.

Thursday morning before the sun rose, the anesthesiologist told me he's clueless about why the epidural isn't working. They administered an unusually high amount of narcotic, and I should have been more than numb. He reluctantly agrees to redoing it. Around 4:00 a.m. he brought in a student who had only inserted a few epidurals. I was clear of my blood thinners for four days, but did not want a student placing a giant needle near my spinal cord.

I suck in fear, shaky and uncertain. Painfully, they replace the steroid catheter in my spine, nervously talking through questions. I sat as still as possible through the pitocin-induced contractions. *After all I've been through, what did I do to deserve a* student *redoing my epidural? Can't they practice on some other laboring mama?* Growing weary, tired, and disappointed, my eyes well with tears. I move past impatience and defeat reigns: nothing is working and everything is out of control.

A consuming contraction clenches my body like a giant hand. I do my best to breathe slowly instead of gasp for air. The picture of our swollen, pasty, white, baby boy placed onto my chest appears in my mind, popping the balloon of pain I am focusing on. The meeting moment will be worth all of this chaos, worth the pain.

I laid in bed with a new epidural, the maximum amount of narcotics dripping into my system, surely making their way to our son who is resiliently fighting with me for three days now. Julia and Loren remain asleep when the doctor comes in.

"Natalie, we aren't there yet...but with how slow your contractions are progressing, even with pitocin, I need you to get into a space where you're thinking about a possible C-section. We aren't there yet, but I need you to think about it." The room spins. Her words knock the wind out of me. She turns and leaves. I don't even know her name. My jaw drops. Eyes wide, I stare at her back as she leaves the room, my mouth draping. The thought of a cesarean had never crossed my mind. I am not prepared to even travel the road of this as an *idea*. I am meant to birth, *vaginally*, through my body, *naturally*. I am made to grow this human, to conceive and carry, and then deliver him. I am going to push this baby out of me.

Tears silently fall from my eyes. I wipe the snot running from my nose. I needed to wake Loren or Julia. They are exhausted, though. I feel more than lonely. I feel isolated and in shock. My body shakes with fuzzy thoughts; I can't think clearly. Unsure and needing reassurance that I would not be cut open, I stare at my midwife hoping she can feel my eyes boring into her. I ache for Julia to tell me this isn't going to happen, that I am strong and will push this baby out of me. I will experience at least one part of this dream I envisioned for years.

Eventually the sun rose pink over the city, and my epidural still was not withholding the pain. The anesthesiologist seemed frustrated with me: "Some bodies metabolize the medication and yours seems to be doing that." I don't know what that means. I am tired. I want rest. I want my whole family together.

Around noon my revised birth team suggests I start pushing with each contraction. More than ready, I am about to push this baby-human out. The urge is strong, and so I push—for hours—and cry. I changed positions, threw up, moaned and groaned and changed positions once more. I was more than ready to meet this little man. I also missed Sage. I wanted our family together.

Four hours passed and I felt my strongest as I laid down. Yet, there is little to no progress. I am hot. I am sweaty. "You seem to have an infection in your placenta. You're going to need antibiotics." The nurse says plainly.

Confused, I look at Julia questioning if this is the right thing, "Will the medicine hurt Ira?" I asked sadly. Everything is going wrong.

"Honey, the risk of not taking antibiotics is much higher to you than the risk of anything happening to him. You need to take antibiotics," says Julia calmly. Her voices brought peace in the chaos.

Defeat crept into me deeply: How can I fight so hard physically, and get nowhere? How can I be laboring and contracting and pushing and my body not yet deliver? In the zone, I fought with everything I had and more. Swollen and fat, pumped full of fluids to keep me hydrated, I was starved and hungry. It felt like I hadn't eaten in days. *But I am about to meet Ira.* Evening came and Loren quietly stands near my head, wiping away beads of sweat with a cool wash cloth.

Julia pulls me out of focus. "You need to rest in between your contractions." Suddenly and what seems unexpectedly, the wind is knocked out of me with her next statements: "You have done as much as possible and even more, honey. This baby is not positioned right. He isn't going to come out vaginally."

My world freezes. I looked at the circular clock above the bathroom door, reading 5:06 p.m. The nurses ask me to consent for a cesarean. My body somehow nods my head for me as everything spinned around me. The chaos of labor takes a turn I never thought to even think about. Julia asked to have a moment with Loren and I. The room is hazy and her words are floating; I couldn't grasp them. I simply know she's offering a space for us to process. A clipboard with consent papers and lines to sign sits on my lap. Nurses point out where to sign. With my signature, I agree to have them put a scalpel to my skin, creating an incision for my son to escape. I am sure I'm drowning.

The moment of meeting Ira continues to emerge, serving as a piece of hope to grasp. The doctor would still hand him to me, and set him on my bare chest. We would still meet flesh to flesh; my handsome baby Ira. Loren will be right there at my head, ready to meet his second-born son. We beg them to let our midwife join us in the operating room. "Please, can she please be present to take photos? Please give us that. Nothing has gone right, *nothing*." They nod as a reluctant consent, pack up our belongings, and begin the trek to the operating room.

I laid on the operating table, cold and naked, stripped bare of not only clothes but confidence. It isn't the first time I find myself in an operating room. Bright lights blind me. My eyes squint to see Loren and Julia scrubbing down. They throw their robes, masks, and hair nets on. Loren sits at my head, his hands on my shoulders. We stare into each other's eyes. I mostly come to peace in those quick fifteen minutes acknowledging that this is our story. The sacred moment of meeting is still going happen. I will cherish the sweet moments to come forever. I fought hard for three days. It will still be victorious as they cut me open, remove my son, and place him on my chest. Tears will still stream. There will still be a level of magic; this is still miraculous, I remind myself.

Unknown hands begin to push and prod at me without real permission or explanation. Hands on my belly, hands grabbing for more veins, hands in my vagina. I'm anxious no one talks to me, scared they'll cut me wide open before I'm fully numb. I did not feel like a person, but a mere cavity from which a baby would be pulled. It was cold, everything felt violent, and I kept trying to picture meeting Ira as my focus. The anesthesiologist explains how the numbing medication works. They will distribute it through my epidural catheter, "If by some crazy reason, it doesn't work, which I doubt, then we will do a spinal. Only 5% of cesareans end in spinals, though."

"What if the spinal doesn't work?" I ask, wide-eyed. I imagine feeling their incisions as they cut into me.

"I don't foresee that happening, but then we would put you under completely. General anesthesia. Only 1% of cesareans happen that way, though. You shouldn't worry." He pinches me, asking me if I feel it. I do.

Worried, I look into his eyes. *Why can I feel his pinch?* After a few moments, he seems frustrated and decides to move on to the spinal. "This should work just fine."

I am cold. There are so many people in the room I don't know, people who are going to be present for the birth of my baby. I wonder if I can still call this a birth. If I can refer to this as "delivery." It sure doesn't feel like either. It feels like an extraction.

"Ow." Startled, I look at him.

"You can feel that?" His tone annoyed, his eyes cold.

"Yes...can you give me more? Is this medicine getting to my son?"

"You don't want to be feeling us cutting into you. You want this numbing medication. Can you feel this?" He pinches. The left half of my giant belly is numb. My right half refrains from submitting to the narcotic.

"I'm sorry, but we have to put you under."

"Like, under completely? Like out of consciousness?"

"Yes. Loren and Julia, you two cannot be present. Please wait down the hall."

Panic rises in my husband's wide eyes. "What? This is my wife. I am not leaving."

"Yes, you are. You cannot be in here."

"No, no I won't." His attempted firmness doesn't matter. They move him toward the door. I look all around frantically, beginning to panic: they *cannot* steal this moment from me, and my husband. This is not the plan; this was not at all our dream, not even a slice of this is our vision. Tears stream down the sides of my temples and into the anesthesiologist's lap.

The room fills with commotion, spinning around and around. I feel unsteady. I heard the rustling of sheets, my hands suddenly strapped to the bed, countless questions run through my mind. There is no time to process what is unfolding. A sudden voice says was urgency, "His heartbeat is rapidly speeding up, put her under *now*." Tears stung my eyes. I faded to black.

[69]

Agony engulfs my entire existence. Nothing matters. I'm sure I am in hell-on-earth or just hell. Screaming at the top of my lungs, I don't realize other people may be wondering what is happening. It seems as if I'm being slaughtered from my midsection, slowly, and being tortured. The nurse tries to calm me as another pressed my raw uterus, pushing leftover blood out of my body. My last blood thinning injection was over three days ago. Pushing on my newly, sewn body is the protocol to prevent clotting. Dizziness makes everything blurry; all I feel is physical torture.

The pain. The torment. The misery. Every part of me wants to die. Eight layers of sliced-through body, eight layers of freshly sewn stitches, eight layers of wound, forcefully pressed to remove old blood. My body metabolized the numbing medication attempted hours ago. I never numbed and every part of me feels the stabbing, burning pain.

"Can you be done with that?" I yell through angry, sorrow-filled tears. I am so confused and hazy.

Her eyes are kind as she says, "No, honey. I have to do it every fifteen minutes."

"WHY? FOR HOW LONG?" I am sobbing, unsure I will make it through the next round of pushing on my raw midsection.

Loren approaches, holding our newest little man with tender eyes. He holds him out to me: "Here."

"NO!" I wave him off, tears gushing, afraid to meet our son in this state. This is not how a mama meets her son: sobbing and wailing in pain, wishing she would die. I don't even have strength to hold him with this giant hole in my belly, this all-consuming agony.

Julia asks if she can help nurse him. He is hungry. I lay there paralyzed, staring at the ceiling. Tears seep out the corners of my eyes and into the hospital sheets. Julia attaches our miracle baby to my breast for his first feed. I want to be put to sleep again. I don't want this to be my reality. But the anguish keeps me awake.

As my child nurses for the first time, my mere existence feels torturous. *How is this our birth story?* I find myself telling him I am sorry, so sorry, as I drift in and out of consciousness.

Robbed.

Empty.

Depleted.

Raw.

Hurting.

I worked so hard to hold this birth experience in an open hand: I acknowledged we might transfer. As we faced the cesarean, all I excitedly anticipated was the meeting moment: my son being placed on my chest. Instead, it was stolen from me. I wasn't even present. I missed both of my son's births.

Pain consumed me. Every bump along the way to our new room feels like pulsing electricity. I wish for lightning to strike; maybe then I could be put out of my misery. I laid in my hospital bed, holding our new son, missing the other, unsure of how I would cope. How am I going to care for two, tiny infants with this much pain? Loren used all his time off when Sage was born just four months ago. He took the weekend off, but then what?

We can't afford more time off. We can't afford to pay anyone to help me with our babies. All my family members have jobs, children, or school. Loren's family lives out-of-state. My mind is tired and broken. My body was brutally hurting. I found myself again craving to escape my own skin. I didn't want this to be my story.

I feared what people will say when they hear our birth story. I don't want anyone to know, not yet. I want to be the one telling only a few, select people. No one can understand the depth. Never in my darkest dreams did I expect to feel such a loss surrounding the birth of my living child. We are smooshed into a tiny room. The circular clock on the wall reads 2:30 a.m.; I decided to look at my phone for the first time in days. A world of hurt awaits me in that tiny device: How do those little things hold so much power?

I sob reading texts between family members in group texts, about me, demanding I tell them what is happening. They're telling each other I better be begging for a C-section. I feel manipulated and unloved when texts read, "She must not care about us because she's not keeping us informed about her labor progress." I read through texts, tears soaking my face and neck. I want to scream, but am hurt beyond exhaustion already. I want to exile them out of my life: how can they make this event about them?

I type up a curt text with a picture of our little Ira. I explain how no one knew what was happening, we weren't ignoring them or trying to keep them out of the loop. I tell them to not text me back, and send out a message: "My birth experience wasn't for, or about you. I am sorry you felt entitled to it. Goodnight." I attempt to click my phone off, but my heart races. I hate disappointing people. Even my beating heart made my body ache. My husband slept on the hard bench across the room while our baby laid in my arms. I wince at the pressure he puts on my freshly-sewn body. I want to disappear. I want to hide. I want to protect my birth story from people who have no compassion, from people who don't understand the depths of pain and loss, from those who diminish suffering. I want to never see or talk to anyone who is unsafe for my fragile heart. I want to disappear.

Rawer than the eight-layered wound that cut into me, my heart broke. My soul is shattered into bits, and I resisted the urge to pummel it further understanding how lucky I was to have a baby to hold. A *living* baby. Guilt and shame take hold saying I should be grateful for the two sons I have, and am horrible for experiencing sorrow. I closed my eyes and attempted to rest. Silently, tears lead me to sleep.

[70]

Friday, Saturday, Sunday

Our first days together blurred hazily. They were a mixture of pain, sadness, gratitude, and confusion. I was told Ira needed resuscitated after they rescued him from my womb. The physical pain was more than I ever encountered. I didn't know pain like this was possible outside of purposed torture. The pain medication was meant to be powerful but failed to work. My heart was broken in many ways. I feared the things people would say to me in response to our birth story. My chest was tight, shoulders stiff, body tense, brain foggy.

Our boys met Friday afternoon, the 3rd of June. I experienced the beginning of what was my new normal: sorrow and joy simultaneously. I was entirely grateful, and had joy beyond expression: we were parents of not one, but two babies in less than five months. But I also mourned the loss of not being present for either birth. I was hurt from all the pain my body was enduring while grieving the loss of expectations. Everything I envisioned my birth to be for years, it was not. It broke me to not be present for my first, and possibly, only delivery.

A few family members and friends visited us at the hospital, but most didn't. I had mixed feelings about this. I wanted to be home, but was struggling to even stand. My hospital days were filled with tears and frustration. I was constipated for days and was scared I would rip my stitches out; that's the by-product of an unnatural amount of narcotics pumped into a body. Well-intentioned people made me feel I was being pathetic, wimpy, and ridiculous when it came to how I felt about our birth story. I felt I was overreacting in their eyes because I didn't want to talk about the birth with anyone except my midwife. I trusted no one with my tender, bleeding, and broken heart.

Julia was the only one to truly sit and listen to my sobbing. She validated the loss surrounding my birth, looked me in the eyes and told me it was okay to feel this way. In no way did she diminish me, the loss of our birth, or my pain. She was kind with her words, and her facial expressions and body language. She was completely validating, clearly hearing me, and seeing my heart for what it was: raw and really pained, begging to be seen. She never tried to tell me how to feel.

There is a stigma about cesareans making women feel "less than" a "real" mom. The few friends who knew about our birth tried encouraging me I was no less a mom because of my cesarean. This notion had not even crossed my mind, and wasn't in my radar that I was less of a mother because I had a cesarean. I didn't think for a second birthing a child made a woman a mom. Birthing does not make you a mom. I was already one to a boy I didn't carry; birth and motherhood are not tied exclusively. Especially not vaginal birth. When these well-intentioned comments attempted to comfort me, I felt icky in my skin once again. I felt unseen, unheard, unknown. I was *already* a mom and the cesarean did not make me feel less than one.

My loss stems from being asleep for the entrance of my son. I hate that I missed his delivery. My loss is from being ripped open with scalpel and knife by people I have never met and to this day whose names I do not know. It breaks my heart remembering waking up to torture-like pain, not being ready or wanting to meet our miracle son. I was stripped of every expectation I held regarding our birth experience. I dreamed of this, and was unsure I would ever have it. If I *could* have it. Having it completely ripped out of my hands is tragic. This false belief I had was proved wrong: if you listen to your body, it will do what it is meant to do; you can birth a baby naturally. My sadness stems from working harder than any other person I've witnessed labor, only to have missed the delivery of my child; the feeling of wanting to die after I woke up bothered me. Experiencing delivery, the hardest labor of my life, was one of the only reasons I wanted a biological child.

"At least you have your son," many reminded me with gentleness. This statement was a sharp reminder society—people—doesn't like to acknowledge the possibility of grief and joy in one experience. This reminder always brought me shame, leading me to feel as though people thought I didn't take into account the actuality of my son's miraculousness. There was little permission to voice the sadness from our birth while simultaneously rejoice for his life. The voice in my head is always there to teach me a lesson, reminding me I am not grateful enough, or I must be missing the reason to be grateful, how *this must be God's plan and I need to smile through the storm.* God's plan. Well-intentioned loved ones always brought it back to how it must have been God's plan. But what if it wasn't? What if He gives us space to experience both joy and sorrow simultaneously, because He too grieves when loss happens? What if His plan isn't loss or trauma?

[71]

June, July, August 2016

Postpartum depression hit hard like a wall of bricks. I mourned the loss of my physical ability to, right off the bat, be the mama I had dreamed of becoming. My body was tender, and moving was treacherous; I had been so excited to not be pregnant just so I could get out of bed without Loren helping. Yet, there I was with eight layers of torso sewn back together, unable to move—still—without his help.

Layers of cuts and stitches from Ira's extraction were intertwined with a humbling grace of being his mama. A photography client sent a check covering our finances for over two weeks, perfect provision for Loren to take time off work. Another glimpse into God's heart for us. Though circumstances and my flesh failed, He didn't. He covers us and sits among us in this mess, providing what we need; He always has. Before Ira's birth I had never heard the term "Homebirth Cesarean" yet I now found myself in this new category of loss. I joined the ranks of a community of women I hadn't known existed. Thousands of women asking, "Why this? Why me? I trusted birth, I trusted my body, and wondered how God could have allowed this to happen?" A world of fresh hurt, broken hearts and matching scars. Mothers yearning for wholeness despite their brokenness.

I spent those first few months on the couch, attempting to care for Ira who wanted no one but me. He screamed for hours on end, colicky and uncomfortable, begging to be put back in my body. The transition to motherhood with Sage came easy, naturally. Transitioning into motherhood with Ira was painful on many levels, and difficult, but the blessing of these two beloved humans made my heart sing joy.

Watching my husband fold the laundry, wash the dishes, keep our house clean and simultaneously be the sole-care-provider for Sage, I witnessed him grow into himself a bit more. Through sickness and health, we vowed. I'm not sick, but I am breaking. My body was bruised from failed attempts of IVs and layers of stitches keeping me together. I ached pain, and I ached joy. Many people anticipatively asked me how our birth unfolded. I wasn't shy to let the world know the confidence I had heading into it. Many knew how long I wanted this. Emails from friends, family, and followers asked me when I would write a blog post about our birth to *share the story*. I quickly shut them down, not able to enter into the pain our story brought. It's not even like I wasn't already in pain over it.

Most assume I had a cesarean and *I assume* to make me feel better, they remind me it's "a good thing I am alive and so is my son." I wanted to protect my heart, so when asked about our birth I always responded with, "I am not talking about it with anyone." This was nearly always met with, "Whatever happened must have been God's plan. At least you're alive." With these phrases come the unspoken pressure of needing to get over it. These phrases pressure me to move on and suck it up. Isn't that how we treat loss of any form in our society? How *could* I be thankful: ignoring grief and pain and loss, just skipping directly to "joy in the morning?"

But I am not thankful for our birth story. I'm not thankful for the loss and pain. I'm not thankful to be stuck on the couch, unable to hold Sage because he is too heavy, and kicks me in my tender places. I'm not thankful walking made me wince, or for the tragedy of our birth trauma. Surely, there cannot be gratitude found in other's comments about "having the easy way out" because of my cesarean. How do I find thanks in the assumptions of people believing I don't feel like a "real mom" because I hadn't birthed Ira vaginally? I hadn't birthed my first son at all, and I am 100% his mama. I'm not thankful people always tell me how to feel. I'm not thankful this loss threw more wedges into relationships once so dear.

I spend weeks on the couch, darkened by pain and loss but brightened by a bounty of babies. Continually and consciously I accept His invitation to carry the cross of loss from our birth.

At times, I give into numbness. I allow my heart to remain shattered about our birth. The voice within me revisited the agony accompanying our little life: years and work it took to conceive only to miscarry; the spiritual abuse and trauma from church leaders; the loss of our ministry-career and sweet community due to said hurt and trauma; the loss of our reputation with our youth group; the loss of relationships with our youth group; the years of serving births as a doula and craving it to be my turn; being unable to continue being a doula and birth photography; not being present for Sage's birth; not being present for Ira's birth; the physical turmoil of Ira's delivery; and not being present as a whole and healthy mama at the start of our virtual-twins journey.

I threw my pain into a shed, storing it away to falsify it. It seemed to be the invitation our culture gave regarding hardships. So much of me didn't want shame to cover me, however. I wanted healing, whatever that looked like, but I knew sometimes healing looked like revisiting wounds. It meant breaking bones to be reset them, and that was painful.

Courageously I faced the aching parts of me, and continued to find strength as I chose to give sorrow space. Strength is found to make it through one moment at a time, knowing I won't always be this tender. In giving sorrow space, I found immense grace. Permission from Him to feel the sadness, yes, but also great joy.

[72]

August 2016

My sister-in-law and her family had driven ten hours to visit us. The highlight of their trip was to go to Build a Bear. Their decision. I didn't ask questions. We finished up at the mall play area and agreed to meet in the parking lot. It was time I lead the caravan to a park.

I don't frequent the mall much, if ever, but I'll do anything for my cute nieces. With both my brand-new baby boys strapped to my front and back, I pick up my diaper bag determined to make sure they don't wait long for me. Unloading two babies from my body and into car seats is no simple or smooth task. Quickly, I walked through the long mall corridor trying not to make a scene. Carrying two babies tends to call for attention. I mean, they're cute, I don't blame anyone.

I'm abruptly stopped by a woman and what appears to be her teenage daughter, just four stores away from the exit.

"Those aren't twins are they?" Her eyebrows raised, her face cynical.

"No," I responded with a smile, thinking what treasures these two are. "Just close in age." I turn to keep going. Sometimes I have time to stop and talk, answer masses of questions, tell the jaw-dropping story. Other times I don't. This time I didn't.

"They can't both be yours then, right?" One hand moves to her hip as she spits the question. Her tone seems to be trying to prove a false point. She stares at me with eyebrows raised and points a finger, trying to peer around me to see Sage who is strapped to my back. He is brown-skinned with wiry dark hair, a face unlike mine. Ira, who is being carried in the front, is white-skinned, with blonde hair and blue eyes. They are not quite five months apart, but are different in size.

Not an unusual question, I attempt to maneuver around her as I say, "Oh yes, actually they are both mine." I believe a kind answer turns away wrath, but also know kindness can be found in firm and calm statements too.

"Well they don't look related at all."

At this point, I'm forcing my smile. I too-kindly say, "They don't have to look related to be brothers," and once again attempt to move on with my day. I don't have time to have this conversation for what feels like the millionth time this day. I certainly don't need to make time for someone who is trying to prove a false point to me.

Unwilling to let me have space and peace, she says boldly and loudly, "Well did you *birth* them both? Because if not, they can't *both* be yours." Her emphases made me frustrated. I neither know her story, nor where her life has been. I don't know her hurts and her baggage. I *did* know what she had said was detrimental on many levels, and I didn't owe her my children's stories. Annoyed and angry, my courteous smile no longer belongs in this conversation. I stop trying to move toward the doors, certain my sister-in-law and her family were already waiting. With all the confidence in the world, I responded with: "These boys are both my sons. Equally, they are mine. Birth isn't the only way to make a family." I step around her and continue walking. Thankful my children are still babies who don't understand; I'm horrified for the messages this world will send them all too soon.

Reaching for the door out, I turn to look at her one last time. She watches me as though I robbed the Victoria's Secret she was about to shop at. What I needed her and the world to know about my boys is that they *are* mine and I *am* theirs. Still under one-years-old at the time, they don't know what countless people ask or say to us every single public outing. Soon, they will have ears to hear and a maturing brain to process the harmful and intrusive questions, comments, and assumptions.

My boys may not share blood or DNA, but they share parents and a family. We love them both fiercely and unconditionally. What I need the world to know about my boys, my almost twins, is I love them the same. I need the world to know we are a real family; we are not playing pretend or house. I love them both as though I birthed them both, but also as though I adopted them both. I am assured with the utmost confidence, I love them with the same fierce and unending mama love. My husband agrees.

I hadn't realized signing up to be an adoptive family meant signing up for unsolicited comments, questions, and statements that weren't other people's business. It is one thing when inquiries stem from some sort of adoption connection, or a genuine interest in adoption. It is an entirely other when the onlooker and speaker is simply trying to prove how *unreal and invalid* our family is, how different we are, how unacceptable it is to have adopted. When we began the journey of adoption, we weren't aware of the invasive and ongoing questions strangers would impose upon us.

"Are you the babysitter?" "You must be the nanny." "Oh, are they cousins?" "Are you his real mom?" "Are they real brothers?" "This one is *clearly* your own." Was she a teen? She didn't want him? Why didn't she want him?" "Is there something wrong with him?" "Bummer, you got a black baby, didn't you want a baby that looked like you?" "I have always wanted a black baby." The hurtful list is endless.

Upon sharing these unwanted conversations with people we love, some nod their head and know exactly the feeling. Others share they have used similar terminology previously, but are thankful to learn what the best terms are. I too am always learning, uncovering ways to use my words better. Yet others dismiss us, tell us in some form or another we are too sensitive, we are over-reacting, "people don't mean it that way," therefore we shouldn't care.

But what is missed with dismissive responses is a way to love others well, better. In dismissing heartache with language and stigmas surrounding adoption, and any other pain-topic, learning how to love fully and selflessly is missed. Humility is missed, pride wins.

Being told I am overreacting or too sensitive only casts shame and blame: *the problem isn't with society, but with me.* But the problem *is* with society: the set and silent standard is families clearly resembling one another: a cute family of mini-me's.

I see this standard slowly but surely being torn down. Sometimes it feels hopeless, like the stigma will never be stripped. But I have to believe it will. I have to believe one day more people than not will know love is what makes a family, so I keep writing and sharing and telling the truth. I do this for my kids and my friends' kids. But I also do this because it is the greatest picture of God's love. His sacrificial, selfless love is what makes us His. Nothing else.

A seeker of grace and honesty, I find myself often being interrupted at the park or grocery store being asked questions. I am perpetually learning I don't owe anyone my story and I certainly do not owe anyone my children's story. If anything, I owe it to them to keep it more private. It is their story and I have overshared far too many times.

I do my best to smile and inform as appropriate, to educate the most loving terms, but sometimes I simply want to be seen as a valid family. Sometimes I have to re-process the loss of being seen as a normal family by society, the loss of being inconspicuous. Sometimes I just want the world to know that it doesn't matter how we became a family, that our skin and hair don't match, that our children's ages "don't add up," because love makes a family.

[73]

Our previous boss' voice morphed into my voice over time. Though I am sure he loved us, our relationship was unhealthy at best. I work hard to uncover the voices in my head continuously shaming me and speaking falsehoods over me. Counseling keeps me almost sane. Somewhere along my journey, *prideful* attached itself as a primary part of my identity, along with an unhealthy sense that *I am selfish and entitled*. Shame is taxing to uncover and then strip off, over and over again.

I constantly question if I am selfish and entitled in choosing to give various losses voices in my life. Something in me exclaims if I give pain, sorrow, and even sadness a voice at all, I am being selfish and unlike Him. My whole heart aches to be like Him.

I sat on a gray Ikea couch across from Carrie, my counselor. She gently asked me week after week what I would tell someone else sitting in my seat. Would I tell them to suck it up, to breeze past the sorrow, to plaster a smile to my face? Would I tell them they are being selfish and unlike Him in giving their pain a voice? Would I tell them they are entitled to a fault? Would I tell them it is their choice to be "offended" or hurt from spiritual/emotional abuse from people they revered? Would I judge them the way I judge myself?

No. I would sit and genuinely listen to their pain. My eyes would be kind and soft, my face muscles relaxed. My entire self would be available as their friend in scary, vulnerable moments. I would urge them to tell me about their pain points, to open up their wounds, both fresh and scabbed, and potentially ill-healed. I would invite them into a safe and sacred space to bleed out their losses, their grief, their shacked-up sorrow. I would invite them to unshackle themselves. I would insist they speak about their sadness, encourage them to uncover old wounds buried long ago because they believed they had to, in order to live a life like Him.

I began doing that. I began listening instead of "fixing" or telling someone how to feel. I invited others into a space of safety and sharing, both face to face and online. I began hearing people's stories, so many stories I cannot count them, as they shared with me the broken bits of themselves, the unfair pain handed to them. The undeserving pieces in their stories. The fragments of their hearts less traveled; parts of their history hidden for so long, they stopped carrying their cross because they bought into the same lie I did: it was less of a Christian, selfish, faithless, and therefore shameful to give suffering a real space.

Emails flooded my inbox from strangers I have never met, and probably never will, bearing their souls to me. They revealed the parts of themselves they had never shared with anyone else. In response to their sharing, I validated their pain and reminded them not to feel silly. Grieving and weeping were things Jesus did, even when He knew everything was going to be more than okay. He *wept* when Lazarus died, though He *knew* He was going to raise him from the dead. I believe He still weeps over loss, right there with us.

Listening to human beings share their losses through miscarriage, health, adoption, foster care, and church, I continue to find my own healing in the permission to be honest. I want my pain to be heard, validated, seen as acceptable instead of shameful and unlike Him. My journey of learning to give loss a voice led me down a path of fullness to a life I didn't know existed.

While I listen to other people's stories, the world is seen through an entirely new lens, new angles. I quickly realize I held a very small view of this world. The world is not as I thought it was; or rather, the world is a lot bigger with a lot of different experiences than the single one I knew and am living. There is much I do not know, but much I am willing to listen to learn and understand.

Before we knew about Sage, we read *Inside Transracial Adoption* by Beth Hall and Gail Steinberg. Inside those pages the seeds of listening were planted. Growing in us was the importance of hearing people's experiences who share our future child's race, color, and culture if different than ours. Since bringing him home, the priority of doing this intensified. Transracial adoption wrecks me in the best and most necessary ways.

This idea of never understanding living in our child's skin sinks in. If my journey is about loving well, who am I to dismiss an entire community's experience? Who am I to invalidate people of color who say their experience in America is different? Those who say their experiences have been oppressed, is not as rose-colored as white America paints it? We do not want to be the white parents who ignore our child's race and culture, raising him to be completely out of touch with whom he'll identify, leaving him unprepared to live a black experience in America. While reading, these words uplifted themselves from a necessary book:

> "What many black and biracial transracial adoptees were not prepared for was that the societal realities they faced were the same as those facing other People of Color. The information that white transracial adoptive parents needed to give their children did not exist in the white world; these parents would have to interact with black America in order to understand the problems most likely to trouble transracially adopted children."

> -Rhonda M. Roorda, *In Their Voices:*
> *Black Americans on Transracial Adoption*

This new lens is worn purposefully and intentionally through the art of listening. It is my new normal. I ask a lot of questions to understand as many people as possible. All I want for my life is to love well; if I don't love well, what is the point? But if I am to love well, *like Him*, I need to at the very least make an genuine attempt to understand the spaces in which other people live. Belittling their voices, shutting down experiences as made-up and illegitimate, telling someone and communities of people they are too sensitive and need to "get over it" is far from loving like Him. I absolutely cannot imagine God—the gracious and good Father—dismissing the pain of people of color, telling the hurting to move on and get over "it."

I no longer explain away why a white person "didn't mean it" the way it came out. Whatever *it* was, if *it* hurt someone, impact quickly became far greater than intent. There is grace on both ends, the intention and the impact, but our job is to worry about where our heart is and how we are loving well and not how someone else is reacting. It is never our job to tell someone their feelings are wrong or incorrect. It is always our job, as Christians, to walk humbly, apologize, and seek to love better. Humility is recognizing when we unintentionally impact someone poorly, in a hurtful manner, and owning up to it. Saying we will do better, and keep going.

The journey to loving well directly correlates with listening well. The walk of loving well, like Him, was beginning to look uncomfortable. But uncomfortable living never turns me away, if it means I will live like Him. The disappointment soon set in when I realized the vast majority of white people in my life don't think this way. I figured more people in my life and the Christian culture felt the same way: if it means loving others well, then yes, I will shut up and listen without defensiveness.

If loving well means listening well, I want to do it every time the opportunity presents itself. From my experiences I feel entirely loved when the people around me listened well. When everyone else in the world could become pregnant by sneezing, I was temping, tracking, becoming a yogi and all the things a desperate, childless mama does. I felt most loved when a friend sat down and listened to my pain. I felt most loved when she heard me with eager eyes, withholding fix-it or skip-it responses, and instead said, "I don't know what this feels like, but it sounds entirely lonely. I am sorry."

When I miscarried and I was sure it was the end of my joy, I felt the opposite of loved when my friend reminded me of Job and all the loss he underwent and *how I could have had it worse. I could have it like Job.* I felt loved when friends dropped meals off on our porch, my sister-in-law gifted me a remembrance necklace, people asked how I was doing without the intention of telling me how to feel better and get over it. I felt loved when my friend came and sat with me on my couch while I cried. She simply listened with a kind face, welcoming eyes, genuine love. You can feel love radiate from some people, you know? This pure kind of love is felt in the atmosphere. It exudes.

When we were fired unexpectedly and quite traumatically, I didn't feel loved when people told us we were running from our calling, or we must have been making up the absurdity of the situation. I didn't feel cared for when we were not asked by the management and elder team what our point-of-view was, or when we were told "real Christians stick it out." I didn't feel loved when people told us not to share what happened, that we had an obligation to protect the leadership of that church as well as The Church. I felt loved when friends listened and heard, saw our pain and instead of discounting and dismissing, embraced us and asked how to help. I felt loved when people offered to buy our groceries when we were suddenly jobless, help pay for our rent, help us find jobs, and simply sit in the pain with us. I felt loved when we were told it made perfect sense to be wounded.

When my hope-filled birth experience turned into one of the most pain-filled days of my life, I felt unheard and unseen and uncared for when the response was: "So when are you going to be okay with this? At least you have your baby. At least you are alive. Can't you focus on the positive pieces? You have to come to a point where you are okay with this." When my midwife continuously validated my pain and the layers of loss we endured, I experienced heaps of love. When my counselor Carrie reminded me that Jesus grieves the broken pieces with us, even the pieces society says aren't worth grieving, I experienced His presence. When I am bombarded with other mamas sharing their birth stories without my asking, He cares for me in the tender, most fragile parts of my heart. He holds with care the pieces I don't want to share with others.

In my experience, I have felt well-loved when I have simultaneously felt truly seen and genuinely heard. When, instead of having someone show me what I am feeling or experiencing is wrong, listened and attempted to sit in my shoes. Instead of telling me how they would walk the journey better, how they would respond to various pains, saw loss and acknowledged the space needed to grieve brokenness.

This isn't to say we need to walk around throwing pity parties and inviting others into our pity parties. This isn't to say we need to be mushy piles of sadness forever and think only about ourselves and how depressing our lives are. This isn't me giving myself permission to reside only in sadness, to wallow in self-pity. This is to say, on my journey towards healing and freedom, and most of all *Him*; I am most empowered to find fullness to life when I experience someone's love wrapping around me without dismissal of loss. Simply solidarity and being seen.

In my experience, when I look at who Jesus is and was, I cannot imagine Him dismissing pain of any sort. I don't see Him telling hurting people to "move on and get over it," or to stop being so sensitive. I don't see Jesus ever responding to someone with, "Why are you so offended or hurt or sensitive?" I hate hating my broken experiences. I hate that I am not wholly healed and don't look upon losses with *only* joy. And yet, I must give a voice to each of these losses. I must give space to acknowledge I am not invincible or perfect, *and that is okay*. We are in a process. We are human.

It grieves me when people are unable to process their losses with anyone, for fear of their tender hearts with being crushed with insensitive responses. No one likes to be misunderstood. We avoid joining the sad parts of other's life, because the sad parts don't often need a "quick fix" or "ten steps to feeling whole." But rather, we need someone to just sit in the sad with us. This is where I uncovered my purpose of becoming a safe person for people's pain. This is where my passion for people's pain has come alive: I began creating safe spaces for people's losses. Spaces for people to simply sit and cry, vent, grieve, and weep. It can be awkward not knowing what to say or not saying anything, but I have been told time and time again my calm and validating presence is just what was needed.

Uncovering how I have experienced being loved well has led me toward learning how to love others well. I have about half a clue, but I'm a work in progress. As my friends of color share with me the little and big privileges that accompany my life because of my white skin, I have learned to quiet my defensiveness and simply listen and truly see. I began asking myself, "Why would I be so quick to prove how they are wrong, too sensitive, whatever?" The answer lies in self-preservation. The answer lies in not truly caring deeply about others, and more about my ego. The answer lies in the inability to have true compassion, to co-suffer, to share empathy.

When confronted with discomfort, bombarded with the privilege my whiteness brings, I ask: What do people of color have to gain from making a bunch of white people angry by confronting white privilege? It must be worth the risk, because making people mad at you isn't fun. If entire communities are sharing their pain and oppression with the slightest hope of being heard, the slightest hope for some sort of change, the least I can do is listen and validate, do my small part in making this world better. In creating safe spaces for my friends who I really do love and want to love well.

[74]

Late 2016

"Does everyone in our family think I'm crazy? Are people afraid of me? Tell me the truth, because this is how I feel." I slowly ask my mom, after months of wondering. I arrange my face to appear calm with gentle eyes. I want her to be as honest as honest can be.

Her eyes widen incredulously like I was silly, she responds, "What? No. Of course not! No one thinks you're crazy," Calm comes over me. *Why didn't I have this conversation sooner?*

A few days later my aunt tells me family members are probably scared to talk to me about things regarding race and adoption because I seem pretty sensitive. This validated my fear that I am a scary person who freaks out on everyone. I feared my mere presence falsely forces people to walk on eggshells out of anxiety. The validation fractured my heart. I'm always working hard to be a space of safety and grace, but also honest in my convictions. Can we not be both gracious and honest in conflict?

Being honest about the way people's language and assumptions hurt doesn't make me a monster. Though it often feels that's what the world thinks. Being honest about pain and different forms of loss doesn't make us weak, simply honest and sensitive. Our culture shames sensitivity. But being sensitive is a sort of superpower.

Choosing to be sensitive is a vulnerable way to live, but a courageous one too. Being sensitive is displaying a quick and delicate appreciation of others' feelings. In my quest of being honest about the way words hurt people, I invite them to choose sensitivity. It is a way of inviting others to love well, especially loving those who are hurting. I want to love well, so I do my best to listen when people share the ways they aren't feeling loved. It's an honor to learn how to love someone better. In being honest with people, graciously correcting because I assume we all desire correction if it means loving better, I invite others to love well. This isn't easy, we are tender and fragile, us humans. Sometimes when we are confronted on how our words hurt other people, we become defensive instead of choosing humility and apologizing. I do this. We all do this. But I am on a journey of perpetually quieting what I think I know, choosing to hear the heart of the person I hurt.

I cannot imagine Jesus telling any of His tender-hearted people, "You are too sensitive; you care too much about my other children. Stop being so sensitive."

PART 2

Undeserved

UNCOVERED

[75]

UNCOVERING UNDESERVED GRACE

Part of the great gift of my grief is unpacking what it means to love others better than I did yesterday. Grief itself is sprung out of deep, tender love wishing to be found and fostered, and kept safe. Wading through grief has taught me both how to love well and what isn't an experience of love; or rather, how to perpetuate pain. Grief taught me both how to respond and how not to respond to other people's hurt. It has led me to loosen expectations of myself, as well as others, regarding where we need to be emotionally, or how we ought to act.

It is constant hard work to intentionally remove my preconceived ideas of how we should feel or act or respond to life. I am constantly uncovering subconscious ideas I didn't know I had.

It wasn't until I was forced to stare my losses in their faces, to grab ahold of my grief, to claim my pain and decide to process honestly that I began seeing the gifts of grief. I wouldn't wish loss on anyone; but we all endure loss.

I wouldn't know how to listen and therefore have true compassion for others while they are in a lonely state of being, had I not encountered loss. Compassion means to *co-suffer*. It isn't compassion unless you decide to willingly join someone in their pain. To sit in all the uncomfortable feelings, emotions, and realities, and experience their loss *as your own* to the best of your ability. You must choose vulnerability and sensitivity to choose compassion. You must walk barefoot over the broken pieces of someone's story, allowing each pointed rock to poke your flesh, forcing you to notice the pain. This is where true friendship lies: among the pointy, pokey, rocks of our story. Where we are broken-up and fragile, thirsting to be seen.

The Christian culture I bought into for many years—the one making me seem ungodly when I was honest—began revealing itself more flawed than ever. The Christian culture I thought was driven by Jesus was appearing to be driven by people who resembled the "religious" and "pious" He rebuked in the Bible. I wanted to move past this created culture and into a life more meaningful, a life set up for more than just myself and my glorification. I want to live a life fuller than the look-good-feel-good, cute Christian status.

I read somewhere that we only love God as much as we love the person we love the least. This includes the lazy homeless man you think "should just get a job;" people fleeing for their lives, becoming refugees, leaving everything they've always known with a small, glimmer of hope to live and hopefully their children too; people who migrate here, illegally and legally alike, who don't share our language, but are hoping to find a life where they aren't constantly *behind*.

Our relationship with God is half of the coin; the other half is our relationship with everyone else. Including people society deems unwelcome, unworthy, less than. We must learn this and believe this without the need to say, "but—" and justify our unwelcome. We must analyze our hearts and notice how we truly see people: are we viewing all humanity, *every* one, as an image bearer of God? Or someone breaking the rules and therefore, unwelcomed?

Picking up the pieces of my heart stuck in Christian culture, I continue toward Him. He is always found among the people who are cast out as less-than, as dirty and filthy, as unacceptable, as lazy and overly sensitive. Look closely, He is there and it isn't a cute form of Christianity. It is the rawness of Christ's life. He lived at the bottom rung of society.

Subconsciously and consciously our white (and yes, even Christian society) has treated the *"others"* poorly for centuries. Native Americans, African Americans, Muslims, refugees, Mexican immigrants, Latinos, people who are part of the LBGTQ community, and more. Since this country's beginning, we have been cruel and unlike Jesus. I refuse to buy into the false notion that our country was founded on Christian principles. Unless, it is "Christian" to come in and kill, steal, and destroy. To cause loss. To break families and hearts. To devalue humanity. To perpetuate brokenness.

Is it uncomfortable leaving behind all I thought I knew, even when most of my family and childhood friends remain in those spaces of belief? Yes. It is uncomfortable. It is another form of loss. I lost the comfort of seeing eye-to-eye with a lot of my family, with people who helped raise me, with previous pastors and leaders and mentors. I lost the comfort of agreeing and solidarity, in thinking we saw the world the same, and viewed Jesus equally. This loss is a loss I chose, but a loss I cannot go without.

Learning more about Jesus means losing more of what I thought I knew. It means me losing closeness in relationships, ignorance, and the ability to sit by and be okay with subtle racism. But learning more about Jesus is worth losing it all. Because in learning more about Jesus, I learned about His love for me and His love for His people. His love is the scandalous kind. The kind I want to emulate every day of my life. The kind that saves lives.

[76]

Sometimes, when I write I stare out the window in a daze. Starbucks is my office for now, and I was staring out the window when I was sure I had seen Matthew.

A chunk of anxiety lodges into my throat, quickens my heart, and twirls around my insides. What is he doing in Portland? The man turns around and it isn't Matthew. Sucking in a few deep breaths, I look around me. Nobody seems to have noticed my sudden panic. Will these triggers ever stop?

Shame, anxiety, pain, and fear are the raw experiences I walk through every time someone asks me "What happened?" regarding our transition out of youth ministry. I often wonder if other people encounter these experiences when asked about their church trauma or spiritual abuse. It's been two years since we kissed the church career and our precious community goodbye. It feels like yesterday, yet also a lifetime ago. We said goodbye to so much more than a "job" or "career."

Are we in a relationship with those we were hurt by? No. Do we believe we need to be in order to fully forgive and reach reconciliation? No. Do I think far too many people leave churches when they should probably stay and work through tension and conflict with people? Yes. Do I think some circumstances warrant leaving, spiritual abuse is not something to tolerate? Yes.

I grappled with grief, wrestled with worry, and wondered if I'm crazy. It is hard, exhausting work to dig ourselves out of the pit of spiritual abuse, or any abuse. But we are not forced to do it alone.

I wrestle with furthering the often too true stigma that the church is entirely messed up, and only adds hurt to people's already pain-filled life. But I grew tired of being held back from honesty, of not sharing purely out of fear. I grew weary of not processing in ways that brought me healing. I was exhausted from hearing countless stories of people hurt in absolutely unnecessary ways from church leadership, only to carry the unnecessary weight of being hidden without a voice, out of fear and shame and anxiety. People need to know it's okay to leave toxic churches; Jesus never intended for spiritual abuse.

I began to uncover the realization that not speaking about our spiritual abuse perpetrates permission to continue unhealthy leadership. In choosing to not be vocal and talk about church trauma and leader abuse, we are telling the abused and world that abuse is not worth giving voice to, abuse doesn't need to be stopped.

There is little permission to speak out and share unfair tragedy done at the hands of The Church. I wrestle with what parts to share and withhold, with whether to share anything more than: "It was an unhealthy environment." Or, "It wasn't where we needed to be." Or, "We never wanted to stay there for more than five years."

Do I share how it felt as though every single "meeting" we had was to address how prideful I was, though I felt I was constantly in a place of being humbled in humiliating ways? Do I share how it felt like every time we were invited to bring an honest critique to the table it was somehow turned to be our fault?

We felt there were no boundaries; relationships were expected to be not just our "boss" but considered family, friend, pastor, even parent. Matthew told me he was disappointed when I didn't buy him a Father's Day card. It was confusing.

We felt unfair pressure was placed on us, "If you leave this community, I will be ruined." It felt we were always to blame: if only we knew hearts better, if only we spent more time with so-and-so, then everything would be fine and perfect? It felt like distancing ourselves was the only thing to do to protect our hearts from constantly being questioned.

Do I share how we felt constantly confused by Matthew, our boss? Every week it seemed we would hear conflicting statements: "You have free reign in your ministry area and I trust you with every detail" met with, "Why didn't you ask me to do this? Send weekly reports of everything you did all day, every day, hourly. Report to me every detail of who came, what you did, what you taught, etc." We wondered if this was normal or if it was "micro-mis-management," as I often liked to call it.

Do I share how we felt every time we brought a personal hurt to the table, we were told it was our choice to be offended; it was our fault we were hurt. I felt a twistedness of unrealistic expectations and pressure to balance one million church-title hats while also being told I "do not corner the market of busy-ness," and I "only have to pursue the parts of ministry that feel natural to me."

While in the thick of grappling with whether or not we were a part of something unhealthy and detrimental, I felt crazy. I started counseling six months before the end of our vocational career and every week brought tears and the unending, ever pressing questions: Am I the crazy one? Does this pain really make me not Christlike? Is this really all my fault? Is it my decision to be hurt from this? Is my hurt valid? Do I need to suck it up, forgive quickly, and move on?

I hope to give the gift of going second. By sharing our story, I hope others feel the freedom to share their own. It's ok to leave a toxic church to find an imperfectly healthy one. Many experience loss, trauma, hurt, and pain while on a leadership team at church. This unfair hurt, trauma, and abuse is just as valid and worthy of a voice as any other loss. The Church is imperfect and my job isn't to pretend differently. It isn't my job to protect His bride; He will do that. The Church is filled with hypocrites: we are humans. It is my job to be honest and search for Him in every detail of this life, accept His invitation to see life through His lens.

When we decide to unpack why shame and fear rule our life when the topic of Church Leadership surfaces in conversation, it is uncomfortable. It is scary. But in unpacking why shame and fear are so prevalent, it becomes clear these were birthed out of fearing people, not God. My story and your story represents the cross on many levels. The worst events in human history, the darkest and most traumatic realities, brought us the greatest good: the suffering and death of Jesus brought us the ongoing opportunity for freedom and joy; in this, we can find complete wholeness.

In my experience, we cannot access full freedom and all-encompassing joy, the fullness of life, until we walk through the darkest, most pain-filled parts of our story. Even when it reveals the ugliness of not only mankind, but of The Church. The entity that should be known for its good deeds and services, but is often known instead for its tragic hurt of others. I can't begin to truly forgive those who hurt us and find reconciliation in the deepest parts of me until I give pain the voice it demands. It isn't enough to just feel the pain; we need to be conscious of it, to face it, to wear it, to claim it as ours.

Not even two months after we were traumatically fired and banned from our church, Matthew's wife emailed me. Sitting in the cabin for my dad's Christmas, I read a long email from her. She is gracious and kind, but the email digs into my raw wounds. "I am sure you have forgiven us," and such statements. Statements assuming fast forgiveness. Forgiveness I was unable to truly access so quickly, if I am honest.

Forgiving quickly, in my experience, is often superficial forgiveness. Fast forgiveness is a way to avoid pain. Fast forgiveness is a way around suffering. Forgiveness happens in layers. Layers running deep, on top of the other, take time to uncover. Sometimes a new layer pops up unexpectedly. Fast forgiveness is a part of Christian culture I want to help change and transform. I ache for a journey of Jesus-like forgiveness. The kind demanding time and suffering in the process. We analyze our faults and sin; I tend to over-own things in my repentance. But I'm learning the kind of forgiveness inviting us to acknowledge the fault of others, the unfair pain brought upon us that wasn't our fault. It's not about sitting around blaming and justifying my hardened angry heart, justifying bitterness turned to hatred; no, it's about softening my heart to feel the pain, acknowledge the deep brokenness of humanity.

When I invite God into these softened, honest spaces of honestly seeing brokenness, I am more sad than angry with those who hurt us. The hardened walls of bitterness are shed and replaced with soft sorrow and an invitation to grieve the loss of what should have been.

Forgiveness is for our healing and wholeness, forgiveness is what launches us into the fullness of life. But I cannot find this freedom and joy until I truly begin to walk through the dark parts of suffering and pain. Time and time again, I find I cannot skip the night to arrive to the morning. Joy comes in the morning, but the morning comes after the dark night. Sometimes the night lasts longer than we want it to.

[77]

We drive down Martin Luther King Blvd. every Sunday morning on our way to church. It's an unexpected trigger each week. I forget to prepare myself for the flood of emotion.

"There's Count Dracula's castle," Loren jokes as he looks across the river to see Oregon Health Science University's buildings nestled into the forest. It's where we ended up during labor, where Ira entered our world. Sage babbles to himself in his car mirror while Ira cries in his car seat. I move my gaze from the dashboard to OHSU, my heart rate picking up speed, the sounds of the present becoming distant.

My eyes gloss over and memories from the night—nearly a year ago—we drove to the hospital consume my mind. I can't help but be sad. As soon as sadness registers and I recognize my sorrow, shame settles in too. How can I be sad when I have my baby? Who do I think I am? Why can't I suck it up and move on?

We pass through traffic lights and search for a spot to park. I am lost in my mind, reliving the trauma of transfer, the tragedy of waking up to torment, the loss of meeting Ira with any joy and only pain. Loren parks the car near church and asks me a question; I don't hear him.

"Huh?" I ask him, being pulled out of my hazy memory.

"Really, Nat? Come on." Frustrated, he opens the door to get Ira out of his car seat. It's not his fault I find myself in my thoughts more than not. I stay in my seat, defeated once again by this birth trauma. Will I ever get over this? Will I ever recover? When will I cross the bridge into downtown Portland and not be consumed by reliving our homebirth cesarean?

I pull open my door, unbuckle Sage. He's smiling and giggling, waving his arms ready to run around. He became a toddler while I blinked.

People are spilling out of the giant building we meet in to gather as a church. There are so many people making up this church, we are always meeting others. Smiling at every family we passed, the overwhelming truth of our blessedness consumes me. How did I get to be this lucky? Two babies turning toddlers. Breathing becomes easy again as I settle back into my current reality, letting my hazy memories fall away.

We check the babies turning toddlers into the nursery. I throw a dribble of coffee into my cup of cream and we enter the sanctuary my soul has grown to love. Seth sits with Maria on the pew against the wall, Lacey must be checking their four-year-old foster daughter into class. *Home.* These are the spaces I find healing, slowly but surely. These are the spaces feeling most at home: church community. Friends.

"No Longer Slaves" is being sung. The song inciting tears to shed for months of Sundays when we first brought Sage home over a year ago. The scar across my midsection shares an anniversary with my son's birthday, which is quickly approaching. I cannot help but let the memories of his birth flood my mind again.

Bringing Sage home felt perfectly right for our story and family, in all its undeniable brokenness. Adoption fit our family and who we were made to be. We knew adoption would be the main source to building our family before we were wed. But experiencing the miracle of pregnancy and the conquering of labor was a desire placed in me many years ago when my first niece was born. The desire only rooted itself deeper as I served as a doula and birth photographer.

All over the sanctuary, hands are raised in surrender, voices singing in unison about His melody unraveling us, surrounding us with a song. His song of deliverance from our enemies, until all our fears are gone. The words, "I'm no longer a slave to fear," is being sung, but I feel a slave to something. Maybe sorrow. How does one live freely in sorrow? What does that look like? Gently, God tells me I am not a slave to sadness: I simply give it the space it demands. Sweetly, He speaks to my soul, reminding me it's okay to not be okay with the loss of our birth. Healing doesn't always look like being okay with brokenness. Healing doesn't mean ignoring or removing scars. It takes time and happens in layers.

Softly, He helps me process why I feel so much sorrow surrounding our birth experience. Why does Ira's birth experience cause me so much grief? I find myself sitting on the pew while everyone else stands. With my face in my hands, I let my tears pool. It's because I knew this might have been my only labor and delivery. I felt stolen from. I *was* stolen from.

I doubt I will ever be okay with the way I met Ira. But my pain and feelings of loss are marks of my deep love and desire to meet Ira in a sweet and beautiful way. Healing looks different for each loss. Grieving is part of my healing, and while giving ourselves permission to do so heals us, it does not occur overnight. Birth trauma is not deemed a valid loss, worthy to grieve. But I continue to give it the space it demands, because in it I have found gifts of freedom and the permission to feel.

[78]

"You're so emotional." I often heard this statement thrown at my mom as an insult growing up. Tears were ridiculed and a sign of weakness, and embarrassment. When a woman ran for president, countless people said a woman shouldn't be in the White House. Why? "They are too emotional. What happens when she's on her period?" They scoffed. Emotionally driven equated shame, until I met Matthew. He was extremely emotional and for the first time, I felt permission to let my deep well of emotions run their race. When a man of deep emotion was praised, I thought my deep emotions and sensitivity as a female would be accepted and celebrated.

Loss of any sort should stir up emotion; if it doesn't, it's because we've trained ourselves to be numb. We've bought into the great societal lie that *emotional* and *sensitive* is bad, is shameful, is weak, and worse yet is unlike Him. Too many men I know experience shame because society places pressure on them to withhold emotion: *emotion and sensitivity is weak*. I have found the opposite is true: emotion and sensitivity is what makes us strong.

When I decided to grab ahold of my pain and look at it, claim it, wear it as mine and shun shame away, I discovered Jesus was more emotional than I realized. Jesus could express raw emotion without shame or embarrassment. Jesus shed tears, was filled with joy, grieved and mourned, became angry, felt compassion—

co-suffered with others—and He experienced sorrow, distress, astonishment, and wonder.

Jesus was neither numb, nor emotionally dead. Jesus could fully separate the expectations of people from that of His father.

When our Messiah came, people had a box for Him to fit into, but He refused it. He didn't fall into the box of perfection and pious and rule following they expected and planned. Jesus came emotional and raw, scandalously gracious. He came confident in who He was, but entirely sensitive to His people. Devouring the pages of my Bible, scribbling little notes along the margins, I found hope for myself and hope for others. As I opened myself up to grieve honestly—as I became more acquainted with who I believe Jesus really is and was—I noticed He wasn't entirely selfless. He of course was never selfish, but He also did not live as if *only* other people were valuable. Jesus knew He was valuable, He was worth. Jesus had friends and asked people for help. Jesus took time to rest and pray and be alone; He modeled healthy introvert time. And hallelujah for that.

Jesus also recognized the value in all people. His life was literally spent and sacrificed for others. He chose to die and bear the darkness of humanity for us. He couldn't tend to others without tending to His own humanity, though.

You cannot care for others in great ways unless you first care for yourself. This is something I am constantly relearning. You must tend to your heart and soul before tending to others. Jesus modeled this. Jesus was courageous, Jesus let people down, Jesus said "no" and set healthy boundaries. Jesus validated loss. Jesus is my hero because He is the greatest example of loving well, of welcoming the foreigner, of seeing value in others without discrediting their journeys and losses. He is the great example of love who addresses brokenness without denying it exists.

Jesus's life was one of loving well and living whole. He wasn't emotionless. He wasn't a doormat. He wasn't narcissistic. He was healthy and whole and an example of the life I want to live. In the life He lived, I see freedom and grace unending. Who doesn't want freedom?

But the piece of rhubarb pie I have tasted is that the sweetness of grace and freedom comes hand in hand with the uncomfortable, bitter-rawness of honest emotions and grief.

The bitter-sweet moments of this life are found in vulnerability, transparency, sensitivity, and big emotions. We cannot experience free joy and happiness without experiencing the depths of pain. Wholeness is birthed through vulnerability and sensitivity, which is often conceived in brokenness. Jesus taught me this.

[79]

You've stuck with me this far. I ask you to give me a chance to unpack this delicate, tender topic. It will push buttons and tender pieces of you: I ask that you press on and press in. There is loss involved, a loss I choose because of Jesus. I invite you into this space of loss because I promise you, you will find freedom. I promise you, you will find grace. I promise you, Jesus is worth quieting our defenses to see clearly and love better.

"He's the cutest little thug."

"Can I call him my little Oreo?"

"Oh, so you've got a nigglet in your family?"

"What a little gangster."

"I want a black baby one day."

"He doesn't even really look black," said in a positive, encouraging tone.

My boys sit side by side each other nearly every time these statements, assumptions, and jokes were voiced. My white son, Ira, never receives these titles or attention, though they wear the same outfits and are nearly the same size. Ira is full of pudge and wrinkle-rolls, creases up and down his limbs from the amount of fat squeezed beneath his skin; the focus on him is his cute fatness.

These are real statements said to us in the first year of our biracial, black son's life. You may read these statements and assume they were said by random bully-strangers, people explicitly racist on a regular basis, someone waving a confederate flag from their truck. But they weren't. Each of these statements were said by people I love to my core, who love and support us, have so for years, who love our family a whole lot, are white, and who fall into the category of Christian. None of these statements were thrown at us in hate.

I find this to quite possibly be one of the most problematic forms of racism. It is the subconscious kind embedded into us from our childhood. Many parents didn't realize they were helping embed racism into our society. It is a by-product of ignorance, one which I did not know existed in me. I had never really experienced it, noticed it, or felt I had a reason to. This racism is the kind people respond to confrontation: "I am not a racist! That's not how I meant it!" They grow frustrated with the slightest suggestion of our society being systemically racist.

I grew up in a tiny, predominantly white, agricultural town of 3,000 people. You know how they say ignorance is bliss? It is. I almost miss it. I almost miss not having to confront the comfort of my privilege, of what our country and Christianity has done to people who are not straight, white people. But once my eyes were opened to the injustices people of color are frequently, if not constantly, faced with I couldn't turn away. I couldn't hide because I knew Jesus came to fight for justice. Yes, I knew racism existed. I knew hate was woven into our country's seams. Our country was birthed from the genocide of a valuable group of people: our country's Native Americans. Until I realized fighting for true justice *for all* was the life Jesus called me to, I did not have a real urgency to truly confront it, or see racism.

It's uncomfortable, realizing you've been living your entire life in complete ignorance. I didn't have to carry around the discomfort of seeing our nation as it is: set up for the success and dominance for white people, especially white men. I could write things off, explain away and dismiss well-intentioned hurts; shout about how all lives matter in response to black lives matter and feel really good about myself. I could dismiss the pain of entire people groups and not feel bad about it.

What a privilege right? To not have to enter this pain and trauma and grief? To have the option of avoiding centuries of oppression and systematic racism? To not have slavery built into my family line, my ancestry, my heritage and culture? To see myself represented in every aspect of my life, to the point I think, "Oh cool, they have a brown baby on the diaper box!" because it is so abnormal? To see myself represented as so much more than athletes on posters in the classroom? To know everywhere I go, my language will be understood and spoken?

Instead of wallowing in unhelpful guilt, I began listening to podcasts and reading blogs by people who belong to communities of color as well as white people who were very aware and educated when it came to systemic racism. I knew the burden to educate me should not be carried by people of color. Initially, confronting my privilege and really trying to listen stemmed from complete love for my son: I knew before we brought Sage home his experience as a biracial black man in America would be different than ours. I just didn't know what that meant; I still only have about half a clue.

We knew adopting transracially demanded humility; it was agreeing to take on a culture that isn't ours, one we may be unfamiliar with. We knew before bringing our son home, if we were going to adopt transracially, it meant immersing ourselves into people groups we did not understand, who were different from us but like our child. It meant choosing to lose comfort in many ways we were unable to fully foresee.

Stepping into other cultures and recognizing differences is necessary. Choosing to "ignore" cultures and color says there is a default; the default ends up being whiteness. Whiteness being a default means whiteness is the standard, which means anything other than white is *less than*. This makes white supreme.

Pretending our child is our same race and culture when he

isn't feeds the systemic racism that white should be default and standard. Therefore, "color-blindness" is the complete opposite of helpful. Denying his race and culture embeds shame into these giant pieces of his identity, normalizes racism, and tells him his blackness is something to be ashamed of. Ignoring race silently screams his blackness is *less than*, blackness shouldn't be noticed or celebrated. Being "color and culture blind" subconsciously weaves white supremacy into our lives and minds.

Uncovering this truth forced me to my knees in prayer. I grappled with Him, asking Him how in the world I had lived all these years buying into this white supremacy and been totally unaware of its evil grip, saturating everything. If I believe God made all races, all cultures, all nations, why would I choose to ignore them? Why would I choose color-blindness? Why would I think defaulting everything and everyone to whiteness was okay? How could I not see this as feeding white/European supremacy?

I began seeking out and hearing from transracial adoptees, Black and Latino and Chinese children raised to adults by White parents. My friends of color share with me ways their lives are littered with loss on so many levels. Individually and as a community. Part of me wonders how I was so blinded from it for so many years; I'm embarrassed. But the ugly truth of the matter is I hadn't fostered any close relationships with people who were much different than I. My closest friends my entire life were white and a part of the Christian culture I wrestle with; until we moved to Portland, which is still the whitest, big city in America.

"I used to deny racism existed," Eva told me through the earpiece of my phone. "It felt like the *Christian* thing to do, you know?"

Eva is black, her parents are from Nigeria. We met in Corvallis during college, but retained our friendship over the years. It's the kind of friendship where you rarely see one another but when you do, it's the best day you've had in awhile.

She continues. "It sucks, you know? As a person of color, I don't want to see or acknowledge the real racism existing in everyday life. It's painful. It's exhausting. It can break me if I think about it too much. But I got to a place where I couldn't keep ignoring it. I remember in high school, I was one of the only black girls. A few of my friends told me I was the whitest, black girl in their class; not my skin color, but in the way I acted. I saw it as a compliment. I still can't believe I thought that was a compliment."

My gut drops a bit. This is the world my son will grow up in: where acting white is a compliment, acting white will get you jobs, because it is "professional." Eva loves Jesus a whole lot. Eva offers me grace as we process together through random phone calls and coffee dates. She initiated these phone calls when NBC started airing *This Is Us*.

"What do you think about people of color who internalize and feed into white supremacy, into the notion that racism doesn't exist in the everyday?" I ask her.

"I mean, I was there too. For years. It's what our society teaches us, it seems nearly impossible *not* to buy into it." Eva shares vulnerably.

We talk about a recent music video released by a white, Christian rapper. The video was supposed to be about love, but instead perpetuates false stereotypes about people of color. It demonizes black people, portrays them as violent troublemakers, while the white police man is humanized by looking at pictures of his kids. I watched the music video with my jaw on the ground; my friends Eva and Angel tell me they aren't surprised by the video. It's nothing new to them. This is how mainstream Christian culture treats and portrays people of color.

This is how my son will see himself portrayed in mainstream Christian culture. As his mama, it is my duty and privilege to fight on his behalf, to love him fiercely, even at the expense of myself. Even at the expense of my comfort.

I join our church's gospel choir, despite how entirely tired I am by 6:30 p.m., solo-parenting our two babies on Tuesday nights. I also can't sing, so there is that. The bulk of the choir is white, but led by an amazing woman of color named Michelle. I stand in the back while wearing both babies, pretending I can sing. Going to choir each Tuesday evening incites so much anxiety in me: will my babies scream and cry the whole time? Will they discover I cannot sing? Will I need to leave early? What if they both start having tantrums at the same time?

Our family participates in community events celebrating other cultures. Seth invites us to a night of refugee celebration. There is loud music, people teaching us the dances of their culture, and food trucks. The mass of people flooding the gymnasium vary from the palest of white to the darkest of black; languages from so many cultures and countries, my heart feels at home: He is here among these people. Among the many tribes and nations He created. This feels more like a slice of heaven than my summer camp full of white kids.

We attend the twenty-fifth annual Good in the Hood: a celebration of Portland's black culture. There is dancing and bar-b-que and music. The majority of attendees are black; this is one of the few times I am in the minority of skin color. The toddlers chase other toddlers, dancing through the grass.

I broaden my reading scope. I read memoirs and short stories by refugees. As our tiny community grows more diverse, I grow quieter and attempt to listen. To hear. Without explaining my or other people's intent, without trying to show another point of view or how a statement was interpreted wrong. I begin the art of simply listening and seeing, without defensiveness. Jesus is among people I had unknowingly and subconsciously other'ed. Someone could have attempted to point it out to me, but I would have waved them off with a smile saying they didn't know what they were talking about. "I just have faith and love people like God," I'd say.

Jesus was, and is, among the communities who are oppressed and tossed to the side, perpetually faced with loss: loss in their feeling of safety, loss in seeing positive racial and identity mirrors, loss in being feared instead of celebrated, loss in being deemed as less than the status-quo.

If majority of an ethnicity, culture, or race, other than my own are saying they feel less-than, or oppressed, maybe I should quiet down what I think I know and listen. The practice of listening moves me forward in the way I see the world, in the way I love like Him. I find wholeness and fullness when I choose to see the world from another's perspective.

When I acknowledged that Jesus leads us in the way of honesty-in-suffering I could truly hear people's stories. I learned any form of loss ought to be validated, and therefore, is worthy of being heard, felt, and respected. It wasn't until I saw the suffering of the cross through a whole new lens, that I believed this. As I unlock the worth of giving suffering a voice, it feels as if I am unlocking the way to love well.

Jesus retained the gnarly scars from His crucifixion into His resurrection, and it reveals how God values our losses. Jesus gives space for our traumas and losses and hurts. He doesn't wipe them away and pretend they never happened, but rather enters with us as we heal and become made new.

[80]

People do not know how to handle suffering, loss, tragedy, and trauma. We don't know how to live with broken hearts, or how to respond to a friend's brokenness. We've lost the ability to sit and listen without trying to fix or force the sufferer to a space we deem "better" or right. It seems easier to tell people how to feel or respond to their pain, you know? We rush to remind people: this must be God's plan, good thing this part happened, we should be joyful in time of suffering, or it could have been worse.

The Christian culture of America doesn't know how to lament. We don't know inside of grief, there are gifts to be unwrapped and discovered. In all the undeserved pain, there is an immense amount of undeserved grace to be found. However, the grace only comes fully by permitting yourself to grieve, and to just *be*.

Here on earth, tragedy and trauma and suffering and pain are inevitable. They are promised, no matter who we are. This earth is broken and has been since the Garden. As Jesus was approaching His crucifixion, He agreed to carry The Cross of suffering. I can't help but think of Peter in these last moments. Jesus rebuked Peter, told him that he was a stumbling block, told him *he was Satan*.

Jesus was explaining to the disciples He was about to suffer; He would be rejected, and killed to resurrect with power. Peter took Jesus aside and rebuked Him; saying, "No, no Lord." Jesus responded by rebuking Peter's words. He knew his disciple did not have the knowledge of God to see the purpose in this future pain.

Peter tries to find an alternative route to suffering on the cross. He tries to find ways for Jesus to go around the pain and trauma. We can't blame him either. We do this too, pointing our afflicted friends in the direction we believe is best. We try to skip the dark night and arrive to the morning where there is joy.

Yet, when we tell people they shouldn't be concerned about their suffering and loss, when we diminish their pain. Like Peter, we become a stumbling block. Jesus understood this. It's why Christ sits with us as we carry the cross of loss and hurt. Instead of erasing our scars, He validates our pain. Yes, He heals them, but in time. Healing happens in layers. Christian culture is constantly attempting to suffocate this beautiful, and godly part of Jesus. Instead of accepting loss as a part of life, and something to address and comfort, it's often disregarded.

Culturally, we have become a people who use the art of distraction to rid ourselves of pain. We use articles and blogs and books, or listen to podcasts, watch Netflix, all to avoid the things we rather not speak or think on. Through experience, I have found ignoring these delicate pieces of life doesn't get rid of them. They remain, waiting to be addressed. Healing can never be found until we begin taking care of the underlying issues within our heart, and attempt to sew the broken pieces that cut us. The rocky road to healing must be walked barefoot, so we feel every sharp rock poking our feet, forcing us to cry out to Him, Abba Father Healer.

Cross-carrying faith is acknowledging your loss, and admitting out loud things didn't work as planned. It's admitting you cannot control every circumstance, smile your way through, or pretend it doesn't hurt. Sometimes, you must sit and admit it feels impossible. It takes faith to hold loss in your hands openly, in full view, and be honest about it. Letting go of control helps us acknowledge the One who sits beside us through each emotion we are experiencing. It's in recognizing Jesus is right there with us that we find pieces of Heaven on earth.

Our ego is tied to controlling it all, just like Peter's: there must be a way around this pain, "just do these steps or say these prayers and all will be well." True surrender silences our ego, and creates a path to trust. Keeping our crosses, our losses and grief, hidden and kept quiet in a random compartment of our brain helps no one. It doesn't make us godlier, or make the Christian faith more appealing. It doesn't bring us freedom. Hiding our crosses shackles us. Maybe we look at them from a distance, feeling unable to enter the pain they bring, and seeing how messed up we are, how far from Him we've strayed. *Our life should be spotless, perfect,* we tell ourselves, *we are Christians.* This is part of the lie that broke the earth. The lie that we should have it all, be it all, know it all. The lie that brings forth shame.

But sitting in the space of shame continues to suspend us. Jesus says there is no shame in cross-carrying. We may think our cross is the biggest cross to have ever been carried; if only our cross could look like *her* cross. We ask why our cross can't be lighter like *their* cross?

He does the heavy lifting and will continue to. Their crosses look lighter and smaller because Jesus is doing the heavy lifting, just as He is for mine; it's just hard to see. I don't know the weight bearing down on another's cross. Everyone's cross is heavy. Everyone's hard is hard. Everyone's grief feels dark and lonely.

Jesus invited me to stop looking at other people's crosses; He invited me to stop comparing. I have a problem with trying to diminish my own pain and suffering, reminding myself I don't have it as bad as "so-and-so." The voice in my head says I am being pathetic, and am *shameful* for giving any sort of loss in my life a voice.

Jesus not only invites us to stop comparing how *light* other people's crosses are, He also invites us to stop comparing how *heavy* other people's crosses are. The cross I'm carrying is the only cross I should be concerned with, when it comes to the weight—I am not to compare mine with yours, and vice versa.

He reminds me repeatedly: crosses and losses are not quantifiable. They all need surrendered and He remains King over all the things. I continue to confess Him as King, craving to trust Him with the losses I carry, with the things I don't understand, the circumstances I cannot control, the things I do not like about our story. In this holy surrender, I deny myself and follow Him. But I also find freedom.

Friends, this is how the Kingdom of Heaven breaks in on earth and in our life. When we stop trying to diminish the cross, stop ignoring the suffering, stop pretending the pain away, and we instead open our hands in surrender and say let's do this, let's face this suffering and cry out to Abba because this is too much for me to handle alone.

The Kingdom breaks through when we end our suspension in shame and enter the pain of the cross with Him. It is the great paradox of life coming through death, of His Kingdom breaking through to earth as He was crucified. Our King hanging on the cross is the paradox of God's victory over sin; the Sinless One becoming sin itself so we can be righteous, and find freedom. That's where the key to hell was taken, where victory was had: in the darkest night, the most agonizing pain, the heaviest cross.

[81]

I sit at a coffee shop, a doula of words, birthing stories from within my soul. The weighty gift is not lost on me. Process. We are in perpetual process of becoming who we were created to be. Our potential is big. We have the capacity to love far greater than we believe of ourselves. The biggest love costs us our ego and pride, though. The biggest love runs red, *it killed Him*. We have far more to give than we ever dare; we can love far bigger too.

Our journey is not a religious one of following rules and jumping through hoops and living perfectly and piously. Our goal shouldn't be to live right. Our journey is one of wondering at the mystery of Christ becoming sin on the cross, His suffering, and Him retaining the scars in His resurrected, perfected body. When we decide to grab ahold of suffering and find Him, we are living out the tragic beauty of the cross.

I am part of a large community of foster families. Did you know foster kids reach a point where they age out of the foster care system? They often find themselves family-less. Too often we reach a point where we feel like we age out of God's love and favor. Especially when face-to-face with suffering. We fear He gets tired of us in our suffering, we fear we aren't behaving right.

We feel we must walk through suffering and darkness in a formulated way and act good enough for Him to accept us, take us in as His; but it *isn't* so. He chose to adopt us, take us in as His own, to love us as His children. I cannot imagine ever telling our child via adoption he isn't behaving well enough, and because he is too broken, traumatized, and sensitive we've revoked his adoption. I cannot imagine ever being disappointed in my son for talking about his pain and sorrow, and any loss he's experienced.

God's adoption of us is even more permanent than any parent-child love. In His adopting us, we get to become who we are meant to be. We are offered a home: a room, a bed, and most importantly: a seat at The Table. We are offered a place to belong. In belonging, we can begin to shed what we initially knew as life. We can forget the street life, the hopping from home to home. We can strip the brokenness off our identity and allow love to heal our trauma; but stripping brokenness doesn't mean erasing it.

We receive the Spirit of adoption, making us a child of God. The fees of our adoption were legally paid for by the Cross, by Jesus giving His very own life. The adoption of us to Him breaks through abandonment, suffering, shame, and pain. It takes time, but as we wade through the trauma in His presence, we begin to really believe He loves us through and through. We begin to really believe He doesn't care how ugly we deem ourselves to be. He loves us. He values us.

His Spirit is so real to me. He offers a life of real joy, peace, assurance, and security unlike anything else. I begin experiencing His very true love. True adoption. Becoming a legal daughter to our Father. This is healing, and the power of the Gospel.

It's not just for me to soak up, either. It's for all the people I subconsciously, and mistakenly, deem as unworthy, less-than, or *otherly*. It's a never-ending ongoing journey of confronting hidden biases and beliefs of precious people I didn't realize I had. It's an open-ended progression of living whole and loving well, unpacking where I fall short but rising where He meets me. It's devastating to find my failures as a human and Jesus-follower; it is disheartening to find a life like His isn't full of world-perfection, ease, and comfort. Following Jesus isn't peaches and cream, beautiful and attractive, *cute*.

I have found the devastating moments are always the beginning of a miracle. I've learned there is something about the wilderness waiting, asking Him to fill us up with a humble spirit. He promises the river of living water will flow through the valley. The logs we carry will indeed be swept up by the gushing water, and His river of life.

Suffering often feels so lonely, and barren. The God of grace uses our barrenness to anchor His identity. It's an ongoing decision to place our hope in Him and His presence, rather than outcomes, situations, and appearances. Somewhere along the way we make life about living by the rules—ethically, morally, politically— we forget God is so much greater than these things. The wilderness of a difficult life or circumstance, the barrenness that suffering brings, can be anxiety-producing. Instead of tensing up and trying to run the other way, I continue to stop and sit in the wilderness. Every time I do this, I quickly notice I am not alone. If we sit still long enough, we notice He is still good. We find the wilderness is still a place of grace; the deepest valleys where the wild, raging river roars.

I once toyed with the notion, "What did I do to deserve this?" I don't ask that anymore. The truth I discovered among pain of suffering is this: no one deserves such wicked brokenness. No one deserves loss. When I believe suffering is not God disciplining me, punishing me, or teaching me a lesson, I experience not only His permission, but also His invitation to grieve. Knowing His plan—His will—is never for loss, brokenness, and suffering gives me the space to grieve. It provides room to acknowledge these sorrow-filled experiences. God is waiting for us in the space, inviting us and beckoning us to join Him.

You should know, though, in accepting His invitation to grieve and to co-suffer with friends; oppressed communities, you are living out a deeper life of faith. One that is in line with the cross, planted within depths you didn't know existed. Is it painful? Yes. However, there you will also find bounds of endless joy. There's space for genuine gratitude there; and, a grace so scandalous, you will be made speechless. Joy coexisting with sorrow allows grace to weave you together. It knits your soul to Him. It's the best kind of life, and a life fully lived.

Now, finding myself living in immense gratitude, I ask Him, "What did I do to deserve *this*?" These two babies turning toddlers, our story being written. This pain that is lavished with joy. I didn't do anything to deserve; it is simply a product of His graciousness and goodness. He loves so well, and His gifts are so good. He indeed turns our mourning into dancing. To tell of our story is to truly tell of Him. I acknowledge I didn't do anything to deserve the pain or grace, and there's freedom in this. It removes pressure on me and my deeds, and on my inability to carry my whole world on my shoulders. Suffering and grace aren't given to us because of something we have done or didn't do. Jesus is so much bigger than what we do and don't; His grace extends so much further than we can imagine.

Over the last two years, I've discovered Jesus intimately cares about the suffering and sorrow, heartache and pain, and the tragic brokenness we experience. In surrendering my sorrow by grabbing ahold of it, I unearthed a ridiculous amount of grace. My sorrow continues to create in me an undeniable hunger to love others well, as He has loved me. And it is in learning to love others well I have discovered the most freedom, as well as the most profound pieces of Jesus's heart.

God is concerned deeply enough to not only notice your pain, but tend to it. He cares about and sees your sorrows continually, without ceasing. There is no shame in accepting grace as you grab ahold of pain. No matter how big or small in the world's view, your aches matter to Him. He is right there, in between the spaces of despair, working thoroughly within them. And if you courageously and daringly permit yourself to experience it all, you'll realize something life-changing: from the brokenness seeps gracious, undeserving gifts. Growing and birthing pains *do* produce gifts. Honest grief is where I—and you—can uncover life's fullness as scandalous grace.

PART 3

Bonuses

Wholeness Despite the Brokenness

A Workbook for Beginning the Process of Grief + Loss

"Then Jesus wept."

John 11:35

"Job stood up and tore his robe in grief. Then he shaved his head and fell to the ground to worship."

Job 1:20

Praise for
Wholeness Despite the Brokenness

"Natalie hits on something very real within the pages of this workbook: brokenness. If we are breathing, we have been — in one way or another — broken. It's the human experience. God has greater plans, though, for our pain. If we allow ourselves to be still, listen, and hear the workings of our souls, we can be lifted out of the hollowness of our broken parts. We can arrive to that beautiful place of wholeness. This workbook is a powerful start along the journey to healing."

—Michelle Madrid-Branch, Life Fulfillment Coach and
Emmy-Nominated Journalist, Writer, Blogger,
Former Foster and International Adoptee, Adoptive Mother
www.MichelleMadridBranch.com

"Natalie's heart for healing is revealed in this workbook's gentle, thought-provoking questions. This book provides a launching pad for those who are hurting and don't know where to begin working through their loss. Natalie uses her own experience to provide a framework for others to process their trials in a faith-filled way."

—Kayla Craig, *Just Really Joseph*
Author and co-founder of *Upside Down Podcast*

"With her unique voice, Natalie shares her personal journey through grief and loss while inspiring readers to explore their own pain, and find hope and healing along the way. Natalie's self-paced workbook walks readers through their individual grief journeys with biblical references and prompts to reflect, learn and grow from their past pain. It offers meaningful insight for anyone who has felt broken, confused or hurt by their past or present life experiences."

—Shelley Skuster, Award-Winning Journalist and Infertility Survivor, www.ShelleySkuster.com

"Natalie shares an inside perspective of loss and grief. She strives to move the reader to recognize their own loss by digging deep into their soul to give the loss a voice, then encourages you to pursue wholeness and healing. A must for anyone that has experienced loss. Also, a powerful tool for a mini group bible study."

—Kimberly R. Miller, Mom via birth and adoption

"This book has the power to seriously help people. People who don't want to go to counseling will have a little piece of counseling to take right into their living rooms. As someone who has just recently experienced a heap of grief, I can say that it really helped me. Thank you for your bravery and your honesty."

—Mariah Petewon, Legal Assistant

This Life is Littered with Loss.

Many of us are walking through loss and fail to recognize it. Whether it is a loved one dying, or the distance placed between someone we hold dearly, loss runs rampant in our lives. We fear if we validate the loss we are admittedly unthankful. If we give loss space in our lives, we are not being thankful for the privileged life we live: for the goodness and the grace.

I believe losses need to be given a voice and space in our life to properly grieve them, and grow around them (for example): *a whole and healthy childhood, a stable home, someone who should have been reliable and never was, a pet, physical objects that held meaning, closeness to someone you thought you'd always be close to, divorce, shedding ignorance and perceived beliefs, miscarriage, infertility, failed-adoptions, church community, deaths, security in one way or another (emotional or physical), relationships, failed expectations of really any event.*

We live our lives, day after day, coated with loss and too often we don't know how to cope with it.

Sometimes it seems easier to ignore our loss, pretend it didn't happen or doesn't exist. Sometimes it feels like the expectation is to disregard the pain, to harbor emotions, to wear a facade of okay-ness.

Maybe we feel silly for being sad about things.

We judge ourselves, comparing our loss to someone else's, shaming ourselves for thinking we have anything to grieve. *Their loss is much more tragic*, we tell ourselves. *It could be worse, suck it up.*

Or worse yet, we tell ourselves acknowledging loss is weak. Only the weak grieve.

I would bargain only the strong grieve.

It takes strength, courage, bravery to grieve.

It takes strength to enter your own pain. Courage to sit in it, to give your loss and sorrow space, and bravery to allow it to consume you, even if only briefly.

It takes strength to acknowledge and validate loss.

Loss is unquantifiable.

You cannot quantify and compare loss.

Acknowledging loss and entering grief is vulnerable. It's dangerous for your heart, for your feelings, for you.

It is scary and frightening. It invites fear, but it is worth all the discomfort.

I would dare to say we cannot launch into greatness and true joy, into a path of healing and wholeness, until we give grief and loss their space in our life.

To fully embrace the goodness in life, we must enable ourselves to feel the bad. Experiencing the beauty of joy requires us to acknowledge our losses, and any sorrow it may bring. It is in the extreme of these experiences that fullness is found. Admitting how hard something is grants us the power to heal.

Do you want to uncover losses you may not have recognized you needed to grieve? Do you want to find healing and wholeness? Do you want to experience the fullness of joy? Do you crave freedom? It starts here. It starts by walking over the broken pieces of yourself.

This workbook is short and simple.

While it does not cover the entire grieving process, as to each person's journey will be different, it provides a healthy way to conquer hardships. Give yourself space and time to work through this.

I am not a certified therapist, or counselor; I am simply sharing the process I have walked through for my life. I highly encourage counseling.

Set down your distractions, pour yourself something warm (or icy if it's hot!), and find a physical space free of clutter, sound, and distractions. Silence is important. Grab a journal and a pen to write out your process. Ready?

When was the last time you sat for at least 30 minutes in silence without any distractions?

We are not short on distractions. We literally carry around a numbing-object in our pockets: our phones. The moment we are alone, the moment there is a lull in a conversation, even while we drive, we pull out our device and distract ourselves. We live in a world that constantly begs us to numb ourselves, to stuff our emotions and feelings by simply ignoring the pain.

Think I'm being dramatic? I'm not. It's hard to sit in silence because *true* silence gives our hearts a voice. It gives our fears, our emotions, and feelings a voice.

Healthy grieving gives many kinds of losses a voice. Not just death. But also, those like failed expectations from an important life event, the loss of closeness in a relationship, or your parents' divorce.

To begin this process, I am asking you to put your phone, and all other devices in a different room for at least thirty minutes. With your pen and paper, jot down the answers to these questions to discover where to begin your healing:

Off-hand, can I name any losses?

What hurts in my life?

What have I missed out on in my life?

Have any of my relationships changed in the past year that I haven't addressed?

Have I lost the ability to trust someone?

What comes easy to other people but not to me, making me feel broken?

Who do I feel I am disappointing?

Was I adopted?

Do I share my race with my family?

What relationship in the last year has changed, causing me to feel bummed?

Has someone I love passed recently?

What makes me sad in my life?

What feels too heavy to think about?

There are no wrong answers. Give your losses a voice.

After you have spent a half-hour or more reflecting upon the previous questions, walk through the pieces of your story that does not feel completely whole.

Why do you avoid thinking about this loss?

Example: off-hand, can I name any losses?

Losing our job traumatically was so much more than losing a job: I lost relationships with people I had built my entire life around. I worked with them, ate meals with them, and built community with them.

Why do I avoid thinking about this loss?

Because I feel guilty for feeling sad when it was I who had initially decided to leave. I fear other people think I am pathetic and it wasn't a real loss. It was our fault and it feels invalid. Sometimes I get angry and anger is uncomfortable. Anger makes me feel I am a bad person and ungodly (although I don't believe that).

Give your loss space to speak without shame.

Write down what comes to mind.

The Avalanche Of Loss

Sometimes, once we recognize one loss we uncover a list of losses accompanying that hardship. Has this misfortune caused you to lose anything else, or had a negative impact on you?

Example: We were consumed by losing the church community we had—the people—and our relationship with them; we felt we had lost our identity. Out of a place of deep hurt, we decided against pursuing a new job in that same career-field, as youth pastors. Vocational ministry was all we knew, but we were losing that part of our identity. We also discovered things we had been believing about ourselves: lies we had embraced because they were said by voices we held in high esteem. We noted the loss of a true and whole identity. We had to rediscover what we believed about who we were. We lost the ease in believing people's offers came without strings attached. Now, I am always looking for strings secretly attached to manipulation. See how this works? The avalanche of loss?

Make a timeline of your varying losses:

Have you given yourself permission to view what you've lost as loss(es)? Why or why not?

Has your loss affected the way you view the world and the people in your life? What about the way in which you openly connect with others, and to yourself?

If you could change the outcome of this loss, what would that look like? What do you wish this experience looked like?

When you recognize you cannot control or change it, what thoughts come to mind?

Example: I often felt it would be much easier to cope if I could blame myself. When I go back in time and try to change a specific loss, I usually come around and realize I cannot change it. Recognizing this, I acknowledge I am out of control. This means I cannot blame myself.

Are you blaming yourself at all? If so, write down what you blame yourself for? What do you feel is your fault?

Share the positive experiences that have occurred because of what you lost. What have you gained, that you would not have otherwise, because of this hardship? Can't think of anything right now? That's okay. Return to this in a few weeks, or months. Sometimes we must sit in the sadness.

What are some things you've learned during this time of grieving? In what way has your "view of the world" changed? Have you gained insight from this?

Example: through our miscarriage and church trauma, I discovered the world does not like sadness. I discovered Christian culture does a terrible job at offering grief and loss a true and valid space. On the flip side, I have discovered Jesus does a great job of inviting us into authenticity, even if it feels ugly.

Let's talk about Jesus and your loss.

Where was Jesus when this happened? What do you believe to be true about him in this situation?

Be raw. Be real and even if you feel it's ugly, be honest. He can handle our honesty. I know this for sure.

Do you feel betrayed by Jesus?

Do you feel "ungodly" if you acknowledge a loss? Do you feel god is disappointed in you when you give grief and sorrow space?

"I cannot keep from speaking. I must express my anguish. I must complain in my bitterness."

Job 7:11

*"My eyes are red with weeping;
darkness covers my eyes."*

Job 16:16

Whose voice is telling you it's not okay to feel sad, angry, depressed, sorrowful? Why does this voice have so much power?

"People who are at ease mock those in trouble.
They give a push to people who are stumbling...
Please be quiet! That is the smartest thing you
could do."

Job 12:5, 13:5

I believe Jesus not only gives us permission to grieve, but is actively mourning and grieving with us. Even when our sorrow and sadness feels *petty* He is with us, feeling our pain. I don't believe He is ever disappointed when we let the brokenness sit heavy within us, when we authentically and genuinely acknowledge loss.

I believe we see Him clearest in the cracks of ourselves. In the spaces where we are all broken up. Where His grace is all that remains as steady and sure. Because I believe that in His mourning, weeping, and grieving *with* us we find grace. He is not disappointed in us as we grieve.

His original plan was for no loss, no pain, no sorrow, or tragedy on any spectrum, but because of brokenness, these experiences exist. Because His original plan was for no loss, He grieves with us every time we experience brokenness.

When you are told "this was God's plan," in response to your loss you can find freedom and hope knowing it was never what He intended. His plan is for good, for life: for wholeness without brokenness. One day, we will get to live out and experience His perfect plan in Heaven.

You have permission to grieve.

Who supports you in your life? Name a few people who make you feel safe.

Who can you share this workbook with to see the broken pieces within your story? Trust them to love you right where you are.

Every time your loss is triggered and you are lead to think about it, I encourage you to acknowledge your loss and grief. I encourage you to take note, to give it a voice, and not shame yourself by pushing it away.

I know, it's painful. It's grief and that hurts. But again, to fully feel the goodness in life, we must address what makes us feel uncomfortable. Not doing so numbs the problem and never helps us heal. Remind yourself beautiful lives contain messy, imperfect parts, but when you work at cleaning them up rather than ignoring them, you experience the gift of wholeness: true joy and freedom.

There are so many stages to grief and there isn't any perfect way to walk through its stages. Sometimes you think you are done with denying the loss that happened, only to return to denial months or years down the road. That's okay. You have permission to walk through grief the way *you* walk through grief.

You are entitled to grieve, feel pain, then heal.

The Absolute Normal
+ Permitted Stages Of Grief

DENIAL

ANGER

BARGAINING

DEPRESSION

ACCEPTANCE

It's necessary for you to understand walking through grief is not a linear process. There isn't any formula, or strategy. You may be in a space of accepting your loss one moment, and next be crushed with anger or bargaining. You may feel like you have "moved on" and accepted your loss, then something triggers and you are back in a state of depression.

You have permission to experience grief as it comes, as it hits, in waves.

Grief is unpredictable and clunky.

It is important to acknowledge your loss.

Acknowledge that it hurts and you don't have to be shameful for feeling this way. We grow around sorrow. If it finds a space to permanently reside in you, that's okay. It is a constant memorial, *an honor*, of the thing, person, relationship, or experience you lost. The broken pieces have not been far removed from your misplaced treasure. Allow sorrow to reside where it begs to have a voice.

> *"I too have been assigned months of futility, long and weary nights of misery. When I go to bed, I think, 'When will it be morning?' But the night drags on and I toss til dawn."*

> Job 7:3-4

Start noting wholeness.

We do not have to wallow in pain and sorrow because we have the opportunity and freedom to grow around it. Does this mean we will have hard days? Yes. Does it mean I may encounter another layer of grieving out of the blue? Yes.

> *"Weeping may last through the night,*
> *but joy comes with the morning."*

-King David, Psalm 30:5

Sometimes the morning doesn't come as quickly as we wish it would.

What are your hopes regarding this loss for the present or future. This can be anything: *I want to heal. I want to sleep well tonight. I want to trust Jesus. I want to find Jesus here. I want to be more at ease.* Whatever it is, when you are ready, mark down your hopes.

> *"The Lord is my rock, my fortress and my deliverer;*
> *my God is my rock, in whom I take refuge,*
> *my shield and the horn of my salvation, my*
> *stronghold."*

King David, Psalm 18:2

List five hopes you have in the present moment:

Take another step forward:

Step into them deeper, rewriting your hopes in the present tense: I am healing. I sleep well. I am at ease. Take a moment before writing your declarations to breathe in deeply, feeling them in your heart and mind.

Note your hope:

When you speak your hopes out loud, where do you feel the most freedom? What insights do you gain? Speak your hopes every day for the next 30 days. Try attaching them to an activity, such as making breakfast or brushing your teeth.

Read these out loud to yourself.

It's okay if you don't yet believe them or if you aren't feeling their grace. These Truths can be used as hope:

I am fearfully and wonderfully made.

Your plans are to bring me good and not to harm me.

You will never leave or forsake me.

You have loved me with an everlasting love.

Nothing can separate me from the love of God.

I am made in Your image.

In You, I am new.

You are faithful.

As I obey You, You will place in me the desires of my heart.

Even the birds are beautifully clothed and fed; You care for me.

You clothe me in strength and dignity.

You uphold the weak and comfort the broken hearted.

Sorrow is for a short while, but your joy will come in the morning.

Your joy is my strength.

Grieving doesn't make you
less of a good person;
it makes you a whole person.

Further Reading on Adoption

ARTICLES ON NATALIEBRENNERWRITES.COM

"Thinking About Adoption? Read This" — Adoption 101 on
    Positive Adoption Language
"Black Culture + Hair Care Go Hand in Hand: Raising Kids of
    Color" by Natalie Brenner
"How to Go from Fearing to Celebrating Open Adoption" by
    Natalie Brenner
"Why + What We Read to Our Toddlers" by Natalie Brenner

ADDITIONAL ARTICLES:

"The Problem with Ethics" by Stacey Stark on
    www.TheStarksAdopt.blogspot.com

BOOKS

In Their Own Voices: Transracial Adoptees Tell Their Stories by
    Rhonda M. Roorda
Adopt Without Debt: Creative Ways to Cover the Cost of Adoption
    by Julie Gumm
Financing Adoption with Fundraising, free through her website,
    by Natalie Brenner

PODCAST

Honestly Speaking by Confessions of an Adoptive Parent

VIDEO SERIES

The Adopted Life by Angela Tucker
Closure on Netflix by Angela Tucker

WEBSITES + BLOGS

www.NatalieBrennerWrites.com
www.ConfessionsOfAnAdoptiveParent.com
www.GraceWhileWeWait.com
www.RhondaMRoorda.com
www.MichelleMadridBranch.com
www.GraceFilledMess.blogspot.com
www.Adoption.com
www.TheAdoptedLife.com/AngelaBlog/

FACEBOOK GROUPS

Not Just Hair: The Intersection of Hair/Skincare and Transracial
    Adoption
{Joyfilled} Prospective Transracial Families
Joyfilled Transracial Families

Further Reading on
Racial Reconciliation and Justice

WEBSITES + ARTICLES

"The FAQs: What Christians Should Know About the
   Alt-Right" by Joe Carter on The Gospel Coalition
www.ReadBrightly.com/picture-books-featuring-black-male-
   protagonists
Whiteness 101 Found in the files of the Be the Bridge's Facebook
   group members
www.WeNeedDiverseBooks.org

FACEBOOK GROUP

Be the Bridge to Racial Unity

BOOKS

The New Jim Crow by Michelle Alexander
The Hate You Give by Angie Thomas
List of Christian authors of color found on DeidraRiggs.com

NETFLIX DOCUMENTARIES

13th
Not Your Negro

PODCASTS

The Black History Podcast
Pass the Mic
Invisibilia
1A hosted by NPR

About the Author

Natalie Brenner's work appears on Adoption.com as the top writer, Pregnant Chicken, Parents, the Today Show Parents, and more. Most recently, she has been a featured guest on several podcasting shows including *Oregon Public Broadcasting, Confessions of an Adoptive Parent's, Honestly Adoption Podcast,* and *The Birth Hour.*

She has also created two invaluable resources as eBooks: *Wholeness Despite the Brokenness: A Workbook Beginning the Process of Grief,* and *Financing Adoption with Fundraising.* Both are free through her website.

After a few, long years in ministry, Natalie and her husband's identity as pastors were shed. Their titles transformed into less shinier ones: Work at Home Mom and Skills Trainer Going to Grad School Dad.

She lives in Portland, Oregon with her husband, Loren, where they raise their two toddlers and a couple chickens. When not writing or taking pictures, you'll find her tickling her babies, sipping a foamy latte, or on a run. She believes we each have the capacity to love far bigger than we dare. Natalie loves people a whole lot: the messier the better. She's courageously honest and isn't afraid to have hard conversations.

Become a part of Natalie's inside readers' circle by connecting with her on NatalieBrennerWrites.com; it's where all the cool people go to get sneak peaks, and the occasional freebie. You can find her on social media too: @nataliekbrenner.

this undeserved life

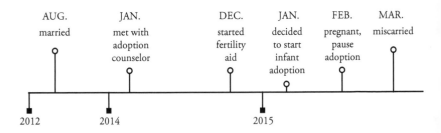

AUG.	JAN.	DEC.	JAN.	FEB.	MAR.
married	met with adoption counselor	started fertility aid	decided to start infant adoption	pregnant, pause adoption	miscarried

2012   2014   2015

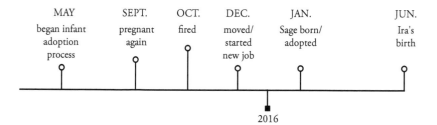

MAY
began infant
adoption
process

SEPT.
pregnant
again

OCT.
fired

DEC.
moved/
started
new job

JAN.
Sage born/
adopted

JUN.
Ira's
birth

2016

Made in the USA
San Bernardino, CA
02 October 2017